Speaking Out

About the Author

Michael Saunders is a retired neurologist and Anglican priest. He is the author and co-author of scientific papers and books on neurology and medical ethics. He was a tutor on an ordination course and a Bishop's educational advisor, assessing the suitability for training of ordination candidates.

His first non-specialist book, *From Certainty to Mystery,* was published by Olympia in 2019.

Michael is married to Irene, a retired psychiatrist, and they have four adult children. He is disabled with muscular dystrophy and is a full-time wheelchair user.

He lives in the Yorkshire Dales.

Michael Saunders

Speaking Out

Olympia Publishers
London

www.olympiapublishers.com
OLYMPIA PAPERBACK EDITION

A CIP catalogue record for this title is
available from the British Library.

ISBN: 978-1-78830-583-9

First Published in 2020

Olympia Publishers
Tallis House
2 Tallis Street
London
EC4Y 0AB

Printed in Great Britain

Dedication

To the parishioners of St Mary's, Masham and St Paul's, Healey

Acknowledgements

I wish to thank Canon David Cleeves, Vicar of Masham and Healey for support during my ministry. This does not imply we necessarily share the same theological positions. Diversity is fundamental to the Anglican expressions of Christianity.

Numerous people have encouraged me. As a full-time wheelchair user many have made it possible for me to take services. As always, I thank my wife for support, including the arduous task of helping me put on my robes and driving me to Healey! The members of the Healey team have enabled me to access the hill church with several ramps and other assistance. My ability to preach and celebrate the Eucharist has been a real team effort. The cover photograph of the outlook from Healey church was provided by Keith Marshall. I thank Jim Heaton for assistance in reading the manuscript. All errors are my own.

Preface

Several people over the years have asked me to print off copies of sermons preached in the parishes of St Mary's Masham and St Paul's Healey. Following my retirement from medical practice my wife and I retired to Masham and these sermons are a selection of those given between 2001 and 2018. I have had to be vigorous in reducing the number in this selection, but even then, acknowledge the tendency for repetition. I think this is inevitable. Whatever passage in the Bible is allocated for a particular day in the Christian calendar, the core features of what it may mean to be a Christian can be reduced to answers to basic questions about why we exist and how we should live. Therefore, whatever the biblical starting point, every sermon has to make connections with the world we live in now.

The title *Speaking Out* has provided some basis for my choice. In preaching I have attempted to be open and honest about the importance of non-dogmatic theology in modern Christianity and this involves saying things that may seem obvious to the 'ordinary citizen', but are not always acknowledged explicitly by the institutional Church; in this case the Church of England, part of the wider Anglican communion.

I am a religious pluralist. I consider that all religions are created by humans in an attempt to explain the great questions of life and that this should be more openly acknowledged by the Church hierarchy. It is perfectly possible to be a 'seeker' within one's own cultural and religious tradition, while acknowledging the equal value of the other great religions of the world. True spirituality is about 'transformation' of the way we try to live out our lives and this is common to all undistorted religious traditions.

The other basis for inclusion reflected in the title is the imperative to *speak out* about the issues that undermine true mutuality in the modern world at national and global level. I claim no expertise in these matters, but I am convinced that religion has to be connected with the 'marketplace'. There is no meaning in 'privatised faith'. It is possible to be 'political' without reference to specific political party affiliations.

I consider the life and work of Jesus is of universal importance. This lies beyond the 'walls' of the Church. Jesus is a charismatic teacher who emphasised the primacy of love in the 'ideal' human existence. Love was focussed in his own life and he is an exemplar for us all. We seek to 'imitate' and follow him in our own lives. These features of his life are brought into focus by his unmerited death and his resurrection in the hearts and minds of people down the centuries. The naming of Jesus as Lord and Son of God are indicative of the central importance of Jesus in the lives of many. Sadly, his example to us has become distorted at times both within and outside the Church. I attempt to emphasise the radical challenge that following Jesus provides for us all.

One might well ask: What is the purpose of a sermon? Although I was raised as a non-conformist and became an Anglican in middle age, I now adhere to the 'ten minute' slot. That time limit happens to be aligned at present with the duration of a consultation with a general medical practitioner

(GP)! Most of what can be said at any one episode may be communicated in that time, although one accepts the occasional exception.

For me, a sermon should contain some exploration of the biblical context of one or more of the readings allocated for the day. Because of my 'dissenting' background I do use a biblical 'text' to start my thinking trail. I may well digress, but it provides a useful starting point and it reminds me that one should examine the context of the reading(s), together with their application to daily life.

Sometimes, I have been accused of being too 'intellectual'. I acknowledge that this may seem to be the case, but congregations contain people of widely differing backgrounds and this must be acknowledged. It is not appropriate to 'talk down' to people and with the absence of other occasions to study and interpret the Bible in many communities, an educational element in sermons is important.

Sermons should comfort, challenge and inspire people whenever possible. In my view the preacher should be unafraid to use personal experience. Stories, of whatever nature, told from one's own life, have greater immediacy than those gleaned from the internet and other people. However, the use of poetry, quotations from historical figures and great literature are useful adjuncts to any sermon.

I accept that my preaching has occurred over a long period of time. This means that some of the 'topical' allusions, immediate at the time, have less relevance and impact now, and their precise temporal relevance forgotten. I have not made any attempt to alter this and the sermons in this book are as preached, with the admission that some extemporary comments will have been made. Although, in earlier years, I used headings and did not write out sermons, I have found the discipline of ordering one's thoughts useful. Punctuation idiosyncrasies within the original sermons are unchanged.

Finally, this book may be read as a companion to my *From Certainty to Mystery* (Olympia Publishers 2019).

Introduction

The parish of Masham is centred in an historic small market town on the river Ure in North Yorkshire. In the sixteenth century it was a wealthy prebend in the diocese of York. Following the abolition of the monasteries, although not specifically related to this, Henry VIII gifted the benefits of the prebend, which at that time included the village of Kirby Malzeard, to Trinity College Cambridge. The college remains the patron of Masham to this day. Masham is an active centre and is popular with tourists. The historic wealth based on sheep is reflected in the annual sheep fair. St Mary's church is central to the life of the community. It has some fine historic features and is well used.

Healey is a small hill village in a large rural parish including the adjacent village of Fearby. It lies at the entry to moorland known for grouse and the area is of great natural beauty. The beautiful nineteenth century church has fine views and the worshipping community are welcoming and lively.

The populations of Masham and Healey are mixed, including retired people, farmers and those involved in local businesses. This is the setting for the sermons preached.

The Church of England lectionary provides a cycle of Bible readings extending over three years. Each Sunday has three readings, with different tracks, including an Old Testament reading, Epistle and Gospel for the main service.

Each year contains an emphasis on one of the Synoptic Gospels; year A Mathew, year B Mark and year C Luke. The Gospel of John is used for all three years at particular points.

It would be impossible to select sermons from all the years for all the Sundays in this book. The selection moves around the cycle for any particular period in the liturgical calendar. For example, the season of Advent may contain sermons from years A, B and C, but does not include the entire possible number of services, if all four Sundays of Advent were covered over the three-year cycle. The explicit Sunday in Advent or other seasonal Sunday is not referred to in the text as the reader gains little from knowing on which particular Sunday in the season the sermon was preached. During Ordinary Time the Gospel used will identify whether year A, B or C readings are being used for much of the time, and the readings are all recorded in the Common Worship Principal Service Lectionary or sometimes the second service in the case of Evensong. As each sermon is headed by the reading used, it is possible for the reader to access them; it is unrealistic to record readings in full.

In the particular Churches I have served it has been the custom to use the Epistle and Gospel and omit the Old Testament reading save in Advent and Christmas. I place on record my disappointment at this trend, as I regard the reading of the Old Testament as a core feature of Christian worship. When possible, I have preached from the Old Testament when it is used, often at Evensong. Sadly, there has been a decline in Evensong in many benefices. Because some added insights may be gained, I have not hesitated to include more than one sermon on occasions such as Christmas Day and Easter Sunday.

A 'text' has been placed at the head of each sermon as well as a general heading. The heading should not be taken as indicating the detailed content of the sermon but is merely a device to gain attention! The 'text' is taken from one of the readings. This does not mean that other readings will not be referred to on occasion, but reflects my emphasis at the time. Although I hope that the reader will be able to deduce my line of discussion from the text and sermon content, there is no substitute for reading the whole passage. The translation used is the New Standardised Version, Anglicised edition, but other versions will contain a similar wording if not identical.

These sermons can be 'dipped into'. They stand on their own.

Advent

The season of Advent is one of the penitential periods in the liturgical calendar and purple is the usual colour. It is customary to reflect on the Advent hope, the Old Testament prophets, John the Baptist and the Virgin Mary, mother of Jesus.

It is a time of preparation for the coming of Jesus. The Old Testament is read preferably if two readings are the norm in the church.

The Advent hope raises issues for modern progressive Christians. Literal belief in the Second Coming of Jesus seems alien to the modern mind after all the years that have elapsed since his original ministry in the Middle East. Whatever Jesus thought about the end of the world, there is little doubt that some of his original followers anticipated that his early return would usher in a new age and reign of God. An alternative viewpoint now is that the Advent hope reminds us of God's continuing presence in the world in the form of the Holy Spirit, or the spirit of Jesus. This is a continuing presence and we are 'judged' and forgiven throughout our lives. The beginning of the liturgical cycle reminds us that a linear view of the world should not be dominant. We return year after year to the point where we first started; 'the end is our beginning'.

Prophesy continues to be an important subject. In Advent we can remind ourselves that prophets speak to their own times and situations. We may benefit from the wisdom of those who spoke out in earlier generations, but we need prophets for our own times who are as courageous as those who spoke to the Jews many centuries ago. Prophets may see the consequences of human decisions and behaviour that have a timeless relevance, but they are not clairvoyants or fortune tellers. It seems that early Christians gained some reassurance in discovering hints to the coming of Jesus in parts of the Hebrew writings. Today many will be less certain about these references that are incorporated in the Gospels.

We know little about Mary. It is likely she had several children. The Magnificat remains a work of great beauty and it is not necessary to believe that she gave birth to Jesus without the involvement of a man. Genuine Incarnation, in my view, requires the same kind of birth as anyone else. The story of the birth of Jesus emphasises the importance of his birth in the history of the world and reflects the metaphors of the time. It should be noted that the Gospels of Mark and John, together with the letters of Paul, make no mention of Jesus' birth.

The reader will note that these sermons refer to topical issues at the time they were spoken. Many issues remain with us. I have not removed topical references. They remind us that preaching has no relevance unless it connects with the world we inhabit.

Room for Hope?

Isaiah 64.1–9 Mark 13.24–37

"O that you would tear open the Heavens and come down."
Isaiah 64.1.

That dramatic phrase is a cry from the heart for God to intervene in the affairs of men and women. Where has God gone? Is God anywhere? Where is our hope? Is life no longer controllable or with purpose and beauty? These are the cries of despair that we can make as individuals or communities. The prophet cries out about the condition of his people, resulting in exile: 'We have all become like one who is unclean, and all our righteous deeds are like filthy cloth. We all fade like a leaf, and our iniquities, like the wind, take us away.' (Isaiah 64.6).

Our Gospel reading, in highly pictorial language, provides the message of hope that is part of what we call the Advent hope, as we await Christmas and the celebration of the birth of Jesus. Our liturgical calendar has come full circle to the beginning of our worship cycle.

The prophet hopes for God to intervene. The Gospel writer, using words from the book of Daniel, describes the coming of the Son of Man in power and glory. We are instructed to be alert and wait.

Although the imagery used in the passages may seem

strange to us, and we are not necessarily expecting the imminent end of the world, we live in times that provide little evidence that we are making progress morally as humans, or moving smoothly towards a world full of love, peace and justice.

The cry of the prophet could be ours today. Come and rescue us, lead us in new ways, help us to sort things out. Such cries have probably echoed down the ages. Have they ever been answered?

Today we are in a global mess. We await fearfully the possibility of a major war with Iraq. We hear of terrorist attacks almost daily in the Middle East. We read of attacks in Kenya. We are warned to prepare ourselves for terror in this country. We could build up very similar images to these apocalyptic ones in Mark's Gospel. In every generation we call on God if we believe in a deity. But our call has already been answered because the incarnation is not something fixed and limited to one temporal event. It is, in effect, a message from God that says to us that He/She is in this world. God has never left it. We leave God.

In Jesus we have a picture of a life and way of living centred on selflessness and love that is the recipe for how to make a decent world.

Our cry to God to sort out this world is immature. We have a model to follow. We cannot opt out. We really must find God within ourselves to make the reorientation that comes from repentance.

Within the Christian tradition, and perhaps in the wider world, there have always been two broad views of the prospects for a 'better' world; in religious language a 'Kingdom of Heaven' on Earth.

Some people take the view that such a kingdom, or more secular pictures of it such as Utopia or Arcadia, are ridiculous. There will never be 'a world come right' where all is peace and harmony. God will judge the world and in a final judgement will gather his own unto himself. The real kingdom is beyond us in another existence. This picture has always had attractions, particularly when we are in the midst of great evil. However, there are serious problems with believing it to the exclusion of all else. It tends to deny the full meaning of incarnation, God with us and in us. It can lead to a world negating view of life, concentrating on a world to come for the righteous. It may lead to a laissez faire attitude to this world's evils and problems; we cannot do anything to make it any better.

The alternative is a firm belief in the 'creation is good' statement. Despite everything we must work to make creation as God intended it. It is possible for the world to become a better place. The Kingdom of God is, at least in part, capable of being realised as present reality within the confines of space and time.

These two views need not exclude each other. But we certainly deny the Advent Hope if we believe that nothing can or has been done. Although we fix the Incarnation at a moment in time, it is not to be fixed in that way. The Advent hope is that we can remember yet again that God is always in creation. God has not abandoned it. He/She suffers the same agonies as we do, but the ultimate hope is that love, peace and justice will triumph. God has broken through the heavens and he can live in all of us.

I love this poem by the neglected First World War poet, Edward Thomas. One might ask what it has got to do with the sermon. I would reply that at its core is the heart of incarnation. God is not in us or with us unless we care about others. There is no Advent hope without that. It is called *The Owl*:

> Downhill I came, hungry, and yet not starved;
> Cold, yet had heat within me that was proof
> Against the north wind; tired, yet so that rest
> Had seemed the sweetest thing under a roof.
> Then at the inn I had food, fire, and rest,
> Knowing how hungry, cold, and tired was I.
> All of the night was quite barred out except
> An owl's cry, a most melancholy cry
> Shaken out long and clear upon the hill
> No merry note, nor cause of merriment,
> But one telling me plain what I escaped
> And others could not, that night, as in I went.
> And salted was my food, and my repose,
> Salted and sobered, too, by the bird's voice
> Speaking for all who lay under the stars,
> Soldiers and poor, unable to rejoice.

Isaiah's Vision

Isaiah 11.1–10 Matthew 3.1–12

"For the Earth will be full of the knowledge of the Lord as the waters cover the sea."

Isaiah 11.9.

This is one of the great poetic passages of the Bible and today we reflect on the word of God in the Old Testament.

This passage in Isaiah certainly seems to be looking forward. It contains a great vision of his world imbued with the presence of God. It certainly seems to be anticipating the coming of one from the stem of Jesse, who will bring harmony and peace and righteousness. The vision is of a new leader who is able to transform people to follow in the ways of God. The animal imagery reflects, in poetic language, how radical this change will be.

For the Jewish people it is a vision of the true Messiah who is yet to come. One can fully understand that from the standpoint of their cultural and political history Jews do not believe this has happened.

For the Christian, this figure in Isaiah is seen to have been realised in Jesus. Because of the Christian belief that the figure portrayed in Isaiah was Jesus, the New Testament has been written to use texts in the Old Testament to justify this. Clearly for the Jew who followed Jesus, it was of great importance that the Old Testament, the sacred history of the Jewish people, should justify the claims made about the first century prophet and teacher who was called Jesus of Nazareth.

Because of this there has been undue emphasis in looking at the Old Testament prophets as telling the future. Prophetic visions are not primarily about telling the future, but they are visions of what the world could be like interpreted through the sacred tradition the prophets have inherited. For the Jew of the time, Jerusalem and the mount of Zion were the physical and metaphorical places where everything that had gone wrong would be restored. Jesse, the father of David, was seen as the root that would give rise to someone who would be the true King of Israel and mend all the agonies and sorrows of the Jewish people.

We need to remember that by the time Isaiah wrote this, the northern kingdom of Israel had already atrophied through invasion and captivity by Assyria; and the kingdom of Judah, the southern kingdom and very much the remnant of the original twelve tribes, was where this hope was focussed.

Yet, at this time we note that there is the beginning of a broader vision that looks beyond Israel and Judah to the wider world of nations. Although Jews believed that they were the chosen people, they had begun to think that they were not the custodians of a tribal god but the God of all people.

As Christians living in the twenty-first century, we may find it difficult to connect with the Old Testament, yet it remains a core literature that is absolutely essential for understanding the development of Christianity before it became radically altered by Hellenisation and spread across the Roman empire.

The Christianity that we know is so heavily dependent on

Greek philosophy that it is very easy to lose touch with its original Jewish origins.

As we prepare to celebrate the birth of Jesus whom Christians proclaim as Messiah, we need to give thanks for the many things that we have inherited from our Jewish cousins in the faith and which we share with our Islamic brothers and sisters. Christianity, Islam and Judaism are all religions of the Book and the Book is the Old Testament or Tanakh.

We share the belief that there is one God, Allah, Jaweh or whatever name we use for God, the source of all being, the ultimate meaning of everything.

We share belief in a divine creation and have all struggled to describe how this happened in words. We believe that everything that *is* has emanated in some way from God.

We believe that humanity is the highest development of creation because only humans are aware of the possibility of God at all. As far as we know we are the only species to be able to reflect and think spiritually and therefore dwell on the meaning of our existence. However, that should not obscure our connectedness with everything that exists.

In some way we believe that humans have free choice and in many of our choices and directions we depart from this vision held up by Isaiah. We go our own way. We hate rather than love. The Earth is not full of the knowledge of God many centuries after Isaiah had his vision.

Christians believe that Isaiah's vision still lies in the future despite the coming of the Messiah. There is potential through following Jesus to change the world and some Christians believe that this is an achievable end; not just through the institution we call the Church, but through human endeavour for good from people of all faiths or no faiths; for

God is not limited to religious institutions. Others feel that the state of the world is so bad that the only thing that will redeem it is the second coming of the Messiah or for the Jews the first coming. Even some Muslim sects look for the coming of a future Imam who will restore the image of the original prophet.

One of the great gifts of the Old Testament to us, is to recognise that true religion is religion of the heart. We read that the one to come will not judge by what he sees with his eyes or decide by what he hears with his ears. Sometimes our view of the Old Testament is buried in the Law. But that is very unfair. The Law was set up to provide a framework for behaviour based on the cultural necessities of the age, but spiritual Jews recognised the importance of the heart well before Christianity split off as a different religion.

It is this change of heart that is the only means of achieving this vision of Isaiah and in looking forward to the birth of Jesus and his great mission. Today we give thanks for all that went before, and which imbued his own life.

Elijah and John the Baptiser

I Kings 18.17–39 John 1.19–28.
"I am the voice of one crying out in the wilderness,
Make straight the way of the Lord."
John 1.23.

In Advent we think of both prophecy and John the Baptist. Our Old Testament, Hebrew Bible reading, recounts the great story of the battle for the hearts and minds of the Israelites between Elijah and the prophets of Baal, the local Canaanite deity. Ahab, King of Israel and Jezebel his Queen had worshipped Baal. The story relates the dramatic victory of the God of Israel as the protagonists attempt to call up consuming fire for the sacrificial bulls. This is a story about a primitive understanding of God, but it was a foundation story for the Jews and Elijah became a crucial figure in the history of Jewish prophecy and you will recall that he ascended directly to heaven in a chariot of fire.

John the Baptist was regarded as an Elijah figure. His dress echoed Elijah and he is presented as the last of the prophets; the forerunner to Jesus, a fulfilment of the prophecy of Isaiah.

Early Christians read back into the Old Testament prophecies that they thought connected with their times. Some scholars consider that they manipulated accounts in the

Gospels to achieve this, what one might call, creative writing. Be that as it may our task is to uncover meaning for today.

John the Baptist is best seen as a prophet who was fearless and who attempted to call the Jews back to a spiritual way of life. He lived in a time of political and spiritual ferment. On the one hand the priestly caste was corrupt, in league with the Romans and suspicious of radical messages with a deep moral challenge. On the other hand, there was a call to a life of greater justice and equality biased towards the poor and disadvantaged. John built up quite a following with his simple message of repentance and the following of a committed moral life imbued with a sense of justice and equality.

We are told he was a forerunner of Jesus, and in the Gospels, he is firmly presented as an inferior person to Jesus. There are hints that it was not as simple as that. Flavius Josephus, the Jewish historian, writes about John as a real person, a good person. He does not elevate Jesus. Some think Jesus was originally a disciple of John. There is evidence that John's movement continued after his death at the hands of Herod. In I Corinthians there is reference to Apollos. He was an Alexandrian Christian who had only known the baptism of John. He was present at Ephesus and Corinth. The Mandean sect in Southern Iraq is an ancient baptismal group knowing the baptism of John who is revered, but not Jesus who is considered a false prophet. We will never know the full picture, but it seems likely that the Gospels have simplified the relationship between John and Jesus.

John is described as a man sent from God. But he was not the last prophet or man of God as he connects with prophecy down the ages. What was it about John and those who have followed him that stands out as an example for us all?

Courage, the desire to speak out against the current of the day, to speak with a message that is transparently good and fair, but that people are unwilling often to follow. We all have our prophetic heroes. I think of Schweitzer with his 'reverence for life', Gandhi for his struggle for freedom in the Indian subcontinent and the personal heroes who influenced me; Robert Cochrane the leprologist, and Paul Brand the reconstructive surgeon at the Christian Medical College Vellore, South India, who prophesied with their skills and exposed the injustices of our world. But today we cannot ignore the voice of Nelson Mandela, fondly known as Mandiba. His death is a profound loss, but his example and his prophetic dream live on as did the dream of Martin Luther King.

Nelson Mandela may not have been a Church member. I neither know nor care, although we know he was a great friend of Desmond Tutu. It does not matter. He was a 'man sent from God'. His battle against racism and injustice inspired the world. Despite twenty-seven years in prison under a brutal and racist regime he was able to transcend hatred and become the focus for forgiveness, reconciliation and justice that has enabled a deeply troubled nation to establish democracy and the beginning of a more equitable future.

But in this world the prophet's job is never done. Every prophet is in one sense a forerunner of one to come. The task of coming near to what we Christians call the Kingdom of God never ceases. There remains much to do in South Africa.

We may think that Mandalas and John the Baptists are rare. They have a major impact on others. They inspire us. But partially hidden from the global view are our local prophets. Women and men who speak to us throughout our lives and challenge us to look at ourselves and change. We must have our ears, minds and hearts opened always to the voice of the true prophet; 'the person from God'.

I have said enough. Here are two quotes from Nelson Mandela — 'a man sent from God'.

'During my lifetime I have dedicated myself to this struggle of the African people. I have fought against white domination, and I have fought against black domination. I have cherished the ideal of a democratic and free society in which all persons live together in harmony with equal opportunities. It is an ideal which I hope to live for and to see realised. But if needs be, it is an ideal for which I am prepared to die.'

'No one is born hating another person because of the colour of his skin, or his background, or his religion. People must learn to hate, and if they can learn to hate, they can be taught to love, for love comes more naturally to the human heart than its opposite.'

Mary the Revolutionary

Micah 5.2–5a Luke 1.39–55
"For the Mighty one has done Great things for me and Holy is his name."
Luke 1.49.

Are we grateful enough and what are we grateful about? Are we, in the twenty-first century, so surrounded by technology and affluence that we lose sight of what really matters? As I understand it Mary is giving thanks for her pregnancy and its special nature. The Magnificat is a song, like the praise of Hannah in 1 Samuel. This ancient hymn of praise is a response to Elizabeth who praises Mary's faith. But the Magnificat is more than that. The word many have used to describe it is *'Revolutionary*'. It turns the world upside down.

I suppose most of us have had experiences of profound gratefulness, but if you are like me, they are not often enough. I think, for me, I feel most grateful when I am on the mend from some health problem, even if it is not full recovery. We need to feel grateful about the basics.

At Christmas we should feel grateful that we have food, shelter and family. Many do not have these gifts. Yet even amidst pretty awful conditions I have been amazed at the ability of people to be grateful for very little. They have not been spoilt by material things; things that are not evil in their own right, but which we turn into musts and needs.

I remember years ago I was in the Kulu valley in North India. This was before there were many tourists there. It is very beautiful; but in winter, snowy and very cold. My friend and I stayed in a small guest house. We sat around a tiny stove. We had to remain completely wrapped up and my Kulu socks were a godsend. Our food was lentils and rice. There was no possibility of undressing for bed. I had come to visit the mission hospital that my wife and I had had an interest in for many years. It was really the fulfilment of a dream.

On the visit we met Nepali road workers with terrible frostbite due to inadequate clothing. Despite the primitive conditions there was an air of peace and calm and love. Afterwards we went to a tiny Kulu house on stilts and drank tea round a small kerosene pan heater with a local Kulu woman and her husband, the manager of the hospital, formally a Muslim from Mumbai; now a Christian convert living in these remote hills. Existence was basic, but there was a sense of gratefulness amidst the joy of Christmas. I went away feeling quite miserable. What had I lost?

Read the Magnificat, the revolutionary song that leads into Christmas and a new way of looking at things. God has looked with favour on the lowly, not the proud and the rich. Mary herself was probably poor. 'He has looked in favour on the lowliness of his servant. He has scattered the proud in the imagination of their hearts.' We are so familiar with the beauty and poetry of the song we take little notice of the meaning. Here we have the agenda for Jesus' mission. 'He has filled the hungry with good things and the rich he hath sent empty away.'

I had lost the revolutionary meaning of the message. How easily we do lose it. 'He has brought down the mighty from their thrones and exalted the humble and meek.'

Year by year we tend to ignore that message. The message of what this special birth means. That is what we need to be grateful for. The path or way has been pointed out to us. It is a way of service rather than acquisition. Remember Mary and her revolutionary Magnificat.

Christmas

The season of Christmas brings many people to church who do not normally attend. Sermons at the midnight mass and Christmas day need to be relatively short but contain some material for reflection.

There are dangers of over sentiment at Christmas, and although the birth stories stir the imagination, they require interpretation to connect with the knowledge and thought of the twenty-first century. There is a reluctance nowadays to accept the value of myth; a story that has profound meaning that goes beyond the rational and is more akin to poetry. It is sad that some of those who continue to accept the literal truth of these accounts feel unable to acknowledge the alternative creative understanding of these stories. For example, the birth of Jesus in Bethlehem, connects the accounts with Old Testament predictions and carries poetic resonance. Whether Jesus was born, as a fact, in Bethlehem, is another matter. Some scholars consider that he was born in Galilee as there is good evidence that Jesus was a Galilean and the historical detail in the Lukan version is not factual, as there was no census at that time and therefore no need for a journey to register for the census. It does not matter where Jesus was born. It takes nothing away from his ministry. Most of us connect him with that mysterious figure on the shores of Galilee summoning people to follow him in seeking and proclaiming the Kingdom of God.

Birth stories aside, Christmas emphasises the concept of incarnation, the coming of God into the world in the form of a human being. This can be understood in many ways and our understanding depends on whether we take an exclusivist view of the Christian religion. For those of us who cannot, and understand Christianity as one attempt among others to provide an account of the meaning of existence, incarnation is one way of saying that the 'One', God, is present in all creation and always has been. Everything is an emanation from God. The Christian focus on Jesus as the expression of this is helpful to many. He is an example of a 'spirit filled person', expressing the fullness of God; a metaphor, but not an exclusive one. Other incarnations fulfil a similar role; for example, Krishna. We all have the potential to be spirit filled.

Incarnation is about God's involvement in the world. Human language is totally inadequate to express this and every attempt to do this 'fails', however enshrined in orthodoxy any particular attempt may be. Jesus is a metaphor, based in history, taken and imagined as God on this Earth. His existence as a cosmic figure coequal with God the Father helps some people to recognise this event as God 'with us', equally one can say God 'in us'; Jesus being an exemplar of what we can be. Rather than emphasise the 'sinless' nature of Jesus we can point to his awareness of God and closeness to God, allowing us to imagine the possibility of following in his footsteps.

Because Christmas is rich in potential meaning, one has to try and speak about it in more than one way. Hence the Christmas selection contains more than one attempt to do this. There are several Sundays following Christmas, followed by the season of Epiphany.

Journey of Discovery

1saiah 52.7–10 John.1–14

"In the beginning was the Word, and the Word was with God, and the Word was God."

John 1.1.

Whether we know it or not we have come here tonight on some kind of journey. We may have some idea how we got here or why we are here. We may not. We could be here by chance.

What we can be certain about is that since we were last here on Christmas eve, or since we last experienced a Christmas, the year has gone around again; we have had another year of possibility, of experience. Some of us have had a lot of years as time goes around and around, bringing us back to the end but also to the beginning.

I know Christmas has many attachments, but if we do seek some form of spiritual enlightenment, we have to ask ourselves whether we have come to any conclusions about the birth of Jesus and what impact that birth has had on us.

I used those words 'beginning and ending' because they remind me of the first and last sentences of the TS Eliot poem, *East Coker*. Eliot's family left for America several hundred years ago, but he came back to Britain, became a citizen and in the end was buried in the wall of the church his family attended several hundred years earlier in East Coker. He came full cycle. But Eliot's poetry is not just about the physical or historical elements of beginning and ending but about the spiritual journey one makes. For the end of one journey always heralds the beginning of another. So, each year end in the Christian calendar, we look back at what has happened on our spiritual journey and start off again.

As we come tonight to meet the infant Jesus at his beginning yet again, we may ask ourselves whether we have seen beyond the surface to engage with the significance of his life and join him on his journey.

I want you to hold in your mind's eye for a minute or two the idea of beginning and ending and the old life and the new. Because what one seeks as a follower of Jesus is new life. Life lived at a level beyond the superficial trappings that increasingly identify Christmas. If one reaches that point one is at a new beginning. There is no finer Christmas poem than the *Coming of the Magi* by Eliot, and although we have not reached Epiphany, I want to tell you about it. It is too long to quote but I suggest you read it.

Using the story of the Wise Men, Eliot describes his own personal, spiritual journey. The poem uses the images that might be associated with Middle Eastern sages or astrologers, but underneath is Eliot's own story that culminated in his joining the Church of England in 1927.

The journey was initially hard. It took time and there were obstacles on the way. It would have been easy to give up and return without completing it. Then life became easier; they arrived at an inn and the weather improved. We read of allusions to the crucifixion (three trees against the sky), and other references to the Roman soldiers dicing, and the betrayal of Judas. They see a white horse; a potent Christian symbol in this context. There are vine leaves over the inn door that symbolise Jesus the true vine, the Exodus 'passing over' with blood. Then there is the arrival and that odd word 'satisfactory' describes their eventual journey end. It is a very important word but what does it mean? Let us see.

The story, told by one of the magi, is looking back on something that happened a long time ago. He arrived, but it was not the end. He would do it again but it was hard, very hard. He had to virtually die to find this new birth. This was no casual trip. The magus returned, as Eliot did to his previous life. But it was never the same again. He felt out of place in the world he inhabited. He longed for another death. What did he mean?

He used the word 'satisfactory' because his journey had reached the point of meeting Jesus. It had cost him a lot. But he had not yet discovered joy. That for him required another journey. There is a reference to St John of the Cross here and what is called the 'dark night of the soul'.

And so, it is with us, whatever our experiences of God. We never finally meet the end, but we discover new things with each journey. We are back to the beginning. This year may have been very hard for us, like a death, but now we have come to the stable anew. We too, can find new birth and start our journey towards God afresh.

God with Us

Isaiah 52.7–10 John1.1–14

"And the Word became flesh and lived among us, and we have seen his glory, the glory as of a father's only son, full of grace and truth."

John 1.14.

Christianity can be understood at many levels and this applies particularly to the great doctrines of the worldwide Church established many centuries ago. The birth of Jesus, sometimes called the Incarnation is one of these. In Mathew and Luke, we have pastoral stories, illuminating to many if we do not over sentimentalise them. In the prologue to John's Gospel, possibly written separately from the Gospel itself, we have an early attempt to turn the Christian story into what we would now call theology. Reflection on the events of Jesus' life produced a more abstract account of the meaning of the birth and life of Jesus.

Judaism is a down to earth religion. Jewish thinking of the time would not have produced this kind of reflection. It is the influence of Greek philosophy, particularly that of Plato, that has fashioned this passage.

You will be relieved to know that it is far too late for me to explain what I mean and so I have chosen those few words of the 'text' because they connect with the birth stories that we are familiar with. 'lived among us.' 'lives among us.' Note that

I have turned the past tense into the present. We cannot just be here to celebrate a past event.

And so, we cannot avoid asking the question: Why do we bother to celebrate the birth of Jesus? The stories about his birth are 'magical'. They may make us feel empathy for the harshness of his surroundings where he was born, rather unlike the modern maternity ward; but we need more than that to keep on remembering the birth of this child. There have been many other difficult births.

One may argue that he grew up to become a famous prophet whose followers founded one of the world's great religions. Through the political power of the Roman Empire, Christianity has grown into a world faith. We do remember the births of famous people. All that is history, but that is not enough.

God with us. What does this mean? Because that is at the core of Incarnation. It is why we are here. God with us now, dwelling among us.

Everything must start with God. You either believe there is a God or if you prefer, the terms 'the ground of all being', 'the source of everything', or the many other words used for God. At the end of the day the word God is a shorthand for the fount of all existence.

If we accept that there is a God, we ask ourselves: Is this God remote and unknowable, way above the ways of women and men? If God is, we have a problem because he appears to be disconnected from creation. And so, we move to the word incarnation. Christianity considers that God was uniquely present in Jesus. But for many Christians this is not enough. The birth of Jesus, so long ago, is a positive symbol of God's presence in the world as a whole. But this presence has been there for all time. It has been there from the beginning of the

Cosmos; long before humans and animals emerged from the creative process. Jesus has focused this presence.

It may surprise us to realise that God is present in everything; for if God is creator, creation is an emanation, an outflowing from God. God is part of everything and beyond us also. We are all part of the divine process.

So, what we call Incarnation, God embedded in the world, God dwelling among us, must never just refer to the historical person of Jesus; although for Christians Jesus is unique. God is present in everything, and as the Bible suggests we are created in God's image. The prologue of John's Gospel states clearly that we too can become sons and daughters of God.

We can then celebrate this birth of the person called Jesus because it symbolises that God is with us in everything, including our suffering and our joys, our terror and our love; now, today, in a world so different to the times of the birth of Jesus. Jesus suffered as we do yet God was in him. We call him Son of God, Son of Man, Emanuel, God with us

We often think of God as omnipotent, all powerful, although perhaps unsure of what this really means. We then, understandably, question how this omnipotent God can tolerate all that is wrong in this ambiguous world of ours. The answer is that we have imposed our idea of omnipotence, as we do with other attributes, on to God. It is far better to know that God, in the world, shares our vulnerability. That God hopes that creation, in some way set free, will come to be what is intended, rather than be overcome by destructive forces.

This birth that we celebrate tonight is mysterious. It is right that it fills us with awe. For us, it can be a symbol of God's engagement with us, and a picture of what human life can be.

Going to Bethlehem

Isaiah 62.6–12 Luke 2.8–20

"Let us go now to Bethlehem and see this thing that has taken place, which the Lord has made known to us."

Luke 2.15.

Let's do this or that. The words suggest enthusiasm, get up and go. I was reading Dylan Thomas's magical prose piece *A Child's Christmas in Wales* this week. One or two of the ideas in that are certainly full of verve, even if a little misplaced!

'Let's post snowballs through Mr Daniel's letter box. Let's write in the snow, Mr Daniel looks like a spaniel.'

'Let's go to Bethlehem and see this new baby.' Of course, we could get on a plane and go there now, but I am not thinking literally. Certainly, the shepherds went, we are told, and they went not just out of curiosity.

Birth is a beginning. We rejoice in birth, in new things. Some of you may have had births in your family this year. This will have filled you with joy and enthusiasm. It is unlikely that you will grow tired of this new life and all that it means. You will be part of it down the months and years.

But it is very easy to lose enthusiasm, that freshness that we experience when anything new and exciting breaks into our lives. We are worn down by the terrors and hostility we see in the world today. We are saddened by all the bad things that happen to us. We easily become cynical about trying. 'What's the point of it?' we might say.

‘Let’s go to Bethlehem.’ ‘Not now, I’m tired, it’s too late, it’s too far,’ and so on.

Going to Bethlehem is a metaphor for seeking God. Perhaps we are tired of God and God talk. It’s kind of intrusive and gets in the way of what we want to do. There is a serious possibility that looking for God could change things. Those shepherds dropped everything; they even seem to have left their sheep, but do we want to do that?

Each time we come to Christmas we can renew our pledge to seek God, to get up and go and find him. Of course, we don’t necessarily have to get up and move at all, but we make the mental assent to finding God in ourselves, in others and in the world.

When we greet a new life coming into the world, we are very happy. Yet we know at the same time, that if we are truly committed to our new son or daughter, grandson, granddaughter, nephew or niece, we will have to be with them through all the vicissitudes of life.

So, it is when we ‘go to Bethlehem’. It is not just a day trip, a nice outing with no follow up. If we really do go with enthusiasm, we are called to follow up our encounter, to embark on a journey following the Christ child into his adult life and his ministry and mission. Our lives will need to be mixed with his. We will not return to things as they were.

Our religious festivals are part of the seasons in the northern hemisphere. In the dark of winter, when there is a longing for light that illuminates, warms and makes the earth come alive, there is the breaking through of the possibility of spiritual illumination; the possibility of a new beginning for us all following the path of the one who is God with us.

‘Let us now go unto Bethlehem and see this thing that has taken place.’

The Man Jesus

Hebrews 2.10–18 Matthew 2.10–23
"He had to be made like his brothers in every respect."
Hebrew 2.17.

The mystery of the Incarnation is with us always. The quotation from Hebrews states that Jesus was like us in every way. If we take that at face value, it means that he was an ordinary man who became extraordinary. His legacy is undisputable evidence of that.

In the New Testament we have layers or pictures of Jesus that are different. They represent a developing view of his nature. The new Christian community struggled to describe the importance of Jesus in words. We would use different words and different thought forms today and sometimes the pictures we have of Jesus do not appear to add up. That is not surprising when we try to distil into words experiences that are not really capable of such reductions. We cannot reduce to ordinary descriptive or propositional language experiences that are emotional or mystical and thus beyond words. And that means that when reading the Bible, we have to accept that what we read is some kind of proxy for experience and may even represent an attempt by the writer to embellish, in order to give weight to particular opinions.

In the first chapter of John's Gospel that we listen to each year, we hear the words, 'In the beginning was the Word.' In this book written around 90-100 CE at the end of the post Jesus second generation (a generation is counted as forty years), we are told that Jesus is the pre–existent Word or Logos and we can substitute the word Logos with Sophia or Wisdom. Jesus is equated with the Creator; all things stem from him.

John does not need to discuss what Jesus was or became because he was there in eternity. He had no need for accounts of shepherds and wise men. The Jesus that walks and talks through John's Gospel appears to speak in a totally different way to the figure in the other Gospels. We may wonder if this is the same person. The layer we have in John is later and in a different thought form.

This picture of the Incarnation makes one wonder how the quotation from Hebrews could be true. How could someone from eternity be the man Jesus?

It is, of course, logically possible for a god to give up powers and live in human form; one of the epistles speaks of God emptying himself and being born in the form of a man.

One of the central issues in thinking about Jesus is the amount of self-knowledge of his importance and mission he really had. We may warm to the picture presented by John, or we may consider that Jesus became Son of God, Son of Man, the Christ, because of his life on Earth, rather than being a pre-existent figure.

Whatever we believe about Jesus I do think it is important to hold on to those words in Hebrews. Jesus has little connection with us as a brother unless he lived just like us, and many would want to say, was born just like us. That is the essence of true incarnation.

In our collect today, we are reminded of these words: 'As

he came to share in our humanity, so we may share in the life of his divinity.' Paul, in Galatians 3.26, writes: 'For in Christ Jesus you are all children of God through faith.'

This means that through following Jesus in our lives and relationships with each other and with God, we have the potential to become like him and share in the life of his divinity.

Although some parts of the New Testament may be reluctant to express this, we all have the divine spark within us. That is why we are worth saving. There are many creative ways of looking at Jesus, but one is that made like us, he showed the way and achieved special status. Our goal is to follow him on the same path, reassured that he was made like us in every way.

The Point of It

Galatians 4.4–7 Matthew 2.13–23
"'I don't see the point of it,' said Micky through
much imbecile laughter.
'Don't you?' said Harold with curious distinctness. 'Well you
will someday.'"
E.M. Forster: *The Point of It*.

For once I start with a quotation from English literature rather than the Bible.

These words from the famous short story by E.M. Forster have haunted me for many years. Harold is rowing a boat against a strong outgoing current threatening to take them out to sea. He is a recovering invalid. Michael is in the boat. He thinks the boat will win. Harold gives his all and as he utters the words, 'You will someday', he collapses dead in the boat. Michael lives on. He is respectable and quite successful. He is very reasonable and sees all points of view. But he lacks passion and purpose. He dies and finds himself in his own hell of shapeless sand and nothingness. Eventually he emerges on the other side because he learns that through his own efforts he can return to that ebbing river and reach the other side, to the light and warmth of the farmhouse he and Harold had struggled to reach. He discovers, eventually, that there must be a point and a purpose. Micky's enigmatic remark became relevant.

We are nearing the end of the Christmas story. Next Sunday at family service we will celebrate Epiphany, but today's Gospel is after the wise men have visited and describes the return from Egypt and settling in Galilee.

What is the point of this story of birth we hear about each year? We read similar lections each year, pass through the same rituals and begin another year of living. The Archbishop of Canterbury has reminded us that it really does not matter whether we see the stories as legend or literal history. In each case we must go beyond or beneath the account and use our imaginations if we are going to see any point at all. If it is just a 'fair fancy', let's forget it all. There are far better ways to spend our time.

Of course, when we celebrate the birth of Jesus, we are in the position of knowing something of what this led to. We can look back on our limited knowledge of his life recorded by Bible writers and a few other people. Many of these people decided he was special and found ways of expressing this, including founding a religion he did not start himself, but which has spread across the world.

Jesus was a religious man with a passion for bringing a new spirituality to Israel. He spoke of a kingdom that he believed was nigh and that would be dwelt in with God reigning. He was very urgent about this. He gave his all. Some people thought he had military or political aspirations, but they were mistaken. Jesus wanted his world to be transformed in the days he lived in. Like any person he was a man of his time. He may have believed, and certainly his follower Paul thought, that the end of the world would be soon; but we must carry on because they were wrong about that. We must remember that in first century Judaism there was a great deal of apocalyptic fervour about the coming culmination of all things.

I suggest that each time, in our age, when we celebrate this birth, we join Jesus in a new beginning. It is quite appropriate that Christmas comes at the end of the old year with the prospect of something new around the corner.

The point of Jesus' life is not just his death or indeed his resurrection. Paul may have made us think like this for he showed virtually no direct interest in the earthly life of Jesus, although there may be implicit references in his letters. However, the synoptic Gospels of Matthew, Mark and Luke show us something explicit in that earthly life.

It is the quality of that life that should inspire us. We cannot say it was a long life. He probably died when he was just over thirty. The short span of ministry that we know about, barely more than one year, was intense, full of courage and single mindedness. He made a difference to our world in an incredibly short space of time.

I think whatever our age we are continually called urgently to follow him and work out how we can help to make his Kingdom of God real. We must not wait for some future Nirvana or Heaven. Each year we have a chance to review our lives and do something about how we live.

No one can tell us what this means for us. We each have to examine our own lives. It certainly means usually going beyond our comfort zones. We cannot live by agreeing with everyone about everything. Living like Jesus does mean standing out from the crowd and taking risks.

This week Benazir Bhutto was killed tragically by a suicide bomber. You may not agree with her about all things, but she was a woman of enormous courage who longed for a democratic Pakistan and was not afraid to be controversial. She probably made many mistakes, but she was driven by the values she espoused.

She was famous. We are not. That is not the point. Each of us has to discover the point that drives us on, that animates our vision of the world and our place in it.

Perhaps restlessness and striving do not appeal to you, but we have to accept that Jesus was a driven man; he was restless to bring in the Kingdom of God. He did not give up. How do we use what energies we have?

Christianity can be very passive. If it has a point, we need to be re-energised by the birth we celebrate each year, as we have the opportunity for a new beginning again.

Epiphany

The Epiphany season varies in length and content between denominations. In some branches of the Church, Epiphany extends to the eve before Ash Wednesday. The core events are: the coming of the Magi; the Presentation of Jesus in the Temple; the baptism of Jesus; and the 'calling' of the disciples. The sermons I have chosen relate directly or indirectly with the idea of an epiphany, as well as the baptism of Jesus and his Presentation in the Jerusalem temple. I have included the Transfiguration. It is placed in Epiphany in those denominations that regard Epiphany as extending to Ash Wednesday. Otherwise it is in Ordinary Time in the Sunday next before Lent.

The word epiphany means a disclosure, dawning or a revelation. In the context of this period in the Christian calendar, the journey of the Magi symbolises the dawning that the birth and life of Jesus is for all people. Yet, at the same time, we must acknowledge that this disclosure, fundamental for Christians, must never be allowed to negate the disclosure of the experience of God through other figures in other faiths.

An epiphany is not necessarily sudden. The dawning may come over months or years. My own realisation that my conservative upbringing was not the understanding of Christianity that suited my temperament and knowledge base came over many years and was precipitated by my experience in India. I was fortunate enough to have tutorials from people who had an undogmatic understanding of their faith, but remained committed to the Christian way within the culture they inhabited.

I think we have to view the baptism of Jesus through the medium of experience. The Gospel writers presented their story many years after the event and they were influenced by attempts to explain the significance of Jesus. If one starts with the premise that Jesus was a man, albeit a spirit-filled person, but without pre-knowledge, his baptism remains a significant moment at the commencement of his ministry. The Gospel of Mark records the event as follows: 'In those days Jesus came from Nazareth of Galilee and was baptised by John in the Jordan. And just as he was coming up out of the water, he saw the heavens torn apart and the Spirit descending like a dove on him. And a voice came from heaven, "You are my Son, the Beloved with you I am well pleased."' On the surface this appears to be a mystical personal experience. Either this was communicated by Jesus to others, was heard by all or was placed in the Gospel by the writer of Mark as a hallmark of the importance of this event. Whatever the truth of this the baptism marks the commencement of Jesus' ministry. It does not mean necessarily that Jesus was a pre-existent member of the Godhead, but the account attempts to signify the adoption of Jesus by God because of his spirit-filled life. I have found in rural ministry that committed Christians who experience Jesus as 'Lord' are not unduly concerned about the later doctrinal elaboration. There is often a gulf between the faith of the person in the pew in traditional rural communities and the over educated cleric in the pulpit!

A New Dawn

Isaiah 60. 1–6 Matthew 2.1–12
"For darkness shall cover the earth, and thick darkness the peoples; but the Lord will arise upon you, and his glory will appear over you."
Isaiah 60.2.

Epiphany is a moment or period of great revelation or realisation. In the context of the Gospel reading, it is represented by the revelation of Jesus to the Gentiles exemplified by the Magi. More personally, it is a time or period when you feel that you understand or suddenly become conscious of, something that is very important to you. It is not about belief, but experience. I have used the more general poetic statement from Isaiah because it emphasises the sense of mystery, of dreamlike quality that this story represents. There is a timelessness about the dawning of new light, but likewise darkness, and we have ended a dark year. What hope do we have? What realisation will come to us? That may sound morose, but we need to be honest about the state of this world. Misplaced optimism is as bad as pessimism.

As I think most of you realise, I am not a person for neat solutions, doctrinal certainty. How can one be in this age of science and global cultural awareness? I remain a Christian because I consider that the broad framework of Christianity, developed within our cultural history, is part of us and challenges us to lead lives that are free from selfishness and that recognise the importance of service, and the dignity and value of all aspects of creation. I am not over concerned about my personal salvation and immortality. We humans are part of the world. We live in the world. We are intimately connected with all other life. Sometimes one hears the phrase that we are created 'in the image of God', assuming that we are special and somehow distinct from the rest of life on Earth. But if there is a creator at the root of the Cosmos, that 'Spirit' is the source of everything, not just us. If God is all, his image is in everything. That is why when we seek light at the commencement of this year, we must consider all aspects of earthly existence, not just the human element.

One of my grandsons, studying theoretical physics at university, gave me a Christmas present of several brief lessons in physics by Carlo Rovelli, a noted writer on the subject. At the conclusion of his book, Rovelli remarks that he does not think that the Homo sapiens species will be long lived. All our Hominid cousins are extinct and we possess the ability to destroy our environment and this world. Without agreeing necessarily with him, as we enter this new year, we might list some of the issues that beset us. These include our treatment of the environment and other life forms in the illusory search for progress; the adverse effects of religious intolerance and exclusivism on peaceful coexistence, exemplified by terrorism throughout the world and even attempted genocide; the gross inequality that exists within most societies. There is a rise of separatism within nations and between nations, rather than a coming together, and pollution overwhelms us.

We do live in an age of darkness and seem to have lost our way. At moments of insight we long for a saviour, a guide, someone to enlighten us as to how we should live in this world. We know so much more than those who lived in the days of Isaiah and the early followers of Jesus, but we lack wisdom. We seek instant gratification and avoid the 'long haul'. It seems a black picture.

Yet surely there is some light. We see moments of light in acts of love and caring and self-giving. There we see the possibility of change. The light is always there but hidden by our stupidity. Jesus came to guide people into new ways of living. In his Sermon on the Mount recorded in Mathew's Gospel 5.14, Jesus said: 'You are the light of the world. A city built on a hill cannot be hidden.' That is surely what has to dawn on us; that must be our epiphany. To be lights, to be enlightened, must start at home however minute we are in this vast Cosmos. In our treatment of God's world in all its many forms we must live with a sense that unless everything around us is treated lovingly and is healthy, we are heading for catastrophe. It sometimes takes a profound shock to bring us to our senses. In Isaiah's day, captivity and transportation to Babylon brought about radical change in the Jewish people. Yet when Jesus came, he still saw his fellow Jews as captives. That is why he told them that he came to fulfil the law, not abolish it. Much that is good in Western society is imbedded there through Christian ideals. Yet these values often lie dormant or overwhelmed by materialism and greed.

There is a well know text from the epistle to the Romans 13.11 that says this: 'Besides this, you know what time it is, how it is now the moment for you to wake from sleep. For salvation is nearer to us now than when we became believers.'

Paul aims this passage at those of us who profess to be Christians. He is telling us to wake up. Wake up before it is too late. That is our Epiphany message. Become a pilgrim again: go metaphorically with those Persian Magi and rediscover the Christ child who first called you to follow him.

Beyond Reason

1 Corinthians 1.10–18 Matthew 4.12–23
"For the message about the Cross is foolishness to those who are perishing, but to us who are being saved it is the power of God. For it is written,
'I will destroy the wisdom of the wise,
and the discernment of the discerning I will thwart.'"
1 Corinthians 1.18–19.

It has been one of those weeks. After sitting hearing the wisdom and opinions of many during the working week in Newcastle, I wonder what wisdom is and certainly would not object to it being destroyed. There are so many wisdoms, so many opinions. One important aspect of Christian worship at the Eucharist is that each Sunday we can bring our week here and lay it on the altar before God. Our weeks differ in content, but collectively we bring our world before God in all its ambiguity and problems, seeking healing, peace and reconciliation. If I had them on me, I would place on the altar the many papers I have had to read, wishing that many of them had never been written!

This statement by Paul in 1 Corinthians raises fundamental issues in relation to faith. Paul had had difficulty while preaching in Athens. He had tried to beat the Greeks at their own game of reason and had found the whole experience frustrating. Paul realised that the leap of faith is not rational. It is based on personal experience as he understood it. The driver to belief in God is experience of the Holy, whatever the context. The German theologian and anthropologist Rudolf Otto drew attention to this. It is not rational but based on much more primitive and basic urges within us.

Today we have read about those early disciples, called by Jesus. He must have been a charismatic teacher. They responded to him at a very basic level without fully understanding what the kingdom he preached was all about. Has the world of science and reason made this leap of faith more difficult? Can we readily ignore the claims that science will explain everything and explain away God?

I have been trained as a medical scientist and done my spell of laboratory research. Over the years of study, I began to learn that there is more to science than reason. There is inspiration and feeling involved. The question began to arise as what was the real scope of reason? Was the human mind able to unlock the mystery in everything? I spent two years studying philosophy at the University of Wales. This eventually led me to realise that the nature of maths, the basis of much science and reason itself, might not be the absolute I supposed. Reason and maths may not be sitting out in the universe explaining everything. We have used the mechanisms of our brains to produce effective means to live successfully in the material sense, in this world. But reason will never tell us ultimate truth. In my view that is beyond human attainment. We do not have the equipment to know what ultimate reality really is.

So, the great decisions of life are not rational. Strangely, after the foundation of the Church, rationalists tried to reduce the religious experience of people into a highly convoluted set of doctrines; the nature of Jesus, the Trinity, the meaning of the Cross and so on. This was bound to fail because of the limits of reason, and we have placed too much emphasis on the words of religious language. They are vehicles, but inadequate ones that attempt to say what cannot be said and we should remember that.

Jesus said some very simple words in Mark 1.17: 'Follow me and I will make you fish for people.' It is a metaphor, but we all know what it means. It was and is a summons, a very radical one. After all, why should those early disciples leave their jobs that provided the basic goods for survival and follow this man? This is the leap of faith, the irrational jump into the unknown. What draws us is not easy to put into words for as I have intimated already, these experiences are beyond words. Somehow, we glimpse the possibility of love, a life beyond the events and ways of living that shackle us. We glimpse something ultimate. We are drawn beyond reason.

The word epiphany means a great realisation or dawning. The scales preventing true vision are parted. The world is seen in a different light. The one who is in all and beyond all is glimpsed; the ideal of humanity is revealed in Jesus.

In the great poem, the Journey of the Magi, surely one of Eliot's finest poems, we find a picture of three Orientals, perhaps Persian kings or wise men, making a journey. They were expecting to find a king in their mould, but on arrival it was very different. They experienced a dawning, a realisation that changed them, encapsulated in the two lines: 'We returned to our places, these kingdoms. But no longer at ease here, in the old dispensation.'

That is what can happen when we encounter Jesus. Everything is changed. Our perspective is altered. We are no longer at ease in the world we once inhabited.

Exploring Sacrifice

1Corinthians 13.1–13 Luke 2.22–40
"And they offered a sacrifice according to what is stated in the law of the Lord, 'a pair of turtle doves or two young pigeons.'"
Luke 2.24.

That may seem a strange way to commence a sermon! Why lift that reference to an obscure and perhaps forgotten Jewish practice? Sacrifice. The word, the concept, has been at the heart of much religion since time immemorial.

Jesus' parents take him to the temple for dedication. They make the prescribed sacrifice. They are firmly within the tradition of Temple Judaism. Why make such a sacrifice? Because it is pleasing to God?

Deep at the core of religious practice has been the idea that God demands sacrifice. Indeed, his wrath can be abated by sacrifice. Sacrifice may influence God's decisions about the weather, disease, crops and so on. All kinds of animals or humans have been sacrificed in the name of God.

The story of the Exodus tells us about how the sacrifice of a sheep or goat and the sprinkling of blood on the door lintel caused God to pass over the Jewish people and save them from destruction. At one level it is a primitive story. At another level it has had a massive influence on Christian thinking and theology. The idea of sacrifice, sacrifice of something pure has influenced us all.

We may no longer believe in a God who needs sacrifice to influence the weather or assure our victory in battle, but the use of the word sacrifice in everyday language is not dead. We speak of sacrificial giving of money or time. We refer to scapegoats being sacrificed to satisfy our awful need to blame someone when things go wrong. Government reports are littered with 'sacrificial lambs'.

The death of Jesus is seen by many as a sacrifice and we continue to argue about what this really means in our modern world. The doctrinal area around this debate is called the Atonement theory.

One popular idea within Christianity is that Jesus' death is a substitutionary sacrifice. He died to save us from our sins. His death has, in some way paid the price of human sinfulness or alienation from God. Several of you here this morning may well think this. But how can this be the case? What kind of God demands this kind of activity? What kind of chemistry is at work to make this real? Is it healthy to consider that we are liberated through the activity of one person? We may well consider that the sacrifice of many young men and women in battle has been an important factor in keeping this country free from tyranny; yet at the same time we may mourn the wastage of life, when the cause they die for is less clear, and the motives for sending them to war, dubious.

It is easy to see the theological coherence with Jewish theology in the sacrifice of Jesus. Jesus is the final sacrifice. God requires no more appeasement. Jesus' death takes away the sin of the world. Does it? If only it was as easy as that.

One can look at the sacrificial death of Jesus in several

ways. His death was a result of his being true to the values or mission he followed. He would not compromise. Therefore, in his life and the way he died, he is an example to us all. We are challenged to follow him, and that kind of life may be connected with the idea of sacrifice.

Jesus is seen as the victor over sin and death. He has shown us that in following our father God and walking in his way, the Way of the Cross, we may overcome sin. In one sense this is a life of sacrifice because we do not follow the path that necessarily pleases our egos. On the other hand, it is not sacrifice if we walk with God, for God's will becomes our will. We want and like to follow God in Jesus. That is the ideal. Of course, it is naïve to think that is easy. That is why Christianity contains the doctrine of grace so beloved of Paul.

Palestine in the days of Jesus was seething with sects and political turmoil. It is probable that Jesus and his followers were one of many groups causing the Roman authorities concern. Even Jesus' group contained at least one Zealot, a violent military group. Judas Iscariot may have been a member of the Sicarii, a group of secret assassins who stabbed people in the crowds in Jerusalem and then silently faded away. It is not surprising that the Romans thought Jesus might be leader of a very dangerous group and executed him. The Gospels have tended to present the death of Jesus as the work of Jews. In this way they made the emerging Christianity more agreeable to the Roman Empire. The reality is that Jesus was executed by the Romans, but his death was still a sacrifice for him.

What can we make of sacrifice in our world today? Should we value it? It is a rich subject to think about. It is obvious there are a lot of awful sacrifices. Do we admire the suicide bomber who gives up his own life for Islam or any other cause? That person may be deluded, thinking that God will welcome him to paradise and many virgins will meet him. We do not want sacrifice like that. Is martyrdom ever a good thing? It is fashionable to praise it if it meets our cultural image. The suicide bomber is a martyr for God or an evil deluded man, according to your view.

Some images of the Atonement have influenced much Christian behaviour. Martyrdom in early Christianity was fuelled by the death of Jesus although Gnostic Christians condemned it. We are wiser to look at more prosaic examples. The mother who willingly gives up much of her personal ambitions to bring up children; in one sense this is a sacrifice. But sacrifice is in the eye of the beholder. The daughter who cares for elderly parents, the overseas worker who is motivated to work with needy people. We can all provide examples.

We can call this behaviour altruistic and there is a link between the idea of sacrifice and our understanding of altruism. Perhaps you follow the theory that we are hard wired to be altruistic or selfish, willing to abandon an egotistical life or not. Recent publicity has suggested that the posterior temporal sulcus is the seat of altruism, of the sacrificial life. It is unlikely. It is better to assume that we all have the capacity to serve, to follow the example of Jesus in serving others. There is little more certain in this life than that the person who follows the path of greed and selfishness will end up unfulfilled. The choice, as always, is ours.

We have moved far from the turtle dove and two small pigeons. Let your mind take off when you read the bible. Let it float free.

Light of the world

Hebrews 2.14-18 Luke 2.22-40

"Master, now you are dismissing your servant in peace,
according to your word; for my eyes have seen your
salvation, which you have prepared in the presence of all
peoples, a light for revelation to the Gentiles
and for glory to your people Israel."
Luke 2.29-32.

To be a light. The prophetic last words of Simeon. The much loved Nunc Dimitis has been chanted or sung over the centuries by untold numbers of people; worshipping in this church and elsewhere. To be 'a light to lighten the Gentiles' connects us with Candlemass, a festival of light that symbolically underlines the theme of Epiphany, enlightenment or illumination of the heart and mind.

In our cultural history this festival has been aligned with many hopes, expectations and fears down the centuries, some of them predating Christianity. Candlemass marks the halfway point between the Winter and Easter solstices. It was a time when some predicted that future weather would be determined by todays weather. 'If Candlemas Day be fair and bright Winter will have another fight. If Candlemas Day brings cloud and rain Winter won't come again.' Look outside and predict the weather for the rest of Winter!

More importantly, Candlemass tradition marks the blessing of candles. We can think of those on the altar here. Lit on most occasions when we come to worship. We light a candle over there in the corner when we offer prayers for others or ask prayers for ourselves. The candle is a deep seated symbol for us. It has been used to ward off evil spirits; we give a candle to those baptised; we fall back on the candle when we have a 'blackout'. You may think all these little customs are trivial, but they are not. The candle has become a metaphor for many things.

Luke is the only Gospel writer who relates this story. Regardless of its historicity, the theme of light, enlightenment, is focussed on the words of Simeon, who spoke filled with the Holy Spirit. Luke is unique in his many references to the Spirit. In this passage it is the vehicle that guides into truth, an emphasis made elsewhere in the Bible in other ways.

The Presentation of Jesus in the temple is part of Jewish custom. It is not specifically Christian. It is important to take on board that Mary was a Jew. Jesus was a Jew. The subsequent religion of Christianity, however, is bound up in this prayer of thanksgiving of Simeon's: 'To be a light to lighten the Gentiles and to be the glory of thy people Israel.' Jesus *is* a figure of universal significance. Christianity spread from Judaism, through detaching the story of Jesus from much Jewish ritual and culture, thus enabling it to spread beyond the boundaries of Israel to the non-Jewish, Gentile world. Simeon, predicting this, is held up as the spirit-filled holy sage who was enlightened to 'see' beyond his own culture. But we must never, never, abandon the Jewish source of Christianity. Paul had a struggle with this. There are accounts of genuine dialogue at that famous Council of Jerusalem, between Paul, representing Gentile Christianity, and James and Peter representing Jewish Christianity; that is very different from Paul's polemic against Jewish Christianity in the epistle to the Galatians, but he is more accommodating again in the epistle to the Romans.

Returning to the presentation of Jesus, I was brought up as a Baptist and many aspects of the liberal Baptist tradition remain in my blood. One of them is the presentation of a child in church known as 'Dedication', not baptism. The child is offered to God, as Jesus was by Mary, and Samuel by Hannah. The Baptist custom stems from this story and that of Samuel.

Regardless of the difference in emphasis in many of the Christian denominations, we can see how important Candlemass is with its many allusions and traditions. The humble candle signifies how important the metaphor of light is in Christianity.

Mary's need for purification seems alien to us. It no longer connects with our understanding of women and their role in society. Perhaps there remain elements of this ancient male prejudice. The tradition that men did not require purification, and women did, may lie in the subconscious of some males, and lead to the attitudes we sometimes find in those unable to accept the ordination of women. Lack of inclusiveness leads to evil and the dimming of that light that we celebrate today. Antisemitism, focused in the annual remembrance of the Holocaust, is an extreme example, but lesser acts of diminished inclusiveness, exemplified in an ignorant misunderstanding of the complexities of human sexuality, continue to undermine the ministry of the Church, including our own Church of England.

Candlemass must be about seeking a level of illumination as to how we should live in the 21st century if we want to make Christianity connect with the many who no longer feel they can attend Church. Enlightenment must occur in each generation. It is not frozen in time. We can no longer accept some of the moral positions expressed in the Bible. We must not parrot expressions of love divorced from genuine pastoral commitment and inclusiveness.

I just want to quote a few words from the Bloomsbury Central Baptist Church mission statement. They express what my personal view of what Christianity should be, and I want to say it to you as I contemplate retiring yet again!

'We are progressive in our theology, reverent in our style of worship, and active when it comes to social justice. Those who find their home here believe there is no one 'right' way, but rather we search together for a deeper understanding of Jesus, and what it means for us to follow him. We aspire to be inclusive and accessible.'

One thing we may agree on is that Jesus is a light in our world, so often full of darkness.

A Beginning

Isaiah 43.1–7 Luke 3.21–22

"Now when all the people were baptised, and when Jesus also had been baptised and was praying, the heaven was opened, and the Holy Spirit descended upon him in bodily form like a dove. And a voice came from heaven, 'You are my Son, the Beloved with you I am well pleased.'"
Luke 3.21-22.

The baptism of Jesus is something we can state probably happened. One may want to ask why he was baptised. It rather depends how you see Jesus prior to his baptism. Is it reasonable in any quest for a picture of the historical Jesus to ask these questions, or does our piety prevent it? Are we even afraid of asking?

We know little reliable information about Jesus prior to his baptism and the start of his ministry. Mark and John do not mention his birth and neither does Paul. So, we must be careful in concluding too much from the birth stories. None of these writers thought an account of Jesus' birth was relevant to a presentation of the gospel.

There are some very curious, even amusing, extra-canonical gospels that portray the young Jesus as a rather objectionable, miracle-working child. These writers obviously thought they needed to fill in the gaps and make Jesus special in view of his adult life. We can safely disregard them.

I think the most reasonable way to look at him is that Jesus was a deeply religious young man who had a vocation to lead his people to a new level of spirituality; he wanted to present to them what he called the Kingdom of God, a way of living that went beyond the Jewish law. It fulfilled the law and that wonderful Old Testament image recorded in Deuteronomy and Ezekiel of a 'heart of flesh' rather than a 'heart of stone'.

I see no reason to doubt that Jesus was baptised by John because he was moved by his message and wished to identify himself with the baptism of repentance.

What happened subsequently was something rather special. Here we go beyond ordinary human experience and observation. Luke tells us that God identified Jesus as his son and that he was pleased with him. Somehow, Luke and others are seeking to put into words something that they cannot really express about this start of Jesus' ministry. Looking back, they can see that this baptism signified so much about Jesus. At this point he seems to have been identified as 'special'. Whether Jesus had foreknowledge about his life and work is a matter of dispute. Theology breaks down here; perhaps faith suffices. That, I think depends on what sort of person you are.

For some people the humanity of Jesus is vital. He is not a god dressed up in human clothing. Early theologians struggled to sort this out just as we do. For as soon as we give Jesus special powers, he ceases to be one of us and we become bogged down in a whole variety of complex arguments.

At the beginning of another decade I want to say this. The ministry of Jesus and the choice to follow him is as important now as it has always been. Any analysis of the past decade must leave us profoundly dispirited about the state of our planet. I need hardly mention the issues of war, religious bigotry of many kinds in many religions, including Christianity; the apparent moral decline in many societies, associated with no clear framework for living out life. Much of what we hear and see is banal and sickening.

But Jesus still calls us to rise up and follow him. This is a huge challenge because it means nothing less than transformation of ourselves, our church and our society. We can only start here locally. We may want to ask whether our PCC (Parochial Church Council) is helping us focus on how we become a church that owns that vision of the Kingdom of God and how we translate any vision into daily living.

As individuals we have a fresh opportunity to rededicate ourselves. Last Sunday we renewed our baptismal vows. We lit a candle to signify the new start we were making at the beginning of another decade. To achieve anything as a Christian community we need to know each other better. There are still barriers to break down, new friendships to be made and common purpose to be identified.

The other evening in bed I looked back to my baptism and the baptism of the young people I grew up with. I was not an Anglican, but a Baptist, and therefore was dedicated as a child and baptised as a teenager one Easter Sunday when I was about sixteen. Let me say, I have no problem now with infant baptism. My baptism was a moving occasion for me. At our church as we rose from the immersion, the congregation would sing: 'Be thou faithful unto death and I will give thee the crown of life.'

Much has happened since then. My views have changed a lot, but that moment started me on the path I have taken. My life would not have been what it has been without it. I am sure many of you will say the same.

I thought of the young friends I was baptised with; people of both sexes, my friends in that community. What happened to them? Of course, we were young and impressionable, but the amazing thing is that moment changed most of us. One became a solicitor and married another of our group; they have lived committed Christian lives, latterly in the Anglican Church. Another fine young person became a Baptist minister, someone who I admired greatly. Another became a nurse and married an Anglican priest. Their lives have been directed by the call of Jesus and identifying with him in baptism. One couple married and sadly had a severely disabled child and have been great witnesses in their local community. I could go on.

Imagine that occasion so long ago; Jesus baptised by John, following his vision and calling his disciples to follow him. The call has gone down the centuries to every kind of person. When they have responded they have started on a new life, a new journey. From time to time they have been renewed and continued on their way. Let us seek renewal now.

A Gospel for Today

Isaiah 60.9–22 Galatians 1.11–24
"For I want you to know, brothers and sisters that the gospel that was proclaimed by me is not of human origin; for I did not receive it from a human source, nor was I taught it, but I received it through a revelation of Jesus Christ."
Galatians 1.11–12.

This statement by Paul in Galatians, if it is taken seriously, has far-reaching implications for revelation in our time and for how we read the Bible.

I want this evening to try and provide you with a glimpse of what I mean and to do this we have to go back to Judaism in the first century.

Paul was a Jew and he thought like a Jew, but he had a vision well beyond the bounds of Israel and the Jewish people. He was brought up in the Diaspora, the Greek speaking world of Tarsus.

We may think it was amazing that he could claim that he did not need to talk to anyone who had known Jesus or discuss his teaching with them. His claim is that the revelation came straight from Jesus himself who taught him everything.

That is a bit like us taking no notice of the Bible and depending on our knowledge of Christianity from some direct revelation from God. Actually, not really, because we must remember that Jesus was a Jew and Paul was imbued with all the knowledge of the Law, the prophets, and the many other Jewish writings that were available. This knowledge base was the soil on which Paul grew his new theology.

After the fall of the Jewish Temple in 70 CE and indeed before, there was a great revival in Jewish thinking and theology. The world of temple sacrifice was waning; Jewish thinking had to change and new ways of being Jewish had to emerge. Many outstanding rabbis left Jerusalem and lived in Yavne (Jabneh) in the community. They discussed and debated their faith and re-examined much of their ancient understanding. They were not afraid to regard previous interpretations as wrong and they were not hidebound about questioning the Torah. Judaism has never had the same problem with reinterpretation that orthodox Christianity has had. That is because those ancient rabbis were sure that they could enter the Shekinah or presence of God in the writings they studied and would be able to see new meanings for their day. Out of this study, after many years, came the text known as the Mishnah. The Mishnah is the outcome of years of Midrash (interpretation or exegesis) of the Tanakh or Jewish Bible. The two Talmud's, the Babylonian and the Jerusalem, are commentaries on the Mishnah, the Babylonian being pre-eminent.

Paul was in the same mould. He reinvented Jewish Christianity in a Gentile context with great creative genius. The outcome was to take Christianity away from Judaism but make it a more suitable vehicle of faith for the wider world.

The reason I am saying all this now is that this should never be a process that stopped with Paul or anyone else. One of the principles of genuine theological thinking and scriptural study should always be: If that is what that meant for our ancestors, what does it mean now? We have to indulge in the same creative leaps that Paul did and rabbis of his day. We even need to be able to say previous interpretations were wrong.

Painfully, the Church has had to acknowledge many of the findings of modern science, for example evolution. We have a different attitude to slavery and racial tolerance. We no longer believe that the world will necessarily end shortly. We are no longer imbued with concepts of sacrifice and therefore find the sacrifice of Jesus less congenial than our ancestors, while acknowledging that less dramatic understandings of sacrifice continue to have global significance. The Church has had to change but it has been very slow and is generally out of step with modern culture and thinking. Some may suggest that is a good thing, but I suggest not. We have to create thought forms that cohere with our times.

Sadly, Christianity is easily stifled by the orthodoxy that constrained it after the conversion of Constantine in 312 CE and that had been instituted by Church fathers such as Irenaeus round 180 CE in his *Against Heresies*.

Unless we show equal creativity and look critically at our scriptures and seek the revelation that is open to us, Western Christianity will not survive long term. It may appear to thrive in Africa at present, but in the West institutional Christianity is dying. Dying, in my experience, because there is great fear about fresh expressions of Christianity. I do not mean making worship livelier or using modern liturgies and so on. I mean helping people connect with God in a way they feel comfortable with.

Who was Christianity invented for? Do we ever ask that

question? God did not spout some pre-packaged faith that fell off a tree. We are meant to seek and find ways of connecting with God through using our minds and hearts to engage with the Divine. Christianity should never be some kind of obstacle trap that we have to negotiate and say yes to, to get into the club.

This whole question of 'I am a Christian and You are not' is a major problem. We are united by our culture that includes religion and we cannot separate the two if religion is to survive. The problem is that the separation is going on apace. We are both culturally confused and religiously confused. The Church has largely lost its way in relating Christianity to twentieth century ideas and knowledge. It speaks in a language that is foreign to all but a few people. The ideas so familiar to our forebears are now strange. Ordinary people do not dwell on words such as atonement, resurrection, redemption, eternal life and so on.

The task is enormous. But if we believe one thing: that revelation is not dead and that modern people, like Paul, can be enlightened, there is hope. We need to listen to some of the voices that are crying out to be heard on the fringes of orthodoxy, who want to rekindle the desire to follow Jesus but present his message in a way that speaks to us today. We too can continue to find Shekinah today if we open our minds to God's word.

Crossing the Jordan

Joshua Chapter 3.1–8.14–17 Luke 3.15–22
"So that you may know the way you should go, for you have not passed this way before."
Joshua 3.4.

Those words take me back many years to the preaching of a famous Baptist minister, Alan Redpath, who wrote a book on Joshua. I have always found them inspiring and challenging. It is the sort of passage that makes your hair 'stand on end' and takes you near to the primary experience of awe that is the basis of all worship.

Topically perhaps, both our readings are linked in some way with water and in particular, the river Jordan. They are both of huge symbolic significance.

In Joshua we read about the passage of the Children of Israel led by Joshua across the river Jordan into the Promised Land. The Ark of the Covenant symbolising God's presence with them goes ahead. Just as at the crossing of the Red Sea during the Exodus, the waters of Jordan part and allow the crossing. In following the Ark, they follow God. They will only arrive at their destination by doing so: 'That you may know the way you shall go, for you have not passed this way before.'

In Luke we again read about John the baptiser and Jesus.

John baptised and Jesus himself is baptised. The site for these baptisms is again the Jordan river. This is no coincidence.

If we recall Jewish sacred history, we remember the Exodus led by Moses, then the wandering in the wilderness; the gift of the Ark symbolising God's presence and leadership and the entry into the Promised Land. But there follows spiritual decay, the destruction of the ten tribes by the Assyrians and then the exile in Babylon.

Even the return from Babylon did not heal the spiritual decline and by the time of John and Jesus, Judah was a vassal state of the Roman Empire. There were many groups at this time exploring both spiritual renewal and political ambitions. There were the Sadducees, a corrupt priesthood interested in rapprochement with Rome and furthering their political power. The Pharisees were not priests but seeking to follow the law through the synagogue and rabbinic teaching. Most of them were conservative. There were the Essenes, who lived apart following their own rule in the desert, probably near Qumran where the Dead Sea Scrolls were found. They sought spiritual renewal but were set apart. Then there were John and Jesus appearing with their ministries.

John, in his baptismal ministry was reawakening echoes of that original passage across the Jordan described by Joshua. In a sense, people had to cross the Jordan again to reach their true home. They had to repent of their sins. Yet John could not complete the task. Just as Moses would not see the full realisation of the journey of the Israelites and the mantle was passed to Joshua, so John passed the mantle to Jesus who would lead his people out of darkness into light. The very names Jesus and Joshua are essentially the same.

Whenever we start on a journey it is a new and fresh

adventure. Perhaps the route may seem familiar but there is always something novel about it. The spiritual journey that is at the heart of these stories is always fresh: ‘We have not passed this way before.’ But we always need someone to go ahead and guide us. Otherwise we get lost.

In our own lives we are faced with a constant challenge to break new ground and travel beyond where we are spiritually at any one time. The journeying of the Israelites is a paradigm for all spiritual journeys. We start out on the way, we lose our way and we wander in the wilderness. God finds us and tells us to follow him. We start out again, we make that crossing of the Jordon. Yet even then, when we think we have arrived we get lost again, side-tracked, losing our focus.

But perhaps along comes another guide, a John, who will prepare us again for that final crossing that takes us into the arms of God.

‘For you have not passed this way before.’ These words can challenge, thrill, bring fear and trepidation. Metaphorically, the river Jordan is always there for us to cross. Even if we thought we had crossed it before, it is always there for us. We stand on the banks; the God who knows us by name beckons us to step out into the deep and follow him to the further shore.

The Call of the Galilean

I Corinthians 1.1–9 and John 1. 29–42
"We have found the Messiah."
John 1.41.

Those words take us firmly to the heart of the ancient Jewish faith; the expectation of a Messiah.

As many of us reflect on the years of following Jesus, we may well want to ask ourselves what it is all about.

One wonders what was in the minds of Andrew and Peter. The Synoptic Gospels and John do not tell exactly the same story. The historical background in John is different, but despite the very different nature of John's Gospel and the Synoptics in some historical matters, some scholars prefer John, despite his portrait of a far from human Jesus.

In the Synoptic Gospels, Andrew and Peter are called as fishermen on the shores of Lake Galilee. In John, they appear to be in the Judean wilderness already disciples of John the Baptist.

There are theological reasons for this difference. In the Synoptic tradition, Jesus is recorded as starting his ministry after the imprisonment of John the Baptist; in John's Gospel, the ministries are parallel.

This is just another example of the important point that the Gospels are not history books, but theological works written by humans for particular communities. They were never intended for posterity at the time and that is why we find them intensely frustrating at times.

We can never know why these early disciples decided to follow Jesus. What was in their minds? We know that the land of Judah was in turmoil and that there was a renewed longing for a messiah. What we can be sure about is that both John the Baptist and Jesus caught people's imagination and challenged them to new ways of living.

The context was probably that many people were disillusioned with politics, corruption and the meaningless nature of their existence. Some saw escape from this in revolution, overthrow of Roman rule. Others saw it in an emphasis on the rigid following of the Law. A few withdrew and lived in communities, such as the Essenes. But finally, there were those who wanted to break through to a new reality that transcended all these things. We cannot know to what extent either John or Jesus thought there was to be an imminent end of the world as we know it, adding a dimension of urgency to the messages that Andrew and Peter responded to. There are undoubtedly apocalyptic elements in the New Testament and great scholars such as Albert Schweitzer have certainly seen Jesus as a prophet of the imminent end of the world.

That need not matter to us because as Schweitzer so movingly said, we should all live in the end time. That removes complacency from the call we receive.

Even though we cannot recover the minds of those earlier followers we need to ask *ourselves* what made us set out on the path of discipleship? What were the reasons? Unfortunately, it is possible to hide behind phrases such as Jesus is my saviour, or he offers me eternal life, or he has saved me from my sins. I want to suggest that there are other basic and understandable reasons that connect with ordinary people.

The only way I can explain what I mean is to go back to my own experience. As a young person I was certainly an idealist. At school, along with friends, I studied pacifism, including the biblical aspects; I pondered in the way that young people do as to how I should spend my life in a pretty unfocussed way. I went to church but was not clear how this really impacted on my life. I was never thrilled by the prospect of eternal life; that did not seem a good reason to follow Jesus at all. After all, youngsters do not really dwell on death and the concept was incoherent in any form of propositional language. That had to be left in God's hands. I could understand that it was a source of comfort, but surely personal survival was not the core of the gospel. Likewise, although the reality of evil was undoubted, I thought there was an excessive emphasis on sin in the Church I knew. Then I had to go into hospital and have an operation and that literally changed my life. I think there were two elements in that experience. The first was the awareness of other people's service and commitment to me. One could say that they were just doing their jobs, but I have never thought that. I was acutely aware of their commitment. My second reaction was one of gratitude for what was done.

I connected these experiences with that figure that I imagine on the shores of Galilee calling people to follow him. Calling one to follow him in a life of service, however inadequate. In my case this was medicine, but I firmly believe that it could be anything providing we seek to fulfil our potential. One might be anything; in our diverse lives, we are all able to respond to that call to serve others through following Jesus.

In responding in this kind of way we are doing the work of God. I have come to realise Christianity is not lived out in church but in ordinary life. Jesus did enter synagogues, but he was removed from temple worship. His ministry and service were carried out in homes, towns and villages. He did speak in synagogues, but he basically went where people lived their lives.

For us that means the place of work, the home, anywhere we are. When I was ordained, I became what is known as a Minister in Secular Employment, a real mouthful! I was encouraged to carry on my work as a doctor in a perfectly ordinary way and be a representative of the Church in daily life. On Sundays, we all bring our world of service in ordinary life to God and lay it before God. We are renewed and challenged. At the end of each service we say: 'Go in peace to Love and serve the Lord.'

That is the heart of our calling. Andrew and Peter responded. In our way, we are summoned to the same calling in a very different world. It is our challenge to work out what that means today as we go about our lives in Masham, Healey and beyond.

Mysticism and Metaphor

I Corinthians 1.1–9 John 1.29–42
"Here is the Lamb of God, who takes away the sin of the world!"
John 1.29.

The writer of John's Gospel has John the Baptist speak these words about Jesus as he comes towards him. There is no direct evidence from this gospel that John baptised Jesus, but we have these highly significant words.

The title 'Lamb of God' is one of several applied to Jesus in the New Testament. We read of the titles 'Son of God', 'Son of Man', 'The Christ', 'Messiah' and so on. These all have complex meanings, only understood with reference to Judaism.

The title 'Lamb of God' is not widely used in the New Testament. It is not used at all in Matthew, Mark and Luke. It is used, indirectly, without the full title in the book of Revelation, probably produced by the same school as the Gospel of John, but the word 'amnos' used in John is not used in Revelation, but the word 'arnion' and the full title 'Lamb of God' is never used.

If we are to use these titles in our own spirituality or consider whether we can, we need to explore their rich symbolism. We are not in the presence of fact, but of mythos, culture and the mystical.

In temple Judaism that continued up to 70 CE, lambs were sacrificed on a daily basis for the expiation of sins by the officiating priest. This sacrifice was also deemed to have saving power. The obvious link is with the Passover story, when blood was sprinkled on the door lintels in Pharaoh's Egypt to save the Israelites; although the imagery is not specifically related to their sins.

Jesus is thus presented by John as the Passover lamb and this expresses the two ideas in Mosaic sacrifice, of expiation of sins and salvation. The power of this symbol in John is enhanced by the way he deals with the crucifixion of Jesus. In this Gospel Jesus is crucified on the eve of Passover, differing from the Synoptic Gospels. This is the exact time at which the Passover lamb would be killed in the temple courtyard. Jesus is therefore explicitly identified in John with the Passover lamb. He replaces it.

An interesting additional symbol refers to an ancient Aramaic legend related to the story in Exodus when Pharaoh has a dream in which Egypt is weighed in a pair of scales, with a lamb on the other. The lamb outweighs the whole of Egypt. The dream interpreters tell Pharaoh that a Jewish boy will be born who will destroy Egypt and all its power, namely Moses. Therefore, there are allusions to two saviours in this metaphor, Jesus and Moses.

There is another very important allusion understood by Jews, in the 'Lamb of God' symbolism; and that is the binding or sacrifice of Isaac, a story of great significance to Jews. Isaac is metaphorically the 'Lamb' of Abraham and the story is narrated in Genesis twenty-two. Early Church Fathers too, used Jewish legend that this sacrifice occurred on the day that became Passover, thus symbolising again the death of Jesus on the Cross.

Paul, in the development of his theology of the Cross, made important use of the Isaac story; and traditions in inter-testamental Judaism, that is, between 200 BCE and about 100 CE, or a bit later, made similar uses. The Isaac story is changed and we see this in the Dead Sea Scrolls, the book of Jubilees and Josephus, the Jewish historian.

In this different account Isaac is no longer a boy not knowing what is going on, but a full-grown man, aged around twenty-five in Josephus, and thirty-seven according to the rabbis. He was told by his father of God's order and ran joyfully to the altar placing his neck upon it. This act therefore became the unaccomplished, self-immolation of Isaac.

In Jewish tradition every time God recalled the sacrifice of Isaac, he would also show mercy to his children. First century Jews would be familiar with this prayer that was used at times of crisis: 'If Jews are guilty and are on the point of being slain, remember Isaac their father who stretched out his neck on the altar to be slain for your name's sake. May his immolation take the place of all his children.'

I think this helps us understand how the imagery associated with Jesus, the lamb symbology and the Cross has been developed.

Our identification with these symbols in the Eucharist, a development of the Passover meal, and the words of the Agnus Dei that we sing shortly, can be enhanced by understanding how our worship and Christian culture has evolved from another ancient religion. These symbols are mystical. They do not become real to us through logic or reason. We have to surrender ourselves to our tradition to absorb them and become part of them.

But today, perhaps there is another challenge for us. Is it possible to imagine other symbols and stories that relate to us and our time and Jesus? One of the problems that this generation has in relation to Christianity, is a poverty of symbols and metaphors they feel they can connect with. First century Judaism is a long way off. Yet we let go of ancient symbols to our peril, because we say goodbye to centuries of culture and tradition

Our Church needs to continue to exercise that imaginative genius that gripped Paul and other people of his age, so that the symbols we have been brought up with continue to live in our lives.

A good example is the rich use made by black people of the Exodus story in their path out of slavery to freedom, and how Martin Luther King, for them, has become a figure like Isaac or Jesus; but not replacing Jesus. That is why when Mrs Clinton referred to a President needing to change the law to make things happen, she caused such offence. Black people did not want the sacrifice of their hero to be diminished by some white woman talking about laws.

May God help us all to rediscover the rich symbols of our tradition and apply them creatively in our world.

Action not Hesitation

1 Corinthians 12.12–31a Luke 4.14–21
"The Spirit of the Lord is upon me, because he has anointed me to bring good news to the poor. He has sent me to proclaim release to the captives
and recovery of sight to the blind, to let the oppressed go free."
Luke 4.18.

Here today we read and hear some of the core of the gospel of Jesus. It is radical, challenging and counterculture. It opposes so much that seems prevalent in our world today. It is this kind of gospel that has called many people over the centuries to follow Jesus and attempt to change the world.

Let's take this last week. The employees of three national stores have lost their jobs or are likely to lose them; Jessop's, HMV and a DVD rental company. Honda are about to lay off over one thousand people, probably our son among them. Benefit cuts are likely to make many people with disabilities suffer further. Many ordinary families face difficult times with cuts in child benefits. Cuts in the NHS are going to affect patient care. Many wards are understaffed. Violence is everywhere and we have seen an example of vicious extremism in the Algerian hostage drama. The whole of North Africa appears unstable. There is profound disagreement about our future in Europe. All this and more you can obtain from reading the news or hearing the radio or watching TV.

All this amounts to a distinct lack of harmony. The context and details were different in the days of Jesus and the known world was smaller, but the lack of harmony was there. In those circumstances he wanted to encourage the poor and needy, the captives and so on.

We always seem to live in an unequal world. Why? It is easy to blame governments, but governments reflect the will of the people in true democracies. The fact of the matter is that political parties become paralysed by indecision, through fear of offending significant opinion and losing their majority.

Jesus had a vision of a different kind of world. He mixed with poor people, promoted equality and condemned usury. He told the rich that they had to be careful of 'losing their lives' because of their attachment to money. He called this transformed world the Kingdom of God. He called people to change.

As Christians we are all followers of Jesus. In each generation people are summoned to follow his example and bring about change in the world. We may not be in government, but it is through thousands and millions of small changes that harmony comes. Christians do have differing views about doctrine, but there really cannot be any confusion about the core of the gospel. Surprisingly, for some it is not about an individual ticket to heaven. It is actually about losing yourself in the daily service of others.

Sadly, we are made cynical by deceivers. Someone who has been helping me over certain aspects of disability told me the other day about his brother. He had bad hips and could not walk well. He obtained a 'blue badge', Disability Living

Allowance and a Motability car on very favourable terms. He had operations. His new hips worked well. He could go for walks. However, he did not inform the authorities, kept his Disabled Living Allowance, his Motability car and his 'blue badge'. He is over sixty-five now and is unlikely to be reassessed. He is robbing the taxpayer and the poor.

I have no magic bullets to suggest how we promote harmony in our world in any detail. I would say one thing; we must not lose our spontaneity. If someone needs help, help them. Our complex world has led to indecision, over-complication and lack of direction.

Glory Revealed

2 Corinthians 3.12–4.2 Luke 9.28–36[37–43a]
"They saw his glory and the two men who stood with him."
Luke 9.32.

The dawning of awareness, or put in another way, the realisation of something new, something that will change your view of many things and for which there is no turning back. There may be further revelations or special moments of awareness that take you in another direction, but the point of all profound periods of insight is that they make a fundamental difference to how you view the world.

We sometimes use the words 'paradigm shift' to refer to profound insights. These may occur in any discipline including that of religious experience.

In science the development of quantum theory was a paradigm moment in physics. Newtonian physics was not superseded but physics would not be the same again.

Religious experience is somewhat different because it is more individual. Our revelations are not the same and therefore cannot be generalised in the same way. All spiritual journeys in life are different. We may sit together in this congregation, but our own journeys will differ markedly as will our understanding of religion.

In the experience of the Transfiguration, only a select few

were present: Jesus and the ones perceived as his core group of disciples. The whole setting is imbued with symbolic significance.

Jesus goes into a mountain just as Moses did to receive the Ten Commandments. Indeed, the disciples have a vision of the two great Jewish figures, Moses and Elijah. Jesus was thought by many to be one of these prophets returned. In this episode there is emphasis on his being the new Moses. But there is a difference. Moses wore a veil when with others, to prevent the shining of his visage reaching the people. On this mountain, Jesus' face shines and the disciples see it. There is no veil. The glory of God is revealed. In high symbology we are told that Jesus is indeed the new Moses and he ushers in a new covenant, a new Israel. There is no discontinuity between the old covenant and the new. Jesus stands with those who went before him, but there is a paradigm shift in the way Israel should be understood, and even then, understanding was not immediate as we see from Peter's reaction.

Now we cannot mimic that experience, but it is a model for religious understanding; the moment when our eyes are opened and for us nothing can ever be the same.

I do not believe we can legislate about what those insights will be. It is true that we all carry with us a background and history of understanding that is unique to us. However, if we are completely open, our minds free to imagine and see, God can take us in many surprising directions.

I suppose all I can do is to give two brief personal examples. The first was the whole issue of the relationship between Christianity and other faiths. I was brought up in a narrow exclusive tradition of Christianity. During a period living in India and visiting India subsequently, I was exposed to an ancient culture and an old and living religious tradition. Initially it seemed very strange, but closer contact with Eastern religions and Indian culture helped me to see the importance of the many insights within a religion other than Christianity. This culminated when I was visiting the house of an eminent Hindu family. I was not very well. The mother, a lady of charm and wisdom, said that she would pray for me. That was a moment of illumination and was part of a journey that has taken me to my own particular understanding of my own faith and those of others.

The second was during a period of prolonged illness. I was tired of 'God talk' and the pettiness of Church politics and religious nit-picking. I was not sure I wanted to have anything further to do with the Church at all. And then in the midst of the turmoil I became aware of God's presence with me. It was not connected in any way with the Church or doctrine. It was fresh and liberating. God was God. He/She was beyond religions and argument and how you felt or what you thought. God did not need explanation. After that I ceased to be frightened about the content of my belief and whether I was approved or not. God was beyond culture or systems.

You will have had your own moments and they are worth reflecting on. When we seek the truth, we study, reflect, pray in whatever way we understand prayer and exercise our imagination. Within our own tradition God will reveal himself to us and we will feel that deep liberation and assurance of being in Divine presence. We may want to prolong the moment like Peter, but it will go. We will come down from the mountain. Our lives will continue, but if we have truly absorbed that privilege of dawning, nothing will be the same again.

Lent

Lent is the season of travelling with Jesus in the wilderness, through his temptations and the disciplines of prayerful reflection and fasting. By the end of Lent we are on the outskirts of Jerusalem after a brief ministry, and the drama moves on to Holy Week. In the liturgical cycle the chronology of Jesus' ministry may appear confusing. John's Gospel does not record the Temptations and they appear to have the form of a Christian myth rather than historical event. John's Gospel seems to have Jesus' ministry extending for some two years, compared with the one year of the Synoptics. Despite any confusion, Lent provides an examination of the type of messiahship Jesus espoused, and provides us with an opportunity for self-examination of our motives for action in the world we live in. The climax of Jesus' ministry is always Jerusalem and the events of Holy Week. This is the final testing ground for the path he took following that period in the wilderness.

Beginning with Ash Wednesday we are faced with the choices concerning our lives. Everyone has the opportunity to follow the example of Jesus or go their own way. It is important to recognise that. But because we are human, we fall short of any kind of exemplary life in most if not all cases. Bitter experience has taught us that any picture of holiness is usually flawed. This provokes the enquiry about the 'sinless'

Jesus. What does this mean and is it a valid statement? It is best to view sin in terms of relationships; with God, our neighbour and the creation around us. It is the positive or negative aspects of these relationships that determine individual actions. I do not find the sinlessness of Jesus helpful. If he was human, he exhibited the usual human traits. It is his spirit-filled life that matters, lived in the historical context of his day rather than an analysis of all his thoughts and actions that are beyond our ascertainment. An understandable reaction to Jesus' humanity is to move him to the status of 'heavenly being', 'sojourning' on Earth. This paradox lies at the heart of the debate about the nature of Jesus that occupied the developing institution of the Church for hundreds of years and continues to exercise us today.

Mothering Sunday on the fourth Sunday of Lent enables us to celebrate the love and sacrificial lives of mothers, a symbol of the life that epitomises Christian service. It is no coincidence that our churches are supported by a majority of women, a stark reminder of the foolishness of male dominated clergy, only recently in the process of correction.

Real Bread

Romans 5.12–19 Mathew 4.1–11
"It is written, 'One does not live by bread alone,
but by every word that comes from the mouth of God.'"
Mathew 4.4.

The temptations in the wilderness of Judea may or may not be an historical event, but the episode has many literary allusions. Mathew and Luke contain the most complete accounts. Mark has a summary, but he does not mention fasting. John does not mention the temptations.

The episode comes just after Jesus has been baptised and is designated 'Son' by God. Some argue that in the temptations the nature of Jesus' Messiahship is tested, others that it is more a searching analysis of the relationship of Jesus to God. Is his ministry to be one of short cuts, abusing his relationship to God, or is he to live his life like anyone else, subject to the 'the slings and arrows of outrageous fortune?'

Today I want to dwell for a few moments on the first temptation. The duration of the temptations, forty days and forty nights, connects with the pivotal event in Jewish sacred history, the Exodus. Moses was on Mount Sinai for that time, although the number forty is purely figurative, meaning a long time. The Israelites journeyed in the wilderness for forty years.

The Judean wilderness is a barren place; scrub, dry land,

some succulent plants and little water. To survive there requires 'know how'. We are not told whether Jesus drank or not, but it would be an act of extreme foolishness not to drink, and survival in that environment without water would be unlikely. That is why we must use this episode as a pictorial account of the quest for the spiritual dimension of life.

'One cannot live by bread alone', but we need bread or nutrition to live at all. Many people in our world continue to starve to death. When we worked in India in the 1960s it was commonplace to find starving people. Even now your rickshaw wallah may be wondering whether he will have the money to feed and clothe his family on the streets of Kolkata. When we were in India people used to moan about *Rice Christians*. They meant that people were claiming to be Christians to get food. So what? When you are starving or profoundly dehydrated you will do anything to survive.

If I were sitting preaching to a group of starving people what would I do? Like anyone with feeling, I would stop preaching or not start at all, and go and find food and drink for them. How can you talk about spirituality to the starving? Indeed, can you talk at all to anyone bereft, for whatever reason?

Yet there is something beyond the simple narrative of life if we can discern it. Life is more than a sequence of events, good or awful, banal or stimulating. The crux of the first temptation is that we can drift through our lives without ever going beneath the surface of events, missing the moments of enlightenment and revelation that give meaning and substance to earthly existence. Through joy and pain we discover what it means to be human.

The problem with high flown spiritual talk is that it has no meaning divorced from the practical. Spiritual masters such as Meister Eckhart recognised that although the journey into ourselves, that we find pictured in the temptations, may lead us to spiritual insight, it means absolutely nothing if we do not return to this world and its messiness and try to make a difference. Jesus was concerned about ordinary people, the poor, despised; he ate with publicans and sinners.

Our world has always been a profoundly unequal place to live in. People have dreamed of utopias where all is well, but that has never happened because we are innately selfish as well as kind. Why do we talk of globalisation in a situation where millions starve? The wealth of creation is not shared across our planet. Our greed causes untold suffering. Is there any salvation for individuals when this is ignored?

One of the advantages of Lent is that it does provide us with an opportunity to go into that wilderness, strip ourselves of our pretensions, the false pictures we adopt of the neat confines of our religion, our faith, and learn afresh what it means again to be a follower of Jesus. He discovered there is no place for preferential treatment. God is not there to give us a special deal as Christians, or adherents of any other faith. We must not expect God to protect us from the vicissitudes of life. That simply does not happen. We all need to be stripped bare and allow the purity of God's presence to enter our lives and renew our purpose of serving others.

As we live, things may happen to us that we find deeply distressing. All we can do is hang on to each other in solidarity and concern, avoiding the platitudes that come so easily. Practical help is what draws us together in a bond that transcends words.

At the end of Lent the idea of sacrifice looms large. We

may find it difficult to connect with some of the ancient language and customs of sacrifice, but I do find the word scapegoat illuminating. The ancients had the custom of casting their sins, their burdens, on to a goat and sending it into the wilderness alone, the metaphorical carrier of their failures. The language of sacrifice comes to life when we picture that ultimate willingness to give oneself for others, regardless of consequences. It is the ultimate vision of service, and the Jesus who returned from the wilderness to begin his ministry had learned that there are no short cuts to avoid the challenge of earthly living. He determined to live his life with a clear vision and purpose without special treatment. He calls us to follow him in discovering a renewed clarity of our roles in His service.

Faith in the Market Place

Jeremiah 22.11–17 Luke 14.27–33

"Whoever does not carry the cross and follow me cannot be my disciple."

Luke 14.27.

I want to talk for a few minutes this evening about what this statement from Luke chapter fourteen might mean in today's world. Alongside this New Testament passage, we will consider what Jeremiah twenty-two has to offer us.

I have in mind today, particularly, the world of politics and government and how we should all behave and count the cost of a life which is consistent and marked by integrity.

In Jeremiah we have a clear denunciation of the King of Judah. 'Do what is just and right' says Jeremiah (22.13-17):

> 'Woe to him who builds his house by unrighteousness,
> and his upper rooms by injustice;
> who makes his neighbours work for nothing,
> and does not give them their wages;
> who says, "I will build myself a spacious house
> with large upper rooms",
> and who cuts out windows for it,
> panelling it with cedar,
> and painting it with vermilion.

Are you a king
because you compete in cedar?
Did not your father eat and drink
and do justice and righteousness?
Then it was well with him.
He judged the cause of the poor and needy;
then it was well.
"Is not this to know me?"
says the Lord.
But your eyes and heart
are only on your dishonest gain,
for shedding innocent blood,
and for practising oppression and violence.'

Leaving aside the ancient idea that if you are good God rewards you, and if you are bad, she punishes you, we are left in no doubt that living life as a religious or spiritual person requires high standards, honesty, and integrity. The cost of being a disciple of Jesus in Luke's Gospel is high. People should count the cost because it excludes ruthless personal ambition. There has to be a caring approach to people. We have to be servants and humble.

We still have a queen, but our government is in the hands of an elected parliament. Virtually everyone in this country is profoundly disillusioned with our elected representatives. Why?

In general, we think they have not behaved with integrity. We think they have shown a level of self-interest that does not sit well for those who seek high office to serve the people. The various 'scandals' that occupy the media give us the strong impression that much time is taken up with internecine warfare rather than public service. Approval ratings for any politician have reached rock bottom.

Has all this got anything to do with Christianity? I think it has a lot to do with it. Some people think that because Jesus said that we 'should render unto Caesar the things that are Caesar's and to God the things that are God's' we need not connect religion and politics. Religion is a private matter. That text is taken out of context. If we do not make connections between our faith and daily life we make a profound mistake. I have no hesitation in saying this and am very grateful to the Archbishop of Canterbury for speaking out, as he does, about issues in public life.

I am not referring to any particular politicians or parties. People do have party affiliations. If we differ about which party to support that does not matter. The issues I am referring to transcend party boundaries. No party has a coherent political philosophy. They deceive themselves if they ever thought they did.

The current state of our political systems is deeply unsatisfactory from a Christian perspective. Reading the passages we have, and reflecting on the whole nature of Christian discipleship, one can come to no other conclusion. Unfortunately, our politicians reflect the current status of society in the same way as our doctors, dentists, lawyers and for that matter, all of us. They are probably no better or worse than we are. Abuses and behaviours reflect how we operate in society, meaning that we all might be just as bad if we were politicians. Therefore, we should be wary about being self-righteous. Humility is the one characteristic that we should all hope for. As T.S. Eliot said: *'Humility is endless.'*

What can we do about all this? The first thing is to ensure

that our lives are lives of genuine discipleship whatever our religion. In general, the great religions take a similar view of the moral core of a genuine spiritual life. Next, in any way we can, we have to make it clear what we expect of our leaders. One way we can do this is through the ballot box. Fortunately, no one can tell us how to vote. We should vote, but this time we need to reflect very hard on how we can best send a message to those who are involved in politics, whether in opposition or government.

Our world needs the right kind of role models. When we look at the influence of celebrities on young lives it is easy to despair. Who can we seek to follow? The one answer is to follow Jesus, but we do need modern role models to inspire us. People who exhibit the spiritual qualities enshrined in Christian discipleship that will inspire people. We desperately need them to turn our society around. I suppose the one modern politician who has risen above all others because of his life and service is Nelson Mandela. There are few others. Role models do not have to be famous. When I was young, I suppose Albert Schweitzer was a role model, because despite his academic brilliance and high musical skill, he chose to train as a doctor and serve in Africa. He did not need to do that, but he was compelled to do so by the arresting figure of Jesus, sometimes called the 'Stranger of Galilee'. He was a very liberal Christian and a man of his time, but an inspiration to many.

The 'Stranger of Galilee' asks us to count the cost of discipleship hoping that we will choose to follow him, because in doing so lies the power to change ourselves and society. Without those standards, society drifts into chaos, selfishness, dishonesty and meaninglessness. Jesus was not a 'yes man', he had clear opinions and teachings. He stood up to the prevailing culture. We have to as well. I think it is a good thing that Jesus has that mystical remoteness about him. People sometimes sing ‘what a friend we have in Jesus’, but it his compelling figure on those distant shores so long ago that calls us and continues to do so. We may have to count the cost, but it is worth it.

Known but Not Known

Romans 4.13–25 Mark 8.31–35

"For those who want to save their life will lose it, and those who lose their life for my sake, and for the sake of the gospel, will save it."

Mark 8.35.

On the surface those words might appear to refer to martyrdom, a feature of the persecution of the Church when they were written around 70 CE. Even if these actual words were spoken by Jesus prior to the foundation of the Church, they would have been uttered in the context of a highly inflammatory world of the Jewish state under Roman rule. But do we find a deeper meaning more relevant to our times? That is what I want to explore.

What I want to say may seem a bit obscure, even tortuous, but first I put before you a number of scenes or personal experiences, and from these attempts, connect with the whole business of finding a true humanity or losing it.

I have referred before to the strangeness that can come upon me when I look at a word, phrase or sentence for any length of time. My mind goes blank. I begin to feel a bit uneasy. What does it all mean? It would seem that the closer I look at something the more slippery it becomes; the less I seem to understand. Then I reach that point when I begin to relax. I start the task of trying to go deeper and trying to understand and make connections. One could have that feeling with our text today. I think it is true that the closer one looks at something the stranger it seems. But paradoxically it is then that we really have the opportunity to engage. GK Chesterton famously referred to the utter 'muddiness of mud' or the 'wetness of water'. There is a strangeness about these things if we look hard enough. Some would equate this with the spirit of poetry. Have you had that kind of experience?

The second scene is more personal, but each of us may connect with it. Being by nature an introspective ruminator, and therefore inclined to look inwards, I get a shock when I have a deep look inside myself and sense that there is nothing there! Quite alarming when you have spent some time discussing the nature of the person and giving talks on personhood. If I look at someone else, for example my wife, there is a related problem. We have been married for fifty years this year. But I suddenly realise that I am not sure I know her at all. We are very familiar with each other after all these years, but do I know her? After all I cannot get inside her head or she mine.

By now you may be thinking I am completely mad. I want to take you to a promontory overlooking Swansea Bay. Seated on the grass is a teenager reading a book. He finishes the book written by Wittgenstein, perhaps the greatest philosopher of modern times. The boy was Rowan Williams, our Archbishop of Canterbury. He was engaged with the whole issue of words and meaning.

What Wittgenstein discovered and Rowan learned, was that words have no meaning on their own. Meaning is only conferred in a social setting. The good life or the life committed to God is not found in the words. The meaning is found in the interaction of that life with the world in its social and cultural setting. Your lives and mine achieve meaning in the world. We cannot find them inside us. We are out there ultimately, even though the thoughts and feelings inside our heads dictate our actions. But instead of going outwards we can build up a self so big that it becomes the be all and end all. What matters is this self and what can make it bigger, better and more important. But in reality, there is nothing there. It is all a mirage

Our Gospel is saying that the whole idea of the autonomous individual is not a picture of what it is to be human at all. It is what it is to be fallen, and the image of God is not somewhere inside but outside. We reflect God only when we pull away from our own interests.

Rowan Williams was greatly influenced by Russian Orthodoxy and his doctorate was a prolonged analysis of Russian orthodox and literary thinkers. Even his appearance reflects this. One of the theologians who influenced him was called Lossky, who remarked that the autonomous self is a kind of blasphemy.

'For those who want to save their life will lose it, and those who lose their life for my sake, and for the sake of the gospel, will save it.' Now, perhaps, we can begin to see what this text might mean.

The good life only has content and meaning when we connect with the world we live in now; the everyday world of the twenty-first century. But because we are believers in God and Christian virtues have entered our society over the centuries, we are able to use our Christian tradition to tease out what this text means today.

I am going to start some definitions in negative terms. One way of getting somewhere near the truth in theology is known as the apophatic or negative way. Instead of what God is we say what he is not. Instead of saying what we have to be and do to find true life or the Good Life, we say what we must not be and not do.

The life saved is not selfish.

The life saved is not careless.

The life saved does not contain false gods.

The life saved is not dependent on time.

The life saved is not risk free.

We could go on. We tend to recognise the qualities that we want to call goodness and often agree about them.

Although I used to think one might be able to define a person, I now know that we cannot. It is always the personal element that remains unknown in another being. God is unknowable and so is Jesus, and so are we all sitting in this church. Because we say we are made in the image of God we are unknowable and the way we are called to is the mystery of the crucified selfhood.

My life and your lives are imprints on the world, incapable of definition, but part of the fabric of creation, a part of the whole for good or ill.

Intimations of Truth

Joshua 1.1–9 Ephesians 6.10–20
"Only be strong and very courageous, being careful to act in accordance with all the law that my servant Moses commanded you; do not turn from it to the right hand or to the left, so that you may be successful wherever you go."
Joshua 1.7.

"Put on the whole armour of God, so that you may be able to stand against the wiles of the devil."
Ephesians 6.11.

Our first reading today is a piece of sacred history. Joshua stood on the brink of something great. It was his duty and his privilege to lead the Israelites across the Jordan to a new life in a new land. This is how the Jewish people have understood their destiny. Others will have seen it differently and still do. Their protection is adherence to the Law provided by Moses. Obeying it will keep them together, maintain their identity and give them success in conquering the land. They saw God as their personal protector. He was their God. He would look after them.

In the epistle to the Ephesians we have moved on. This is an epistle to the early Church. There is dispute about who wrote it, despite a specific reference to Paul. Whether it was directed to the Ephesians is disputed also. However, this is only relevant to scholars. The epistle is directed to Gentile Christians not Jews and therefore moves beyond the scope of Joshua. The Body of Christ, the Church, is much of the subject matter. Unity and purity are emphasised. In this last chapter of the epistle, the Ephesians, like Joshua and his followers, are encouraged to be strong and courageous emphasising the anticipated struggles they will experience living their faith. The armour of God is truth, righteousness, the gospel of peace, faith and finally the helmet of salvation and the sword of the Spirit, which is the word of God. The detail is expressed in metaphorical language.

The essential issue is that only the life and spirit of Jesus, imbued in them and bringing them together, will protect them from cosmic forces that seek to destroy them. The language is pictorial. Translating into today's thought patterns and images one might suggest that there are major problems living as a Christian in any age, because there is always much that will challenge one to depart from ethical and loving principles in one's daily living.

Distorted individualism is the enemy of communal flourishing, leading to selfishness and all kinds of behaviour that are inimical to a life lived honouring the Divine Good as the creator and sustainer of this world of ours.

I suppose the big challenge for us is whether we can connect at all with these passages. Do they have any meaningful impact on our way of thinking, or do we live in a world where religion has become so diluted, other than in the minds of extremists, that we can no longer use ancient scripture as a reliable guide for anything?

Let me say that I no longer think that Christianity carries a level of exclusive access to a spiritual life and quest, and that other faiths practised in a spirit of love and peace provide an appropriate framework for other people. Many Christians, but not all, would say the same thing nowadays.

If one makes a detailed study of the development of Christianity down the ages one can be left in no doubt that much of the man-made doctrines of the Church are misleading and certainly do not stem from Jesus. We have to try to go back to the core of his teaching to discover what still works for us today.

The search for truth is everything. One of the key issues in the teaching of Jesus is that truth is beyond rules and regulations. It is discovered in love. Truth is elusive, but if we make that our quest in a spirit of honesty and peace within a community of searchers, we have made a start. We will never discover absolute truth; that is beyond us. However, we obtain glimpses of truth; not in concepts, but below the surface of ordinary events. That may sound obscure, but perhaps a little domestic scene will provide a hint.

We telephoned one of our daughters to wish her a happy birthday. She had had breakfast in bed provided by her four children, each one bringing a component of this delicious meal. That is not rational, but lurking somewhere underneath that little piece of life is a gateway to truth.

Peace and faith in how we live our lives are part of the quest for truth, embedded in the life of Jesus. When we use the word spirit, for me, it is the source that enables us to go below the surface of life's narrative and using our imaginations discover elements of truth in our life-long quest.

Yes, we can use these passages. They speak to us now if we take the trouble to reflect and use our imaginations. Life is not easy. In many ways it is tragic. To live it fully we have to live in the Spirit and be strong and very courageous.

Living Water

Exodus 17.1–7 John 4.5–42
"Sir. You have no bucket and the Well is deep."
John 4.11.

When I was in my early twenties, I listened to a sermon based on this text. It deeply impressed me although now I remember nothing of what was said! Since then this passage in John's Gospel has been a special one for me. Jesus asks for some water while his disciples are away getting provisions. The lady is surprised as she is a Samaritan, someone despised by Jews. She is told by Jesus that if she knew who he was she would be able to receive 'living water' that would never need replenishing. She responds with those famous words.

The Samaritan lady at the well was practical. Her knowledge of water was practical. She had no idea what this Jesus was talking about. How could he give her living water without a bucket? What was all this weird nonsense about springs of living water welling up inside of you, meaning you would never be thirsty again? Like many people today, the language of metaphor was unfamiliar to her. This creates profound problems in understanding the Bible and religious language in general. We have become bogged down in what one might term 'literal truth' as the touchstone of religious belief. We forget that spirituality is about the inexpressible and resorting to metaphor is a way to provide a point of contact to start us on our approach to the Divine.

In the Old Testament reading for today there was a problem with water. What was it? There wasn't any. Why not? No rain. The scene was a desert.

Why is water so important? Because we can't live without it. We consist mainly of water. If we are mainly water, who do you think has the most water in this church? You do not need to go and point at them, just a general statement; the biggest person. Water is the ideal subject matter for metaphor.

In winter we have spent time by the river Nile in Egypt. Egypt, with its great historical civilisations would never have existed without the Nile and the annual flood. Otherwise it is desert. It seldom rains, although once there were thunderstorms for forty-eight hours and hailstones the size of olives; almost unheard of.

Sitting in a small shelter looking at the Nile, my mind tended to wander to the contrast between the Nile water flowing, seemingly there forever, and the frailty of human and animal life. Of course, the water I look at is never the same in the flowing river. For me it becomes a metaphor that stands out against time and the frailty of human life and love. It points to the need for something beyond time and unperishable. Time and the 'timeless' river make me think. Life can be a blessing but how?

Jesus seems to have been thirsty when he was by the well at Sychar in Samaria; the well that the Patriarch Jacob built. He asked for some water, but he used the occasion to explain to the woman at the well and to us all that there is something deeper than pure physical life and physical water, H_2O. He used water the necessary ingredient of physical life, to explain that if you really want to be alive in every sense of the word, you need to live in the presence of God. That is not a time-dependent phenomenon. Is that the blessing that we all seek?

Jesus said to the woman at the well: 'Everyone who drinks of this water will be thirsty again, but those who drink of the water that I will give them will never be thirsty. The water that I will give will become in them a spring of water gushing up to eternal life.' (John 4.13-14).

He used ordinary words to convey a meaning that is beyond the usual use of the words. In English grammar we call that a metaphor. He may well have been thinking of that spring gushing out of the rock in the wilderness when he said those words.

He was trying to tell us that if we trust in him, in God, we will live our lives in a way that is real life, because our motives, the way we live, will have a quality that truly satisfies, a blessing. Many people in the world find themselves unhappy despite the fact that they are well off, with lots of food, drink and money. They feel dissatisfied. They yearn for something more. What they need is the 'water of life' that Jesus refers to. Jesus lived for others and that is a good starting point. We cannot see or drink the water of life. It is not in a bottle, a well or a rock, reservoir or river. As Jesus said, it is inside us, in our very beings, gushing up into eternal life; life that is timeless.

Citizens of the Light

I Corinthians 1.18–25 John.2.13–22
"The Jews then said to him, 'What sign can you show us for doing this?'"
John 2.18.

If you examine John's Gospel closely you will quickly realise that on the whole, the Jesus portrayed in John is radically different to the Jesus in the Synoptic Gospels.

The Jesus in John is described as the man sent from heaven and in John chapter seventeen he talks of his returning to heaven. The prologue in John at the beginning of the Gospel leaves us in little doubt about his exalted status. The language of Jesus in his various discourses is completely different from the Jesus of the other Gospels where he rarely talks about himself. In this Gospel we hear Jesus say: 'I am the light of the world, the bread of life, the water of life, the true vine' and so on. At various times Jesus seems to say that he and God are one, at others that he is closely connected to God. There are no parables in John at all. No pithy tales so beloved of Jewish rabbis. The miracles are few but all powerful, and they constitute the so called 'signs' that are present in this Gospel. These miracle signs appear to be used as evidence that Jesus is who he says he is. In other words, this Gospel is a carefully worked out piece of writing that is attempting to persuade us that Jesus is the pre-existent eternal Word or Logos who came to Earth as a man, but who returns to God. We can think of miracle signs such as the turning of water into wine, the feeding of the five thousand, the healing of the blind man, the raising of Lazarus.

In the passage read, the Jesus in John is not speaking of the temple itself when he states: 'If you destroy this temple it will be raised up on the third day.' He is talking about himself. He will die in one sense but he is returning to the Father.

In Paul's epistle to the Corinthians he is trying to address various problems that occurred in the early Church. One of these was the thought patterns of the existing Greek culture of the day. The Greeks invented philosophy and did not warm to weird stories about someone dying for the sins of the whole world.

John and Paul, taking the writings as a whole, have a very different perspective on what one might term salvation, a word we can read as 'healing'. In Paul, the Cross is everything. He barely mentions the life and work of Jesus explicitly. For Paul, Jesus is the one who has died to pay the human debt of sin. In his creative understanding, Jesus is the one who has paid the ransom to free us from sin by his sacrificial or atoning death on the Cross. He has paid the price for us and taken our sin upon himself. If we accept his sacrifice through faith and identify with him, we are liberated. We should understand that Paul assumed, probably, that with the coming of the Messiah the end of time was approaching; in common with much Jewish messianic expectation. He was concerned with issues related to the end of the world.

John, writing some fifty years later, does not have this perspective. 'The end of the world' debate has been watered down. We have no passages as we do in other Gospels or in Paul, about end of time imagery. In John's Gospel, although we have a passion story, salvation is about being 'born again', as in John chapter three in the story of Nicodemus. Eternal life is to be lived now, 'In the light', as opposed to darkness. We become citizens of the light by experiencing Jesus and following in his way of light. He has the knowledge and spiritual insight to enlighten us through the Holy Spirit as we identify ourselves with him. The difficulty with Paul has always been that he writes in a world where there was no ordinary future. John has moved beyond this.

Although his picture of Jesus may seem rather weird; more of a God dressed up in human clothing, John does provide a different picture of how to live that has a greater impact on our lives today. His message is difficult to put into words, but he is saying that to live a life on this earth properly you need to be a person of the light. That light cannot be extinguished. He alludes to this as he describes his picture of the 'temple of his body' and life being destroyed and raised up on the third day. For John, people of the light will return to God as Jesus returns to God, but they must live enlightened lives in this world by following him and being born again of the Spirit.

Although we can think of many examples in life where one person 'carries the can' or is the scapegoat for others, we find much more difficulty in accepting that one person can actually be required to pay the judicial debt of sin. Paul, after all, talks as if we are justified before God because Jesus becomes the scapegoat for us all. That is an interesting picture of God and nowadays many people find it very difficult to comprehend a God that requires this kind of restitution.

Christianity has never been a uniform faith. There have always been many different understandings of the life and meaning of Jesus, the founding figure of our faith. As we come to reflect on the passion story, I want to make one suggestion to you. Do not just reflect on that single week. Reflect on the whole meaning of Jesus' life and work. The New Testament is a treasure of differing, but not necessarily mutually exclusive pictures as to how we should view Jesus, and we have to see him through our eyes, living now.

Remember that for us the world seems to go on. We are less interested in dramatic conclusions to our earthly life, but how we live it now, in the spirit and as people of light. Eternal life is light and what happens when we die need not concern us as we are in the hands of the God of light and love.

Maternal Care

I Samuel 1.20–28 Colossians 3.12–17
"Above all clothe yourselves with love."
Colossians 3.14.

Compassion, kindness, meekness, humility and patience. Although the passage does not refer specifically to motherhood, these might be considered some of the hallmarks a mother shows towards her children; these are also features that reflect the outpouring of one person towards another that mirror the image of Christ. But as I have said before these words only reach meaning in acts, deeds or attitudes.

On one of our visits to Australia, our most memorable encounter with a mother was in a beautiful garden on the outskirts of Brisbane. The more formal part of the garden was surrounded by native forest, the home of koalas, wallabies, possums and other marsupials. Our hostess took us on a little walk to a tree where a ring-tailed possum's nest was unusually low in the branches. We peered in; a pair of large brown eyes came and stared at us. We were definitely bad news; great ugly looking creatures. The possum disappeared for a moment and then there she was, running up the tree with one baby on her back and another older one running with her. She had to protect her young.

Protection. That is the word I thought I would dwell on

for a moment. Protection may appear instinctive but it is earthed in love.

The urge to protect a loved one from harm never goes away. I suppose a good example is the situation when older children who have left home and even married get into difficulties or have sorrows. The urge is to protect them from harm, take the pain in their place. The mother hurts with a pain that will not go away.

And that leads on to the notion of sacrifice that is at the centre, for many, of the Christian story. For many people Jesus is the suffering servant who suffers with us or indeed for us. Self-sacrifice is at the heart of what it is to be Christian. The self goes out towards others and we become human. Of course, we often fail and the awful things that happen in this world make us despair. In the great novel by Dostoyevsky *The Brothers Karamazov*, Ivan cannot equate the suffering dished out by evil people, particularly towards children, with any idea of eternal harmony. He wants to give his ticket for eternal harmony away. It just won't do.

Often, we are powerless to make a difference. The forces stacked against self-sacrifice are too great. That is the ambiguity of human existence. It would be easy to give up. But somewhere inside us, there is the will to go on.

I was very sad to hear this week that Archbishop Rowan has announced his resignation; sad because he is a holy man of huge integrity who has been an outstanding figure for good in public life and in the Church. But he has been treated badly. It is widely thought that he never wanted to be Archbishop. It was a sacrifice for someone who is one of the great intellectuals and theologians of recent times. Yet I think it is a good thing as well. Those of us who admire his writing, not necessarily agreeing with him, will be glad that he has more space and freedom to give us his thoughts. He has persevered in difficult times and has sacrificed his own interests.

For many people their spirituality is centred on the belief that Jesus suffered for them to protect them from the ravages of evil. Sometimes I prefer to express this slightly differently. Jesus is a model for how we should seek to protect each other from evil and harm. It is that that brings us nearer to the love that we hope to clothe ourselves with.

Do you like Harry Potter stories? You will recall that Harry survived a curse launched by Lord Voldemort. Why did he survive with that famous scar on his forehead? He survived because the love of his mother, Lily, protected him. She died but her love allowed Harry to live. In the *Goblet of Fire*, Lord Voldemort says: 'It was old magic. I had forgotten about old magic.' That 'old magic' is the primacy of love, found in true motherhood and indeed in all who seek to follow the path of selflessness.

I end with an uncollected extract from a poem by Patrick Kavanagh, the Irish poet. He chose not to include it in his collected poems. It is called *In Memory of my Mother,* I think he captures some of the essence of a grown-up child's thoughts about their mother:

You will have the road gate open, the front door ajar
The kettle boiling and a table set
By the window looking out at the sycamores —

And your loving heart lying in wait.

For me coming up among the poplar trees,
You'll know my breathing and my walk
And it will be a summer evening on those roads,
Lonely with leaves of thought.

We will be choked with the grief of things growing,
The silence of dark-green air
Life too rich — the nettles, docks and thistles
All answering the prodigal's prayer.

You will know I am coming though I send no word,
For you were lover who could tell
A man's thoughts — my thoughts — though I hid them —
Through you I knew Woman and did not fear her spell.

God Talk

Isaiah 40.27–41.13 John 11.17–44

"Have you not known? Have you not heard?
Has it not been told you from the beginning?
Have you not understood from the foundations of the earth? It is he who sits above the circle of the earth,
and its inhabitants are like grasshoppers;
who stretches out the heavens like a curtain,
and spreads them like a tent to live in; who brings princes to naught,
and makes the rulers of the earth as nothing."
Isaiah 40. 21-23.

That is one of the great pieces of Old Testament poetry. It causes my hair to rise; goose pimples to appear. It is one of those utterances that take one to the kernel of religious belief. The idea of the Holy, the sense of the Other. It exposes us as creatures and God as God. Let's talk about God for a few minutes. That might seem an odd statement, but 'God talk' is really quite rare. At least, 'God talk' when we seek to come to grips with who or what God is.

I have just retired from being an educational advisor for the Church of England. This is a role that involves assessing candidates who apply to be trained for ordination. Men and women from all over the country attend conferences, where they stay for a couple of days and undergo a variety of assessments to determine their suitability and vocation.

One of the tests is called the 'Personal Inventory'. One of the questions in it is this: 'What are the first three things that come into your mind when you think of God?' Nearly always one receives rather obvious answers. The candidate often sees God entirely through the eyes of Jesus, rather than the God of Isaiah. The answers vary; friend, love, holiness, judge, mercy, miracle worker and so on. I have never yet received the answer *Nothing*! I expect the candidates would be too wary to say *Nothing,* but why not? If I was asked a question like that, I might want to say *Nothing*. Why? Because God is not a concept that we can reduce to qualities or categories. To say *Nothing* is really quite a good answer. God is beyond our conceptions. As soon as we start giving God qualities we associate with human existence, we reduce God to some kind of superhuman. Many mystics have said more or less the same thing. It is sometimes known as the negative way. 'Have you not known? Have you not heard? The Lord is the everlasting God, the Creator of the ends of the earth. He does not faint or grow weary; his understanding is unsearchable.' (Isaiah 40.28).

But somehow that is not enough. We have a need to try and imagine what God is like. In a number of religions there is always an attempt to give God a human face. In Hinduism, Shiva and particularly Vishnu provide more human pictures than that of Brahma, particularly the manifestation of Vishnu known as Krishna who is the subject of one of Hinduisms holiest books, the Bhagavad-Gita. Jesus is for us, the human face of God; but even then, we make our own Jesus by projecting on to him the qualities we want to see, or the tradition that conditions us to see in a certain way. Can we escape all pre-conceptions and discover God and Jesus anew?

My own view is that we should start with God, the Holy One, the mysterious, the Other. Our starting point is the awareness of otherness, holiness that inspires what Rudolf Otto called 'fear and trembling'. Our passage today may inspire that in us. But apart from scripture, we may experience this mystical otherness in the natural world. It is a basic human quality to experience wonder and awe. A mother or father may have this experience at the birth of a baby, and that experience may recur as we see a baby transformed into a child, teenager, adult.

The second century heretic known as Marcion of Sinope thought that the god of the Old Testament was not the same god as the one of the new. The Old Testament god was inferior, tribal, violent, partial. The god of the New Testament was different. Marcion rejected the Old Testament completely. Marcion's Bible consisted of the Gospel of Luke and seven letters by Paul. Was he right? I do not think so. The reason is that throughout human history our idea of God has evolved. It has not evolved in quite the same way in all cultures. We have moved away from the idea of a tribal god who performs magic and needs to be placated; this god that gets angry and punishes us is a different kind of god. God came to be understood in Judaism and Christianity as the God of the heart, God of love; essentially mysterious but manifested in human form in the qualities of love and self-giving.

Sadly, the Church has often assumed that our understanding of God cannot change and that we are beyond evolving further understanding. That is untrue. We must all continue to seek God. We have had to understand God in relation to creation in a different way. If there is life on other planets we must move from the tribal god of Earth to God of the Universe and that may involve hard questions about Jesus. As part of my education I was always taught to 'think the unthinkable'; only then can one break free of shackles that may be binding us to false beliefs and customs. If we do this, we can be liberated to know God in a purer way.

But in the end, most of us want to return to those two qualities we connect with the New Testament; love and self-giving. We may be able to have a glimpse of God through human agency, but we must remember it is only a glimpse. Why do we choose those qualities? We certainly claim we see them in Jesus but equally we can see them in each other. Our religion would be of no value at all if it did not connect us with some aspect of humanity. Why do we revere some people? We revere a man like Nelson Mandela because of his sacrifice and his ability to transcend his personal maltreatment and seek reconciliation.

The best kind of motherhood is still one of the great examples of love and self-giving. You do not need me to explain this. We see God as ultimate mystery, but we know when we are in the presence of goodness, and somehow feel that self-giving and goodness are at the heart of the Divine.

The Spiritual Laboratory

Hebrews 5.5–10 John 12.20–33
"And I, when I am lifted up from the earth, will draw all people to myself."
John 12.32.

I wonder what that means? Perhaps we think we know. If we think we know, does what we claim to know coincide with what the person sitting next to us thinks? We discover how we are drawn to Jesus through a special kind of research. We learn to make connections; work out a kind of truth for ourselves.

Let's pay a visit to the laboratory. I have been thinking quite a lot about laboratories recently. When I was younger, I worked in a Medical Research Council laboratory and one of our sons has been a medical research worker in his chosen field of haematology. One of the key aspects of medical research is a quest for scientific truth. It is an enterprise that at the highest level requires imagination, question asking and answering, and a lot of application and grind. One must be prepared to modify or even reject received wisdom in order to move forward. The whole exercise can be both exciting but boring, bringing joy and disappointment. In a whole life of research, one can look back and realise how little one has achieved, but also that one is part of a vast chain of endeavour moving towards a goal of universal comprehension of a vital truth.

Have you ever been in a spiritual laboratory? Perhaps you will not call it by that name. It is not a place but more a state of mind. In it we search for spiritual truth; truth that we may or may not feel comfortable with. Perhaps one thing we have to realise before we start is that spiritual truth is simply not an absolute in this life. That is why the way one person owns the truth as they see it is not universal. There is relativity. Fanaticism, extremism and fundamentalism are enemies of spiritual truth because they make absolute claims that are unjustified and take no account of the insights of other traditions.

A life in the laboratory of the spirit requires the imagination, application, question asking and willingness to change we find in any scientific laboratory.

To remain in the 'lab' we have to study, think, imagine and become immersed in the work. Perhaps it is not for all, but those who do live in the laboratory of the spirit need to share their discoveries with others.

I am convinced that each of us needs to discover a spirituality that we are comfortable with. That means that we are integrated and that our spirituality is not in conflict with the evidence and experience we derive from our daily living. It can be very sad to see people who refuse to acknowledge what has been discovered and build a concrete wall around their lives, protecting cherished beliefs from any kind of assault.

I suppose the obvious example of this is the impact that Darwin's theory of natural selection and evolution had on the Church of the late nineteenth century. Creationism still exists today, notably in the USA, but the majority of Christians have been able to adapt their spirituality to new scientific discovery.

The nineteenth century Church viewed from a twenty-first century perspective looks ridiculous, and the famous Oxford debate between Bishop Wilberforce and Thomas Huxley, a farce. It is an example of the danger of a fixed orthodoxy that cannot change but is unfit for purpose for the vast majority of people in the twenty-first century. We live in a fool's paradise if we think we can live in a world view created hundreds of years ago in a different culture.

I am a founder member of a third order group known as the Society of Ordained Scientists. I am no longer able to go to meetings and retreats, but it brings together the laboratory of the spirit and the scientific laboratory. The society members have differing spiritualities and differing views, but they share a common interest in discovering a spirituality that sits comfortably with science and that can be lived out with integrity.

How does Jesus draw all people to himself? We can acknowledge that Christianity is one of the world's largest religions. People from various cultures and levels of development have been drawn to Jesus. But they have not all seen him in the same way. We know from a study of early Christian documents that there were differing beliefs about Jesus from the time of his crucifixion. Sadly, a lot of documents were destroyed by those wishing to suppress alternative views to perceived orthodoxy, but enough remain to discover the rich heritage of imaginative thinking about Jesus and his life and work. One lesson we have to learn from the orthodoxy that emerged triumphant after the council of Nicaea is to avoid dogmatism and live with difference.

Jesus may draw you because you believe in some way he saves you from your sins. You may believe that through his teaching and extraordinary life he is someone to follow, who challenges you through his teaching on the shores of Galilee. You want to follow him in this twenty-first century world of intrigue and hatred as you seek to discover the law of love.

You may think that he is God's Son in the sense that his spiritual relationship with God was very special. But some of you may be less sure that he is the only expression of the Divine in humanity. In this you will pay tribute to other faiths born and sustained in other cultures that you feel you cannot ignore, including the differing views of Jesus that exist in Judaism, Islam, the wisdom of the Buddhas' and Hindu sacred scriptures.

Jesus draws us to him. How he does it is rather like the effect on us of some great poem. We, the readers of this Gospel, immersed in our imagination in the work, find our inspiration, our particular truth, and although connected to the insights of others, it is peculiarly our own. The truth of Jesus drawing us to himself and the insight of a great poem are unique to us individually, determined by our culture, our education, our personalities and lastly by the length of time we spend in that laboratory of the spirit.

I wish you well as we all continue to explore how Jesus draws us and how his inspiration governs our lives as we seek to follow him.

Law in the Heart

Jeremiah 31.31–34 John 12. 20–33

"I will put my law within them, and I will write it on their hearts; and I will be their God and they shall be my people."
Jeremiah 31.33.

"Very truly, I tell you, unless a grain of wheat falls into the earth and dies, it remains just a single grain; but if it dies, it bears much fruit."
John 12.24.

The covenant relationship between God and the Children of Israel is important. Historical studies show that there were two types of covenant treaty in the ancient Middle East: so-called parity covenants between equals and the covenant between king and people. The latter covenant started with a preamble and was followed by specific commitments on either side. It was perfectly clear when the covenant was broken and what the consequences would be.

These ancient covenants were used to describe the undertakings between God, the king and his vassal people. It was made when the law was given to Moses. It was a matter of strict observance. It failed like many others of its type.

Jeremiah writing around the kingdom of Judah's exile to Babylon was well aware of this. As God's prophet he had called upon them to repent. Now writing in a more hopeful tone he envisages through God a new covenant. This covenant is fundamentally altered. Gone is the emphasis on external observance through a rigid treaty.

Jeremiah says clearly that the new covenant is about the heart. It is a covenant that comes from change within. This is a covenant for everyone. How one lives and behaves in the future will come from internal change. It will not be a covenant of fear, it will be followed willingly.

But this does require something radical. The New Testament is ripe with language that points to the kind of change required. The Gospel of John has several arresting images. In the third chapter we have the story of Nicodemus and the need to be born again if we are to live with God in our hearts. One of the images of baptism is of dying to sin and rising to new life as one rises from the water. External rituals symbolise this change of heart.

In the twelfth chapter of John we have the image of the seed or grain of wheat, dying to give rise to new life. It is followed by the image that for us to be true followers of Jesus we have to follow him in dying to ourselves and thus attaining true life.

It is lofty language. Is it too difficult for us? Sometimes we may think that it seems to be something for those who detach themselves from ordinary life in the world, but much harder in the everyday 'knock about world'. The Buddha left his own wife and child. Jesus appeared to leave home and pay little heed to his family. The early desert monastic movement took people away from the world, partly because they considered they were being tainted by it.

Although we cannot dispute the rightness of detachment

for some people, it is not for us all. We are called to be 'leaven or salt'. We are called to work within our world to make it 'come right'. If we believe that God can change us internally, he can do this wherever we are.

There has never been any evidence that the Christian life goes on without struggle. The law written within our hearts has to be fed and kept alive. But it is possible within our human limitations to follow that vision of Jeremiah.

Most of us recognise a holy person when we meet one. They stand as lights for us. They need not be clever, famous or powerful. Jeremiah reminds us of this. A few weeks ago, I went to the funeral of someone in my last parish. He had been an agricultural worker for many years and a church warden for much of them. In some ways he was very ordinary, but in those that matter he was quite extraordinary. I know of no one who did not think he was very special. All the clergy who had worked with him looked up to him. He was a holy man, uncomplicated, but with a broad vision, a great sense of humour. He never complained about his setbacks. He welcomed everyone and shared himself with them.

People like Bob are living examples of the fruit that can come from a life committed to God. As we approach Holy Week and Easter we will reflect on death and suffering, a life surrendered. Death and life do go hand in hand. It is time for us to reflect on the Way of the Cross and what it may be telling us. Paradoxically it leads to life, but it requires a change of heart.

Palm Sunday and Holy Week

During Passiontide it is customary to reflect on the procession of Jesus to Jerusalem, a moment of apparent triumph; and then be a witness to the change in atmosphere, culminating in his 'betrayal' after the Passover meal, followed by his trial and crucifixion. The Resurrection belongs to Easter. There can be little doubt that the core events of this period, perhaps a week, have some basis in history, although the detail varies within the Gospel accounts.

The entry into Jerusalem is not necessarily factual. It is a pictorial account, with Hebrew Bible referents. In Zachariah 9.9 it states: 'Rejoice greatly, O daughter of Zion! Shout aloud, O daughter of Jerusalem! Lo, your king comes to you; triumphant and victorious is he, humble and riding on a donkey, on a colt, the foal of a donkey.' Jesus is presented as a king of peace as he enters Jerusalem on a donkey, an animal of peace. Tradition has it that he enters from the Mount of Olives, after a stay in Bethany. He was popular with ordinary people and was the focus of a movement of liberation, although the evidence is that it was not understood. The heart of the story is that he came to Jerusalem with enthusiastic acclaim. He may or may not have known the city. Some suggest that he was naïve concerning his arrival in the capital, seething with political dissent, with the Sadducee hierarchy wary of any group that would threaten Roman authority.

The ‘last supper’ must have been a Passover meal and the chronology of John’s Gospel emphasises this. Jesus was a practising Jew and there is no evidence that he abandoned his cultural and religious origins. The ‘betrayal’ by Judas is a curious episode. All the disciples betrayed Jesus in one sense, but Judas has been vilified down the centuries. It seems likely that Jesus was betrayed, but what that really amounted to is difficult to determine. The authorities were wary of political agitators, but Jesus appeared unconcerned about politics. Many regard Judas as a ’zealot’ who misunderstood the nature of Jesus’ mission and became disillusioned. Yet this does not really fit in with the notion that Jesus was a threat. The trial material is unclear about what really happened. It seems likely that the Jewish authorities were concerned that Jesus was a rebel and were never convinced otherwise. Pilate, a ruthless man, appears to regard Jesus as a harmless eccentric, but we need to realise that it is quite impossible to find reliable historical data from these stories. They reflect the various agendas of the Gospel writers. It is important to realise that the ‘Jews’ as a whole did not crucify Jesus. Whatever happened, we must never blame Jews, generally, for the death of Jesus. This is one event that has influenced centuries of antisemitism.

The sermons chosen were preached on various days from Palm Sunday to the Tenebrae reflection on Good Friday. There are no specific readings at the head of the Tenebrae reflection as the service involves multiple readings. There is some overlap in the sermons. They are not identical, but some of the images I use are similar; saying the same thing in different ways is at the core of preaching.

Triumph and Rejection

Isaiah 5.1–7 Matthew 21.33–46
"The stone that the builders rejected
has become the cornerstone."
Matthew 21.42.

Palm Sunday is a day of preparation; preparing the ground for what lies ahead. The morning of Palm Sunday is deceptive. At one level Jesus rides into Jerusalem triumphantly, seemingly popular. He is at the head of a group of Galileans; these are not Jerusalem people. In many ways they are 'innocents'. They do not know what they are letting themselves in for. When they arrive, the city is in chaos; a place of ferment, latent political rebellion seething beneath the surface. The political leaders, the scribes and the Sadducees are tense. They do not want trouble. They want to appease the Romans and hang on to their influence.

Matthew covers two days in the temple. Jesus is teaching in parables. He had gone there on his entry into Jerusalem and again on this second day. He appeared to be well received by ordinary people who proclaimed him as son of David, but the scribes and chief priests were worried. Jesus was a threat. The essence of this parable of the vineyard that mirrors our passage in Isaiah is that he will be rejected, but he will become the cornerstone of something new. He is being rejected by the religious authorities that are the power brokers of the Jewish faith.

As we come to consider our pathway to Easter, the word rejection has to be high in our vocabulary. We have to follow the path of rejection to understand the message of Easter and connect with the inner meaning of this foundation event for the Christian Church. In taking our path towards the crucifixion and beyond, we are not just following an ancient story with at least some historical basis. We have to examine our own path of rejecting and rejection. We are required to examine ourselves and our world and reflect on who and what we have rejected in our lives and perhaps how we have been rejected too. Both these are part of what we are, as I hope the next few days will reveal to us. We are a mixture. In the immortal words of the Reverend Eli Jenkins in *Under Milk Wood*: 'We are not wholly bad or good.' We will have rejected bad or evil things, but we will have rejected the good in others, and we ourselves will have been ignored or rejected in our time. Our motives have certainly not been selfless, and our ideas of virtue may have been distorted. So today, inevitably, we should start on a journey inward alongside Jesus.

When we examine ourselves, we are dependent on memory. All memory is in God if we deem him to exist. It is never lost. We may suppress memories we do not want to reflect on, but our challenge is to examine ourselves and discover some of the things we might not want to remember. For us to become 'whole' we must confront our memories, recognise their significance and face them. On Easter Sunday we will recognise why this is important. We might be recalling quite minor events, but with greater significance than we might imagine.

This rediscovery of memory is an important part of preparing ourselves for Easter. I will not elaborate more now as we have several occasions to develop the theme that lies ahead. What is important to emphasise is that rejection is not peculiar to the passion of Jesus, so long ago; both individually and corporately we are all involved in acts of rejection.

None of this is to recommend self-absorption. However, spiritual masters such as Meister Eckhart have pointed to the importance of the journey inward to enable us to move outward into our world in a new way. Meister Eckhart said this: 'A human being has so many skins inside, covering the depths of the heart. We know so many things, but we don't know ourselves! Why, thirty or forty skins or hides, as thick and hard as an ox's or bear's, cover the soul. Go into your own ground and learn to know yourself there.' Sebastian Moore, the monk of Downside Abbey, wrote a famous book in 1963. He recently died at the age of 96. It is called the *Crucified Jesus is no Stranger*. It brings the events of Holy Week into our own world. The title has an obvious meaning. The meaning of the crucifixion is no distant event; it is meaningful all the time, played out in daily life

As I have said, in reflecting on our own lives and connecting them with the events of Holy Week, we are examining ourselves. We are going beneath the surface events of daily life to discover meaning. We may ask what is the self'? Who or what are we? The self is something very elusive.

Sometimes, I wonder where it is. The philosopher John Locke considered our identity indelibly linked with memory that links the past, present and future. We live in time. To be free from time we must rediscover it.

So, in this week we are followers of the Way of Christ and

journey with him, remembering in sadness and awe the intentions of our loving God, and the anguish and pain this caused. But this should be no passive remembrance, but an active one connected to our own inward reflections as individuals and as a community. God will guide us to forgiveness and new life, but first we must travel a painful road.

The Innocent Victim

Isaiah 50.4–9a Matthew 27.11–54
"Why, what evil has he done?"
Matthew 27.23.

Jesus is portrayed in the Gospels as the innocent victim. Whatever Pilate may have said and done he is portrayed in this passage as seeking to protect Jesus from mob violence. His question is reasonable. What had Jesus done to justify execution? Many pious Christians understand this passion story as a divine drama, orchestrated by God to redeem the world. Those who do not take that view are unhappy that the cast in these events are then made to appear as puppets, without ultimate responsibility. Did this all have to happen? We are faced immediately with the question: What kind of God are we 'believing in'? I have put those last two words in inverted commas. Perhaps a more useful question is: Where are we in our exploration of the nature of God? That should be a continuing, shifting journey. For me the issue here is that Jesus did not have to die. His death has more subtle overtones. He draws our attention to the drama of good and evil that continues to dominate our world, despite the ambiguities over our understanding of what is a good or bad act or mind set.

I want to focus for a moment on the universal significance of the trial of Jesus. Rather than reducing this week to the inevitable enactment of a cosmic plan, let us see this as a focus of the battle I referred to. I know we can enter into subtle arguments about these two opposing forces, but for most of us there is an innate sense as to what evil is and the innocent victim epitomises this. And yet we do find, rather too frequently, evil acts perpetrated in the name of a supposed greater good, even in the name of God.

Pilate's question can be answered in a limited way from what we can glean from the possible histories of these events. Jesus was an itinerant preacher, a Galilean Holy Man with an arresting message and a charismatic presence. He drew crowds to hear him, but his message of a new kingdom was not fully understood and certainly not as far as the Sadducees, the political elite of Jerusalem, were concerned. They saw Jesus as a potential troublemaker, someone who might foster rebellion and upset the Roman rulers, who gave the Sadducees an element of autonomy in Jerusalem. That is a partial answer to Pilate's question. We know that Holy Week led to innocent death.

Important as Holy Week is in itself there must be an attempt to make connections between the trial of Jesus and our world. It is the destruction of the innocent that resonates down the ages as an aspect of human behaviour. Major events such as the Holocaust, the decimation of native peoples in the Americas and other parts of the world, and the current tragedies in Syria, France, London and Sweden, point to evil; the suffering of the innocent.

There is a continuing risk of these tragedies being sanitised because they are so common, and we view them from our armchairs. Individual suffering sometimes wakes us up; for example, the appalling attack on a young Kurdish-Iranian refugee in Croydon by a mob of young people. All these events and many more bring home to us our need for repentance and forgiveness. It is so easy for us to stand back and think; this has nothing to do with me. I am not that kind of person. The story of Jesus brings into focus the continuing destruction of the innocent by all of us. We cannot escape our responsibility.

Ten days ago, I had lunch in Northumberland with one of my mentors in neurology, now aged ninety-four. He was reflecting on whether we could see disturbing elements of Darwinian natural selection within humanity. Traditionally, evolution is seen over aeons of time and we tend to discount any current observations. But it is possible to picture a violent subset of humanity emerging. I am not simply referring to Daesh or any other group of extremists, but to the general possibility of the innocent being destroyed by the violent. We cannot assume that humanity is moving in the right direction towards peace and harmony. That may not happen.

Teilhard de Chardin, the French Jesuit priest/scientist/philosopher, thought that evolution was inexorably drawn towards an omega point of maximum complexity and spiritualisation. It is an attractive thought, but it seems more likely that we are continually involved in a battle between good and evil; the outcome not guaranteed. That remains the challenge for us all. That is the challenge of Holy Week and now. Our redemption comes from forgiveness and a turning to face what we are, followed by taking up our cross, determined that hate and violence will not conquer our world.

Crucifixion Today

Isaiah 42.1–9 Hebrews 9.11–18
John 12.1–11

"He will not grow faint or be crushed until he has established justice in the earth; and the coastlands wait for his teaching."
Isaiah 42.4.

Every year, if we are associated with the Christian tradition, we go on a journey with Jesus through the events of Holy Week.

Sadly, for any of us, it can be a half-hearted journey. On the other hand, it may be a journey filled with Christian piety, imbued with the traditional language, depicting the last hours of the suffering 'Lamb of God'. The Lamb slaughtered for us, as those lambs and goats were slaughtered at the original Passover, when God protected the Israelites through the blood of the lamb smeared over their door lintels.

It is impossible to divorce the imagery of the Exodus story from that of Holy Week. Crucifixion was a Roman method of execution, but the creative language that painted the significance of that event is rich in allusion to the inheritance that any pious Jew would be familiar with. This time of year brings us close to the similarity and differences between ourselves and our Jewish 'cousins'.

One challenge for us as we go through the week is to try

to connect with our own thought forms and ways of thinking. Like it or not we live in a post-Christian culture in terms of knowledge of Christian origins. The images we may treasure do not strike chords in the hearts of many. Fewer and fewer people are readily drawn to some of the images or thought forms the Church uses. We may lament this or debate it, but it is reality. The problem is that Easter is for everyone, not just the religious few.

One of the great challenges for Christianity is to make connections with lives today. I certainly believe that unless we face this, Church as institution will wither and be restricted to the more extreme sects that, because of their capacity to attract people, give the superficial impression of success.

The text I chose from Isaiah points to an important element in the last journey of Jesus and it can be a starting point for engagement.

I use the name Jesus rather than Christ or other descriptions very deliberately. At this time, we need to be firmly connected with Jesus, the man, moving towards his death. Other words such as Christ are titles to describe his significance. We need firm contact with the man. Jesus is not the only innocent person to have suffered mentally and physically in human history. Some have been his followers, others not.

We cannot know who the prophet Isaiah was referring to. We may be happy to link these words specifically with Jesus, as many do, or we may see it as referring to anyone who retains their integrity in the middle of innocent suffering. It does not matter. Isaiah's words cohere with important elements in the story as it is told: 'He will not grow faint or be crushed.'

Jesus did not shout and cry out in the streets. He had a

vision of a new Israel, a new spirituality, that led to justice and peace. His vision was a reversal of much of the thinking of his time, obsessed with the battle with Rome and the rise and perpetuation of Jewish nationalism. He may have thought the end of time was near and that focuses any mind. His was a battle against evil in the world.

Jesus stuck to his task, his vocation. It became clear that he was in conflict with the establishment. The picture of the triumphal entry into Jerusalem was soon replaced by antipathy. He was a nuisance. His vision of a world governed by the spirit of God, a kingdom where human precedence meant nothing and love ruled, sat uncomfortably alongside the more political and worldly aspirations of his peers.

It would seem that many people misunderstood his mission. They saw it in a worldlier context. Jesus saw the imminent spiritual destruction of Israel without a complete change of heart on the part of his people. He was not prepared to compromise. It seems likely that he was aware of the likelihood of his own death. He certainly could have backed off. His death was not inevitable. We miss some of the point of it all if we see him as a kind of puppet fulfilling a set plan. He was faithful to the call of God and that resulted in his death. Despite his mental agonies, common to the human condition, he maintained his integrity and died prematurely.

It is not uncommon to turn away from the Good, refuse to listen, desire to snuff it out. It happens all the time. We may feel distinctly uncomfortable when we are challenged to make a complete change of direction and follow God.

All of us can ask ourselves whether we have lost our integrity when we are challenged to take a hard and painful path. We may, like Peter, have given in and tried to hide. It is not difficult to see how this week, special as it is, connects readily with the human condition at any time in history.

The story of Jesus this week, as he journeys to Jerusalem, enters into conflict with the authorities, has a last supper with his friends, is betrayed and executed, is a gripping drama. Sometimes traditional Christology, misunderstood or distorted, detracts from his humanity, makes him superhuman rather than tempted in all things as we are.

The words 'He was despised and rejected of men, a man of sorrows and acquainted with grief,' continue to inspire and move as we journey with him. What would we have done if we were there in Jerusalem? Would we have betrayed him, denied him, executed him? We will never know. But perhaps every time we treat any other person in that way, we crucify Jesus, the spirit of God in humankind.

I have mentioned before, the book *The Crucified Jesus is no Stranger.* I was first put in touch with it when I went for my monthly sessions with the former principal of my ordination course. The basic idea in this book is that our healing, new life, comes when we recognise in the crucified Jesus, raised up upon the Cross, our true humanity, which we reject. That is, we want our humanity to be something different. That should be at the heart of our journey with Jesus this week. If we can accept this, we are at the beginning of being the sons and daughters God called us to be.

Handed Over

Isaiah 49.1–7 John 12.20–36
"Now my soul is troubled. And what should I say — 'Father, save me from this hour?' No, it is for this reason that I have come to this hour."
John 12.27.

Is that quotation the remark of a mortal? We find a more human Jesus in the Garden of Gethsemane; as recorded in Mark chapter fourteen, Luke chapter twenty-two and Matthew chapter twenty-six. But there is no such account in John. It does not suit his theology which has added another layer to the figure of Jesus. For a moment, listen to the Synoptic Gospels: 'And going a little farther, he threw himself on the ground and prayed, "My Father, if it is possible, let this cup pass from me; yet not what I want but what you want."' (Matthew 26.39).

I want to meditate for a few moments on these quotations and what thoughts they may give rise to, linking them with experiences we can bring from our own lives. This is how we can make connections with Jesus. Sometimes human pieties, or what we might call misplaced reverence, prevent us from getting under the skin of these familiar passages.

In the passage from John's Gospel we read of Jesus' awareness of impending trials and tribulations, but he appears in control, he will not cry out for release. He will go through with whatever is required.

In our own experience we can remember occasions when we are close to a difficult time. It may be a very unpleasant experience in hospital, a very challenging experience at work; there are all sorts of ordeals that we can anticipate sometimes, although there are many more that we cannot. They are upon us, there is no warning sign. If we think that it is important, we choose to undergo these trials, or we have no influence over them.

I find it reassuring that we can interpret Jesus as being human in his approach to his imminent ordeal. In the Garden of Gethsemane, in the Synoptic Gospels, Jesus' apparent self-assurance in John has disappeared. He is about to be swallowed up in a process where there will be no escape. I find the synoptic account far more convincing.

Just like us he cries out for relief. 'Help me God!' 'Take this away!' But like many other pious Jews he accepts the will of God.

Most of us will have cried out for God to rescue us from suffering. We long for relief from our condition, a magical disappearance of our woes to a world of peace, calm and freedom. But in our hearts, we know that whatever may happen, we have no choice and we have to go through with the experience. If there is peace and calm, it will not be won cheaply.

We may begin to realise several types of experience that we might term 'suffering' experiences. There are those when something really bad starts to happen to us for no apparent reason or purpose. There is absolutely no benefit to anyone. Then there is the suffering that comes from our own foolish behaviour that we bring upon ourselves. And finally, there is suffering and anguish that we go through for a purpose or a good that we seek to achieve. It is this latter experience that connects with the experience of Jesus and that we need to reflect on.

For Jesus, these last days were the culmination of a life of preparation followed by a very short ministry in which he sought to lead his people out of slavery or darkness into freedom and life, into new life. He had a great vision that he was the chosen one to make this happen. He used phrases like the *Kingdom of Heaven* and the *Kingdom of God* to paint a picture of that new life. Self-seeking, corruption and meaningless religion would become things of the past. He was prepared to go to any extreme of suffering, even death, to bring in the Kingdom, not for him, but for others. At the end, as his people turned against him and all seemed to be turning to dust, he had those moments of uncertainty that he could not go through with it. He did not want to be arrested and die. What human being would ever want that?

But he had gone beyond the point of no return. He was handed over to the chief priests and Pharisees. At this point the active passed into the passive. His fate would be determined by the behaviour of others. How would he be treated? We know the story. He was treated badly. He did not have a fair trial. He was executed. The reasons for his execution may be complex, perhaps it was fear from the religious establishment who wanted no renewal, and perhaps it was fear of affecting a cosy relationship with Rome. But there were reasons why he was killed, and we do him no justice if we stay with the notion it was all part of some pre-determined plan and that the players were robots in some cosmic drama. There is a big place for drama in the mystery of faith, but not at the expense of some contact with reality.

Earth's history contains many examples of innocent humans who have been the passive recipients of human cruelty. When we become passive, helpless, because there is nothing else for us to be, we depend on the goodness of others. Every baby, every profoundly disabled person, every exile, is in the hands of another. Will we treat them with love or despise and reject them? The innocent, the helpless, say: 'Here am I, what will you do with me?'

In the end Jesus was crucified and we too symbolically crucify others who are innocent when we neglect, reject and damage them.

I suppose each of us fears losing control, some more than others. We are terrified of that point when we can no longer run our own lives. As we reflect in Holy Week and dwell on the picture of Jesus handed over; dwell on the agonies we may have felt at being on a path we could barely cope with, that we longed to be released from, we recall the picture of Jesus handed over to the goodness or badness of people. Then, we realise why his mission to change the world must never cease and that we are called to take up our crosses and follow him.

Justifying Betrayal

Isaiah 50.4–9a John 13.21–32
"I tell you one of you will betray me."
John 13.21.

Judas Iscariot has come down in history and entered our language as a betrayer. Whatever recent attempts there may be to rehabilitate him, mainly in North American literature, following the publication of the Gospel of Judas, probably originally written around the year 200 CE, the canonical Gospels cite him as the betrayer of Jesus. Their accounts are different, particularly as to how Judas died. There have been debates about his motives. Were they purely pecuniary or was Judas disillusioned as a possible zealot who misunderstood the mission of the Son of Man?

Acts of betrayal are seldom as simple as they seem. The triumphal entry into Jerusalem was rapidly replaced by a more sinister atmosphere in the seething city. It would not be long before Peter's denial and the early disciples abandoned Jesus to his fate with great alacrity. As we move on in the passion narrative, we are not dealing with the betrayal by one man; we are dealing with the developing antagonism towards an innocent person that ends in his death. I think it is unhelpful to think of all this, as Calvin did, as some predestined series of events, or God's plan being executed as a necessary event.

Many might disagree with me. Certainly, all memory is held in God, but if we are to see the meaning of resurrection that lies beneath the surface events, we cannot reject human responsibility. Betrayal is a very human thing.

If we are to make a worthwhile journey this Holy Week, we must avoid yet another amble through the events and consider how betrayal has entered us, in our relationships and daily lives. Betrayal is the breaking of trust, the erosion of love. It is a state of mind, a desertion. Othello trusts Iago in Shakespeare's play, initially. But Iago has deceived him, nothing is what it seems. Iago uses Othello's vulnerability, his jealousy over Desdemona, to undermine him. This is an example of betrayal in the literature of tragedy.

In classic Greek literature the Oresteia tells the story of Agamemnon and Clytemnestra. Agamemnon and Clytemnestra violated each other's trust. Agamemnon's betrayals were the sacrifice of their daughter Iphigenia to the gods and bringing back a prophetic concubine from Troy. Clytemnestra murdered her husband and in turn was murdered by their son Orestes. This is one of the great breakdowns of family life in literature.

But such examples are not just in our literature, for literature reflects real life and we have to examine ourselves, our family and external lives for episodes or acts of betrayal. They will be there. We may feel we have been betrayed too. The examples may be less dramatic than the story of Judas or those in the great classics, but they will be there. Part of our journey in Holy Week has to acknowledge our role in betrayal in our age and not smugly point the finger at Judas or those early disciples.

One of the essential tasks of the pilgrim is to acknowledge

that the kind of events that led to the crucifixion are not unique in themselves. They are a feature of human existence and every time we betray the trust of another, we are ourselves involved metaphorically in an act that may lead to crucifixion or self-destruction.

Aeneas felt guilty about leaving Dido and tried to do so secretly. When Aeneas stopped at Carthage on his wanderings, Dido took him and his followers in. She offered them hospitality and in particular, offered herself to Aeneas. She considered theirs a commitment, like a betrothal if not a marriage and was inconsolable when she learned he was leaving. She cursed the Romans and killed herself. Aeneas took his orders from his gods but neglected his conscience. If we look at this story carefully, we realise that he made his decision based on a supposed greater destiny; the foundation of Rome.

Life is full of examples of decisions made, that involve the betrayal of one person or group for the greater good of the so-called majority. Crudely put, the end justifies the means. This operates at government level and at individual level. I have always felt that utilitarianism is deeply flawed for this reason. To provide another literary allusion: in Dostoyevsky's *Crime and Punishment*, Raskolnikov, a student, murders a wicked old female money lender with an axe. He attempts to justify this to himself, prefiguring the horrors of The Russian Revolution, by arguing that her death will be for the greater good of many and is therefore justified. His redemption comes through the love of the prostitute Sonia, who truly loves him and leads him to salvation.

It is so very easy to justify what we do by specious arguments. Always, we need to look afresh at what we think and do in the name of some greater good. We will never know why Judas betrayed Jesus. We can understand that the disciples deserted him through fear and lack of courage. Let us have the courage to continue our journey with Jesus to the end of his passion and the hope that lies beyond.

The Servant King

Exodus 12.1–4, 11–14 1 Corinthians 11.23–26 John 13.1–17, 31b–35

"This day shall be a day of remembrance for you. You shall celebrate it as a festival to the Lord; throughout your generations you shall observe it as a perpetual ordinance." Exodus 12.14.

This text is taken from the book of Exodus and we cannot understand why we are here tonight without recalling the Exodus story. God tells the Israelites to prepare young yearling lambs, sheep or goats, and at twilight on a specific day they are to eat the meat in a hurry, fully dressed, ready for action and spread the blood on the door posts and lintel. God passes through the place and the first born of the Egyptian people and animals are slaughtered, but the Israelites are passed over. The sacrificial blood of the lamb protects and saves them. They are told by God to keep the ordinance of the Passover for ever to remember their day of release. And so, the Passover has been kept ever since by Jewish families.

Now imagine the upper room where Jesus meets with his disciples for a Jewish meal. Whatever time of Passover it was, it is clear that Jesus turns the meal into a new kind of Passover. His disciples would have fully understood his references. I think the atmosphere there would have been electric. There would have been a sense of urgency, tension and fear. There would have been a sense that something momentous was about to happen.

Our epistle to the Corinthians is the earliest record we have of the ritual of the Last Supper. It may be the record of a regular memorial meal in the early Church. Paul wrote this letter around 50 CE, probably twenty years before our earliest Gospel, Mark, and approximately fifty years before John's Gospel was written.

Paul tells us that Jesus turned this special meal into a new kind of Passover, as a symbol of the new covenant or agreement between God and Israel and the broader world. Jesus is pictured by Paul and the Gospel writers as the new sacrificial lamb. He supersedes the ancient Passover memory. His death is to be seen as God passing over people who adopt Jesus. He mediates the forgiveness that we need through the shedding of his blood, and it is tonight and every time we celebrate the Lord's Supper that we remember this and give thanks.

What Jesus is stated to have said and done in that upper room is extremely radical. For the pious Jew it would have been an awful thing to mess around with Passover symbolism. His own disciples may have been deeply shocked. Indeed, it may have shaken them so much that they wondered whether they wanted to be associated with him. Of course, we do not know what really happened. We were not there, and our Gospels are not simple history books. But there is no doubt that the language of sacrifice was attached to Jesus' death from an early time, and at the time of Paul, some few years after the death of Jesus, there must have been some kind of memorial meal.

Some people can and some cannot connect with this sacrificial language about Jesus. It may seem alien and from another world. Yet they will want to say that in some way, on this night, something very special happened and that there are many ways of expressing what it was. That is a good thing.

In John's Gospel we do not read words of institution. At the meal we have a different emphasis. The language of Passover and sacrifice is not used. Here we encounter Jesus washing his disciples' feet. Jesus is making them clean through his role as servant. He calls on his disciples and all of us who are present in that room in heart and mind to follow his example of service and love. If we love and serve others we will be purified and those we serve will be altered through our love.

When we meet Jesus each time at the memorial supper or Eucharist, we encounter his purifying love. He serves us as we are called to serve. His new covenant to love one another is renewed. There is no need for sacrifice anymore. He has, through his life and death, removed the need for it. We are free. We sing a hymn: 'This is our God, the Servant King, He calls us now to follow Him, to bring our lives as a daily offering of worship to the Servant King.' This is how we remember Jesus tonight; the Servant King and the Lamb of God who takes away the sin of the world.

Tenebrae Meditation

Jesus was handed over. Despite pious reflection that this was part of a sophisticated, pre-ordained plan that took Jesus inexorably to the Cross, it is more helpful to see this as a situation that had more than one possible outcome. We are sometimes persuaded otherwise by the frequent reference to the fulfilment of prophecy. It is understandable that those early writers, imbued for the most part with Jewish scripture and tradition, would seek to connect the events of the Passion with their early history. They now recognised Jesus as the Messiah and many of them were aware of messianic expectation in Jewish hope. A means of releasing them from bondage.

Jesus was handed over to specific people in a specific historical period; the chief priests, the Roman procurator and the people of Jerusalem. They had a choice. What should they do with this man, crucify him or release him?

When anyone is taken prisoner for whatever reason we have a choice. We can deal with them justly or unjustly. This is not necessarily a judicial situation. We can imagine a refugee, a seeker of asylum for genuine reasons, or a very sick and disabled person who is completely dependent on others. Those people have handed themselves over. The sick person has no choice. How will they be treated?

To understand the situation Jesus was in, it is helpful to remember the image of the scapegoat in Jewish literature. In modern parlance scapegoating refers to an individual, group or country singled out for unmerited negative treatment or blame. In the Old Testament ritual of Yom Kippur (Lev.16.8–10), a goat was symbolically burdened with the sins of the Jewish people. By extension, a scapegoat has come to mean any group or individual that bears the blame of others. Jesus became a scapegoat or a victim.

We decide to make people victims. It does not just happen. Last Sunday we spoke about the need to travel inward to rediscover memory and we used the word rejection as an indicator of how we have rejected and been rejected. Tonight, the word is victimise or victim. We discover that we have victimised others or become victims, most likely both.

If we examine the Church, supposedly carrying the good news of Jesus, we find women, gay people, even disabled people victimised. In my own working life as an NHS doctor I have seen people blamed for a situation to tidy things up. If we have a scapegoat everything will settle down. We can move on and forget about those troubles. Let's blame someone. After all it's so much easier!

Jesus was handed over and he moved from action to passion. The word passion is linked to passivity. W.H. Vanstone wrote two seminal books; one is called *The Stature of Waiting*. By passivity (passion or waiting) Vanstone means that uncomfortable condition of being made subject to something beyond our control: illness, unemployment, frustration at work, old age. These are things that rob us of our power and independence, and thus potentially of our dignity and self-worth. We become dependent on others for better or worse.

Vanstone suggests that the primary purpose of the Passion

stories is not to show that Jesus' death sacrificially atoned for us, but rather that his passion as a whole (his acceptance of being 'handed over' and losing his freedom) gives dignity to all such experiences. 'Glory' is found as much in God's acceptance of passivity in Christ, in his waiting in love for a human response ('Will Israel's rulers turn to him?'), not just in actions.

They do not treat him well. He was crucified. He was crucified by Pontius Pilate, by the Jerusalem hierarchy and by the Jerusalem people shouting, 'Crucify him'. That is not to blame the Jewish people throughout history. That is a great evil. He was crucified by the people of Jerusalem, most if not all happened to be Jews, but the reference to the people of Jerusalem is the better description. As we shall see on Sunday this is most important when we come to reflect on the meaning of the Resurrection.

Vanstone has great insight. The lover is often depicted not as the active one, but as the one who patiently (passably) waits. So, it is shown that the supreme moment of God's glory in Jesus is his surrendering of himself into the hands of men.

Quite deliberately I end with a poem from the great Persian poet Rumi on surrender:

> Joseph is back.
> And if you don't feel in yourself
> the freshness of Joseph,
> be Jacob.
> Weep, and then smile.
> Do not pretend to know something
> You have not experienced.
> There is a necessary dying,

and then Jesus is breathing again.
Very little grows on jagged rock.
Be ground. Be crumbled,
so wildflowers will come up
where you are.
You have been stony for too many years.
Try something different.
Surrender.

Easter and Ascension

The Easter season lies at the core of Christianity; that is beyond dispute. Yet how the momentous story of the resurrection of Jesus is interpreted varies enormously. There are those who take the story literally as empirical fact at every level, considering the Gospel accounts provide an accurate historical picture of what happened. At the other extreme are those who are appalled by emphasis on the rational and empirical trends in religious belief at the expense of myth and poetry. For them the Resurrection is beyond reason and fact; something to be explored from an entirely different standpoint. They take issue with naïve constructs concerning 'eternal life', the 'conquest of death' and the idea that one can accept the empty tomb and the post-resurrection appearances as part of 'history'. A 'middle way' might allow that something happened to Jesus that cannot be put into words and that lies beyond human comprehension.

The Resurrection led to the foundation of the Jesus movement that resulted in the establishment of the Church. Something happened. The mistake is made often that 'facts' lead to 'faith'. However, it is the experience of 'presence' that motivates and drives people forward. Paul Winter, the Jewish scholar, wrote a book on *The Trial of Jesus*. At the end he referred to an awareness of the continuing presence of Jesus with his followers, causing them to continue with his mission, centred around his continuing spirit in their hearts and minds.

Resurrection for many is about renewed life; often after tragedy and disappointment. It belongs to this world and not the next. Such experiences of renewal may be transient, ephemeral, but deeply reassuring. They may result in change of direction, fresh motivation and lasting change.

The Church has mistakenly seen resurrection as the conquest of death; that is a very serious misjudgement. Death gives life shape. It is normal and inevitable. The image of 'conquest' may refer to the belief that we have a future life beyond this one. An alternative is to imagine the 'conquest of death' as referring to pointing the way to an authentic life lived in the Spirit, and Jesus is the exemplar.

Pictures of eternal life may be comforting, but any concept of the 'everlasting' is doomed if we insist on imagining a temporal existence. The words eternal or everlasting have temporal connotations that do no justice to being in the presence of God. Eastern religions provide a more sensitive picture of reabsorption into the source of everything, without encouraging the need to insist that our egos continue to exist. The ego is a time-related mental construct. When we talk about 'self' or 'soul', we are unable to translate these words into anything with a coherent meaning. We are left with mystery beyond reason and neat human evaluation.

The Ascension at the end of the Easter season marks the movement of the Jesus of history to the Christ of faith, present but not seen. Made available to all as a living presence. This is a unique feature of Christianity compared with other great religions. People who seek the transformation in their lives that the power of the gospel enables, differ as to whether the Jesus of history or the Christ of faith empowers them. In our modern era people have been inspired to serve by the mysterious presence of the earthly Jesus calling them from the shores of Galilee. Albert Schweitzer considered Jesus was a failed eschatological prophet, but was inspired to change his life and work in Africa, by the demands on his life by this prophet. Jesus for him was not a god but an inspirational figure and the founder father of Christianity. This puts Jesus on a par with Abraham, Moses and Mohammed. It brings Christianity closer to the other religions of the Book. But many would insist that this is an inadequate and heretical position and condemn it outright. However, my experience of working as a priest in secular employment suggests that in our times this understanding of Jesus remains powerful and is a great deal more than being a member of the Jesus appreciation society.

It may be time for the Church to acknowledge that the concept of what it means to be a Christian is radically broadened. This is long overdue.

Idle Tales?

Acts 10.34–43 Luke 24.1–12
"But these words seemed to them an idle tale."
Luke 24.11.

What is history? Some would say it is an accurate account of historical events, perhaps with some additional interpretation, but foremost it is the record of what actually happened. If one took recording equipment one would be able to capture something resembling the history described. The history of the Bible is different. We cannot necessarily photograph or record it. Here we have sacred history filtered through an underlying view of the world. In many instances the Bible seeks to put into words and images experiences that cannot be expressed clearly. One has to resort to them in an attempt to express something of a core experience that has been transformative but cannot be reduced. Words are dangerous. We must recognise their ambiguity and limitations.

Resurrection is such an experience. You may note that the Gospels, connected by their various sources, vary as to how the accounts of Easter day and afterwards are described. We realise at once that this is not ordinary history, but that in the hearts and minds of those early Jesus followers, disillusionment and sorrow were turned to joy. Lives were transformed, reoriented, renewed.

An account of something very unusual is easily dismissed as 'idle talk'. The account does not necessarily impact on us. The experience is not ours. We do not own it. Without experience, some real connection, history has limited meaning. The history of your life and family has much greater traction than many other 'histories' because they dwell in your heart. They are part of you. They are what you are.

The Resurrection of Jesus has no impact on you or me unless we sense the spirit of Jesus as an active presence with the power to transform our lives; to force us to change and to follow the example of the one who lived so long ago. Resurrection is certainly not about empty tombs or about physical presence. These accounts, whether literally true or not, are a means of expressing the well-known words 'Jesus lives' and lives down the centuries, restoring and changing people. 'Idle talk' becomes living reality.

Resurrection has, historically, two elements. One is the familiar 'idea' that death has been conquered and leads to 'eternal life'. Jesus is seen to be the forerunner of a new creation. The Bible calls him the second Adam. The Fall described in Genesis was seen as the death of humanity. Without the Fall there would have been no death. Sin, perceived as the cause of the Fall, is abolished through the death of Jesus who inaugurates the possibility of a new creation. This notion was imbedded in Judaism and adopted by Christianity. It has been interpreted as an assurance that beyond this world there is another creation, everlasting, waiting for us. But we must be careful in adopting crude and glib pictures of what this might mean. Death in the context of the Bible has varied meanings and much of it is metaphor.

Death in this life is a metaphor for the absence of meaning

and purpose that so easily besets us. We are 'dead'. The word eternal in this context does not mean living for ever but entry into a new mode of living.

We cannot conceive of our own eternal preservation. Eternity is beyond space and time and cannot be measured. It is timeless. So, it is impossible to put into words. In our lives we may have glimpses of the extra-temporal. Moments beyond the world of everyday experience; beneath the narrative of our existence. These are precious.

We must leave what happens to us on our death to God. If we trust in God whatever lies ahead is good. Biological death in itself is not wrong or bad. It is part of life. It gives life shape. It does not need to be conquered. Premature death is bad, but it is through our efforts in this life to overcome disease and the risks that come with creation that we enhance the lives of all on this planet.

It follows that in acknowledging that the only life we know is this life, we must look for resurrection in the here and now and that is what animated those early disciples. They were transformed by the living presence of Jesus, that continues to animate people to this day. In the Gospel of John, written probably at the end of the first century CE, we have the story of Nicodemus in chapter three. Jesus tells him that he must be born again. 'Very truly, I tell you, no one can enter the Kingdom of God without being born of water and Spirit. What is born of the flesh is flesh, and what is born of the Spirit is spirit. Do not be astonished that I said to you, "You must be born from above." The wind blows where it chooses, and you hear the sound of it, but you do not know where it comes from or where it goes. So, it is with everyone who is born of the Spirit.'

That is resurrection. Born again to new life. In baptism the metaphor of death and rising to new life is the true meaning of the conquest of death.

In our Northern hemisphere we are fortunate that our celebration of Easter coincides with the signs of new birth following the cold and dark of winter. We see the season of spring reappearing; spring flowers reviving after lying dormant. Birds making nests again and eggs being laid. We recognise a cycle to everything; new beginnings; renewed opportunities. Resurrection is not a one-off opportunity. It is so easy to see life as linear; an opportunity once past will never reappear. But much of our existence is circular. So it is for our opportunities for resurrection life. We can be reanimated each year by the presence of Jesus, his spirit, in our lives. We have renewed opportunity. We can know that what we experience is not idle talk but real; part of *our* sacred history.

Transformation

Acts 10.34–43 Matthew 28.1–10
"He is not here."
Matthew 28.6.

Those words from Matthew provide a springboard for us to reflect a little on the momentous subject of the resurrection of Jesus and the impact this has on our thinking and lives today. If Jesus is to be meaningful for us, he must be with us now. It is not quite enough, as Rowan Williams puts it, to be members of the Jesus of Nazareth appreciation society.

Before we can reflect on the meaning of resurrection, we may recall what has gone before in our journey through Holy Week. Certain words encapsulate the Passiontide story. We use the words 'rejection' and 'victim'. Jesus is rejected even by his closest disciples. Peter denies him. He is the pure victim who has done no wrong. He attempted to summon people to a new kingdom where God would reign in their lives and they would let go of evil and turn towards the Good.

We can link this passion journey with our own memories, and the rediscovery of ourselves and others we know who have victimised and been victims, have rejected and been rejected. In doing so we bring the events of Holy Week nearer to home. We are linked with those dwellers of Jerusalem who crucified Jesus.

Our word today is resurrection, new life. But before it comes that crucial word, forgiveness. We are forgiven. Before we can talk of resurrection, we need to re-enter Jerusalem and remind ourselves that Jesus was the victim of a group of people, amongst them his disciples, who crucified him as an innocent person. He was sacrificed as a scapegoat to quieten things down.

The only way back from this terrible deed for the people of Jerusalem was to turn around and face what they had done. They must not turn their backs. Turning back towards Jesus, the early Christians repented of what they had done. They were forgiven unconditionally by Jesus and, for them, the Jesus of history became the Christ of faith. Joy and new life were found in him.

Most, if not all of us are here because we are sympathetic to this Easter story. Yet in our era we recognise that there are other great faiths and many nuances within the Christian framework. There is a very broad spectrum of what people understand about Jesus, the Resurrection and eternal life. Our Anglican Church, in general, has learned slowly to recognise this and despite the outbursts of extremists, acknowledges a whole variety of interpretations of these momentous events that took place two thousand years ago.

Many people are either curious or afraid about what may happen to them when they die. If we read about resurrection or any other aspect of Christian theology, we will soon realise how complex all this can be. Even amongst the ancients there was no coherent and accepted picture of what resurrection might really mean or consist of. On the one hand, there was the emerging idea of the resurrection of dead people in a corporeal sense as well as a spiritual sense that emerged within

Judaism from the time of the Maccabees around 200 BCE. On the other hand, there was a purely spiritual view of resurrection derived from The Greeks, particularly Plato, that influenced many Jews and Christians in the Graeco-Roman world outside Palestine, and was epitomised in the writings of Philo of Alexandria.

Most sensible people realise that it is unwise to speculate about what happens after death. Death is real. It happens to us all. It is a biological imperative. However, if you acknowledge God, the One at the heart of creation and the universe, our future should be trusted to Her/Him.

Happily, many of us are more concerned with life as we live it now. What impact do these events of two thousand years ago have on us now, living in a scientific age, and wanting to develop a spirituality that is in keeping with our world and times? People have not stopped being spiritual or having religious leanings but they do want to know what eternal life means in our day to day world, no longer expecting the imminent second coming of Christ as the Thessalonians did; and therefore, less preoccupied with end time events and what would happen to them and their friends who had recently died.

If we note the preaching of the revivified Peter in Acts, we are immediately aware that this is a man who was a traitor to Jesus and like other disciples had been totally disillusioned and dismayed. But here he is, alive with the Holy Spirit and full of hope. He had faced his role in the crucifixion. He had found forgiveness. He had a real sense that the spirit of Jesus was with him. He had preached Jesus and his forgiveness to the people of Jerusalem and beyond. Despite what he had been, God had a role for him in spreading the Good News and he became a new man. He was born again.

You may recall the story in John's Gospel when Jesus confronted Peter fishing by the sea of Galilee. Peter was disillusioned. He thought it was all over. He had returned to fishing with his friends, and then he was confronted by Jesus. There was the formulaic challenge of 'do you love me', mirroring the denials in Jerusalem. He started again on a life of service to the one he had denied. He began to understand that Jesus was not here or there anymore, but the spirit of Jesus would live with Peter as he embarked on a life driven by this presence.

What we are talking about is the transformation of people's lives by this strange arresting figure who lives on, just as the early disciples were transformed. Our inner transformation is memorably put by Paul Winter, a Jew, in his seminal book: *On the trial of Jesus*. In this important and little-known work, Winter emphasises that the Church does not own Jesus. It often chains him, as if he must obey their edicts and doctrines.

'Sentence was passed, and Jesus was led away. Crucified dead and buried; he yet rose in the hearts of his disciples who had loved him and felt he was near. Tried by the world, condemned by authority, buried by the Churches that profess his name, he is rising again, today and tomorrow, in the hearts of people who love him and feel he is near.'

No Barriers

Acts 4.32–35 John 20.19–31
"As the Father has sent me, so I send you. When he had said this, he breathed on them and said to them, 'Receive the Holy Spirit.'"
John 20.22.

"The whole group of those who believed were of one heart and soul, and no one claimed private ownership of any possessions, but everything they owned was held in common."
Acts 4.32.

These two brief passages from our readings point to the underlying meaning of the Resurrection. The early Jesus movement was a group of forgiven and redeemed people; they had faced up to what they had done to Jesus and both in Jerusalem and Galilee they had been empowered to live a new kind of life; resurrection life. This community was empowered by the gift of the Holy Spirit, given by Jesus, to lead them into truth and to a way of life that contained no barriers. This tiny group of people were the forerunners of the Christian Church.

When we look back at this, we need to realise that this community, born out of death, was no easy option. There is no triumphalism here, only a gratefulness that the life of Jesus had pointed the way to what a human community could be; a community without barriers; a community turned outwards to the margins of a world still dominated by inequality, barriers of gender, injustice, abandonment and hatred.

We live in a more complicated world now, dominated by scientific knowledge, individualism, global travel and wealth creation. The Church continues to exist as the Body of Christ and because we are in continuity with those early pioneers, each Eastertide provides an opportunity for reflecting on the health of our Christian community, and whether we are following the path that Jesus pointed to when he breathed the Holy Spirit on those early followers.

Rowan Williams pointed to the primacy of a resurrection community without boundaries as fundamental. There are no limitations in the Kingdom of God. Your 'class', perceived or otherwise, is completely irrelevant. You have to cast off all pretensions of status. Jesus demonstrated this in his social activities. He showed a bias to the poor, the outsider, women and those afflicted in any way. In his parables and stories, he made it clear that self-conscious piety was anathema in any resurrection community. Any examination of the Church leaves us in no doubt that Jesus is with us, but he stands as judge as well as forgiver, as we have fallen far short of what he intends for us.

It is unbelievably sad that some, in Christian communities, are still unable to accept the fullness of women's priestly ministry in the Church. Class divisions and racial hatred continue to distort how we live.

We all have to ask ourselves the question whether we are prepared to live on the edge and be hurt. It is a fundamental misunderstanding of Christianity to think it is about our feeling secure and comfortable. We need to experience discomfort and live alongside the incompleteness of the world.

Last week we went to the Scottish borders for two days to scatter the ashes of a colleague and friend on the river Tweed, a symbol of his Englishness and his commitment to Scotland. His life had not been an easy one, yet he committed himself over many years to sick people.

My mind went on a kind of reverie to a period in my life in the seventies and early eighties when major changes threatened my composure. Overwork, the death of both parents and the discovery that I had had muscular dystrophy since childhood seemed to overwhelm me. Colleagues at work had had violent self-inflicted deaths. I knew what being on the edge was like. I had been a committed Christian, but this did not seem very cosy at all.

Moving to a new community and thinking about the nature of any resurrection community revived me. I recommitted myself through eventual ordination to becoming a 'Minister Secular Employment', at the edge of the Church, at the boundaries between belief and doubt. In my work I continued to experience that curious mixture of pain and fulfilment that seems to me to be essential in the Christian journey, as part of Christ's risen community.

There is no one way of 'being Church'. Many have tried to go back to those early days, abolish hierarchies, meet in homes, abolish churchiness, share everything and so on. In every experiment there is a point where our humanness prevents the 'perfect community' from realisation. Some, by their nature, seek to dominate; divisions occur whatever the model. Jesus certainly showed us what a true humanity is. It is only through his Spirit that we can stay anywhere near the model he set out for us. He is always with us to judge us and set us out again, forgiven, on the path we have chosen through his grace.

The Fellow Traveller

Acts 2.14a, 36–41 Luke 24.13–35
"Then their eyes were opened, and they recognised him; and he vanished from their sight."
Luke 24.31.

The Emmaus road; the Emmaus experience. What is it? It is an enlightening, a fundamental shift in our understanding of things, a revelation that puts everything in a different light. It is something that may change our lives completely and take us in a different direction, turn us around. We can be *Surprised by Joy* to use the title of the famous autobiographical account of his conversion to Christianity by C.S. Lewis. I love this Emmaus story. I never get tired of reading it and pondering on it. It contains so many riches. Defeat is turned into victory, sorrow into joy.

Let us paint a brief picture of what these two Emmaus travellers were thinking at the time of their journey. Firstly, they appear to have been part of the wider group of Jesus followers who thought he might be the Messiah, the one predicted to come by many Jews. But they were now disillusioned; it was a false trail. This Jesus had been put to death by the leaders and people of Jerusalem. Yet they had heard the odd rumour of an empty tomb, an absent Jesus. There was even a rumour he might be alive.

Yet these two were leaving Jerusalem. Perhaps, for them it was all over. They were once the disciples of Jesus, but now they were returning to the old life in Galilee where most of the disciples of Jesus originated. They had lost faith in this mission. It was over.

And then there was this fellow traveller. We do not know whether this is Luke's way of telling us about the new life that entered the disciples or how it all actually happened; but this Emmaus story has entered into our cultural history as a symbolic confrontation. Cleopas and his fellow traveller, perhaps his wife Mary, as Mary the wife of Cleopas is mentioned at the foot of the Cross, had their perspective changed. History was reinterpreted, seen afresh. Finally, as they broke bread together, they understood. Jesus was with them and then vanished from their sight; presence and absence, the recurring theme of resurrection. Jesus is absent but he is present.

The sudden Emmaus experience does not come to us all. For some it is a gradual realisation, for others it is the recovery of something lost. For many of us it comes in what one might call the doubt/faith paradox. For much of the time the Christian life may appear difficult. We are bothered by doubt and the reality of the Christian Way in a world that may appear godless and random in its behaviour. Then in some form of blinding flash we see everything differently. That may not last. The moment of joy, the treasure fades. There is absence again, but we have the memory. It may happen again. It is like a particular way a field is lit by the sun we do not normally experience. We are surprised by it. It is unexpected.

These Emmaus moments may come to us through the normal engagement of our lives. If you are a doctor or a nurse, through your work in the hospital or clinic as you connect with other people through illness. Or perhaps through life as a mother, teacher, farmer or businessman; whatever your role in life is. Jesus is there to meet you suddenly, reveal himself to you. Perhaps negativity will disappear and renewed energy and purpose return.

In this story the experience came in the breaking of bread. This meal was ordinary food fellowship, but it is the forerunner of our Eucharist. We meet week by week to break bread together. We are all different, but we are a community. We share this ritual meal and Jesus comes among us. In each of our minds and hearts there is the possibility of presence, encouragement, fresh light.

One Sunday morning in the 1990s I was a patient in the Freeman Hospital. I had just had an operation. Some young people came to my room and took me down to the chapel in a wheelchair. There, with others, communion was shared. I was low in spirits; my working life was problematic. I was unsure what to do. In that space, at that time, with those people, I received some kind of illumination. I returned to the ward much renewed. Subsequently I made decisions that took me in a different direction towards a different kind of life. It was, if you like, one of my personal Emmaus moments. I may have used this poem before but as I have mentioned a field earlier here it is. R.S. Thomas was the great poet of doubt and belief, illumination and absence:

The Bright Field © Orion books with permission

I have seen the sun break through
to illuminate a small field

for a while, and gone my way
and forgotten it. But that was the pearl
of great price, the one field that had
treasure in it. I realise now
that I must give all that I have
to possess it. Life is not hurrying
on to a receding future, nor hankering after
an imagined past. It is the turning
aside like Moses to the miracle
of the lit bush, to a brightness
that seemed as transitory as your youth
once, but is the eternity that awaits you.

Images of Meaning

Acts 2.42–47 John10.1–10

"The thief comes only to steal and kill and destroy. I came that they may have life and have it abundantly."

John 10.10.

Over Easter we sometimes struggle with what the Atonement means and discover, whatever theory we espouse, it is inadequate. Jesus does not provide theories as to how his death and resurrection brings us life in abundance. Those who wrote in the early days of Christianity provided us with metaphors and imaginative language in an attempt to capture what happened. In this passage from John we have the metaphor of the shepherd, the gate to the sheepfold and the sheep. In addition, we find thieves and robbers ready to undermine the shepherd; those who enter the sheepfold not by the gate but over the fence.

The beauty of metaphor is that it does not restrict. It is up to us to use it. Metaphors stand alongside each other; each in its uniqueness attempting to picture a reality that is not easily captured in words: 'I am the good shepherd'; 'I am the vine, you are the branches'; 'I am the bread of life'; 'the water of life'; 'you are the salt of the earth'. These are not rational statements. They are poetic attempts to give expression to what we may experience.

There has been an alarming attempt over many years to produce an overarching framework, a structure, a rational account as to the nature of Christianity. No one should decry absolutely these attempts, but they can easily deaden the force of Christian faith and mechanise it. Creeds may have their uses, but they are theoretical statements that have no life of their own.

One of the great challenges that we all face is the tension between reason and what we call the heart or our emotional life. Paul spoke of the Cross as being foolishness to the Greeks; seekers after wisdom, noted for their rationality. There is always a tension in Christianity between reason and the heart, our emotions and our intellect.

Jesus states, according to the writer of John, probably writing to a community around the year 90–100 CE, that the result of a life 'in Jesus' is life abundant. That is what it is about. But that phrase itself is a metaphor. On the surface you either have life or you do not. The word abundant might suggest quantity rather than quality; a lot of life. But the writer is pointing to something more profound. He is pointing to something more than the quantitative, a quality of life that is difficult to put into words; a richness, depth, meaningfulness that is beyond the narrative of life lived on the surface. Furthermore, this is not primarily referring, as I understand it, to life after death, but life as we live it in this world. Beyond this, it is up to us, using our imaginations, to come to our individual realisations as to what it means for us, living in the twenty-first century, remote from the times of this Gospel writer.

Metaphors of sheep, gates and shepherds, as well as those who climb into the sheepfold, are essentially rural ones, familiar to the original readers of this Gospel. I was taught a long time ago that a good way of exploring such metaphors is to conjure up some words that help to bring into our minds connections that are meaningful to us. Naturally this will vary. It is the beauty of metaphor. For example, the notion of the Shepherd evokes words like safety, guide, protector and so on. The sheep may be seen as needy, liable to get into trouble, not necessarily good at recognising danger. The gate into the sheepfold represents many things. The passage suggests that Jesus himself is the gate. It is the right way to enter. Other routes are fraught with danger and so on.

But what I really want to emphasise is that we are able to produce our own metaphors and imaginative stories that connect with the living Jesus, with our experience of him. We are dependent on language, however inadequate, to learn the original story of Jesus as recorded in the Gospels. The words written there are an expression of the experience of the writers themselves, dating from around 70–100 CE. Although our Gospels are given names, their dating makes it quite unlikely that the names we know so well actually wrote the Gospels; they may well have been written for communities connected with a particular apostle or disciple. Most of them share common material, apart from John, who writes a very different kind of Gospel, what is widely called the theological or spiritual Gospel. Certainly, members of these communities would never have known Jesus. They are like us.

One of the finest readable accounts of the life of Jesus is by the great British scholar C.H. Dodd. He was the person behind the New English Translation of the Bible. The book is called *The Founder of Christianity*. I do not agree with all he wrote, but it is a moving book. In the preface, the late Bishop

John Robinson described it as 'breath-taking' and 'beautiful'. He did so, in the main, because C.H. Dodd had the gift in his old age of entering that strange world of first century Palestine, sojourning in it until it had become part of his being, and then returning to this modern world of ours and expressing the truth as he saw it for the age he lived in. This is the constant challenge for all Christians. It requires commitment but it is the only way to sustain the gospel we live by. We have to translate our experience into our thought forms so that we can spread the good news of life abundant.

Life in the Spirit

Acts 4.5–12 John 10.11–18
"Then Peter, filled with the Holy Spirit, said to them."
Acts 4.8.

We have read today from the book we sometimes call Luke/Acts. The Gospel of Luke and the Acts of the Apostles is one book written by an unknown person and attributed to Luke and written around 90 CE, probably from Rome. The book is addressed to a high-ranking Roman citizen named Theophilus. The writer of this Gospel and account of the early Jesus movement had a number of purposes. The first part of the section we call the Acts of the Apostles is about early Jewish Christianity. The second part records the activity of Paul, the missionary to the Gentiles and one of the main authors of the birth of the Christianity that we recognise today.

I have used this quotation about Peter because Luke's use of the Holy Spirit is a most important characteristic of this Gospel. Throughout the account, the Holy Spirit is at the core of important moments. Right at the beginning we read of the Spirit filling Mary at conception. Simeon and Anna were Spirit filled as they prophesied in the temple when the child Jesus was brought there after his birth. The Spirit filled Jesus at his baptism and stayed with him to death, when he cried out 'into your hands I commend my Spirit'. The Spirit filled people at

Pentecost, when they spoke 'in the Spirit'. The Spirit filled Peter and later Paul. It is the Spirit that links Jesus with those who followed him.

Luke places far more emphasis on the Spirit of God than on any other doctrine or content of belief or faith. He is far more concerned to link life in the Spirit with a pattern of living. We read in Acts that the early followers of Jesus shared everything in common. The needy and poor were cared for. The Spirit gave rise to a certain kind of life that transcended the law while not necessarily replacing it.

The emphasis on the Spirit in continuity with Jesus has great implications for us all and was a major issue for the early Church. People began to think that they could speak for Jesus as they claimed his Spirit in them. Our Gospel of John, read today, was probably written around 90 CE, although many scholars now consider it to be a composite document. It is clearly unlike the other Gospels and has a particular character. It may well have been compiled by a community who spoke in the Spirit about the life of Jesus and his significance. For the writer of John, the most important thing to emphasise was that Jesus came in the flesh, as a human, despite appearing as an unworldly figure in the prologue and other passages.. This was to counteract rival views about Jesus not being truly human in the early years of the Church, as yet unformed and with no agreed doctrines.

A problem for all generations of Christians has been the diversity of views that have been expressed 'in the Spirit'. How can they all be the truth? Wars and polemical attacks have been with Christianity since its earliest days and continue now.

Paul, in his epistles writes of the gift of discernment, the ability to sort the 'wood from the trees'. The early Church from the late second century onwards sought to establish some level of conformity at considerable cost in terms of exclusion. There is no easy answer to the question whether someone is truly filled with the Spirit when they speak. All sorts of extreme views have been expressed in the name of God.

As far as I can see the only way forward is to be like Luke and emphasise the way of life that results from a life in the Spirit. Paul places a similar emphasis on the 'fruits of the Spirit'. We may be able to reach a consensus as to what they are. In current society there is an awareness of loss of familiar structures and frameworks. Can we possibly agree how to live? What virtues today can we count as evidence of life in the Spirit? That must be important if we believe that the Spirit of Jesus, of God, calls us to new life based on inner change and motives that are not governed by self-interest. I do not intend to name these today. We can all work on them. They are vital in the life of this or any other worshipping community.

Courageous Daniel

Daniel 6.1–23 Mark 15.46–16.8

"O Daniel, servant of the living God, has your God whom you faithfully serve been able to deliver you from the lions?" Daniel 6.20.

We all know the story of Daniel and the lion's den. For us living today it seems a fanciful myth. Well, I want to try and use that myth to get under the skin of the story. A myth is not a tissue of lies or something that is untrue. It is an account or story that can be examined for deeper meaning. We can dig for treasure in myths.

Setting the scene, we have Daniel, one of the people of Judah, a tiny kingdom, taken into exile by the Babylonians and subsequently ruled by the Medes and the Persians, who became the next great empire in that part of the world. The Bible is kind to Darius the Persian king and sees him as an instrument of God.

Daniel rises to high office. His peers become very jealous of him. They seek a way to undermine him and fix on his religion. The king is seen as a god, but he is very tolerant of Daniel and his god. The plotters force the king into making a declaration that all must explicitly worship him. Daniel, although very loyal to the king in every other way, refuses. He continues to worship his god. The king is forced to imprison him in a den of lions. The predicted outcome is death. The next day he is alive and unharmed. He is released.

Daniel is a very important figure in Jewish history and the book of Daniel is a mixture of story and obscure passages about the Son of Man; a title Jesus used himself.

This straightforward story or myth is first an account of integrity versus corruption and jealousy. Daniel remains true to his god whatever the consequences. He is not prepared to compromise over something that is crucial to his whole life and purpose. He clearly likes and respects the king, but he cannot worship him, a false idol. This is the kind of integrity Jesus showed in his life. The kind of integrity we would hope to show in ours. None of us want to be found wanting. Perhaps most of us are not put to the ultimate test for our faith, for the things that we believe in. Others are.

I had a colleague who was an Iraqi consultant physician and specialist in chemical pathology. Both his father and his mother were murdered by Saddam Hussein because they would not be corrupted. In this world there are many kinds of corruption. In the world of work, it can sometimes be very hard to stick to one's own integrity as a Christian. That applies also to non-Christians and those who adhere to other faiths. It is obvious how difficult this is for people in public life. Few of us survive unscathed after a lifetime working in this world, whatever our jobs have been. We need all the help God can give us to survive.

Survive! Can we expect to walk out of a den of lions like Daniel? Of course, there is the banal point that lions are unpredictable and only eat when they are hungry. Perhaps there was a nice juicy carcass in there anyway! None of that matters. The deeper point of the story is that the path of being true to God and maintaining our own integrity is the path to life. That applies even if the threat to us is not to our physical existence, but to our reputation in the world; our mental calm. We can only have the peace of God if we have behaved according to the integrity we have received from God.

Our Gospel describes the aftermath of the Way of the Cross. That was the ultimate result of Jesus being true to his calling. We are told that terrible as this was, it was not a death dealing experience, but in the end a life giving one. That provides us all with hope that following God leaves to life not death. The path taken by Jesus was not in vain.

The Broken Middle

Acts 7.55–60 John 14.1–14

"But they covered their ears and with a loud shout all rushed together against him."

Acts 7.57.

The stoning of Stephen, in the presence of a young man called Saul; St Paul as we now know him. Stephen, the first Christian martyr; but why?

He was a Hellene, someone with a much broader perspective than the high priests and the council. He opposed temple worship. It had no place in promulgating this new world view stemming from the person of Jesus. Jesus had a vision of what an authentic human life might look like. It was not narrow or legalistic and it did not depend on animal sacrifice. The vision was outward looking, global if you like. It contrasted dramatically with the world view of the Jerusalem hierarchy.

Stephen had a vision; he saw Jesus, the Son of Man with God. For him it was an affirmation of his faith and purpose. He wanted to serve his Lord and he knew no other way. He had to 'stick to his guns'.

He was stoned to death but forgave those who killed him. They had closed their ears and indeed their eyes to the Way; a mode of living in the world that transcended the old dispensation. A young man was watching the stoning, the stoners' coats were at his feet. That event may have been the root cause of the young man Saul's dramatic change of direction and indeed the reason we are here today.

There never has been a single world view. Indeed, despite attempts to control the dogmas of the Church, divergent understandings of Christianity have been central to the story of the Church since its inception. Recent news suggests that the Church of England could easily split with a conservative section ordaining its own bishop via an overseas conservative schismatic bishop, with the possibility that a new conservative break-away church might be formed.

In the so-called secular world this country's political parties will be publishing manifestos that underline the significant differences in the world views they hold, and those documents reflect the differences within our society. In case I am accused of being too political I am not going to go into too much detail. However, the idea that faith is a private affair is nonsense. Our faith must be lived in the 'marketplace'. After all, how we live is meant to be based on it.

We are all people that can be described as 'living in the world'. What we call the world is not everything that can be known about the material planet Earth, but the world of everyday living and aspiration. At the most basic level of human existence, induced by poverty, disease and political repression, there is minimal ability to build opinions and views. But for those who are more fortunate, most of us will develop a picture or vision of what the world should be like; not just our own little community, but the global picture beyond our shores.

Is there a general Christian world view at all? It is

debatable. If there is, it might go something like this: Christians believe that the world has at its heart a creator, God, despite any evidence to the contrary. This is an act of faith; a leap, not rational, but based on an experience of God, the entirely other, in our lives. Furthermore, the Christian feels that Jesus, in some way, is the human expression of God and an example for everyone of how to live an authentic life of love and service. The Christian aspiration is to follow in the footsteps of Jesus and, interpreting with the aid of the Spirit of God, present in the world, the way to live in any historical period. But beyond that we have a problem. The problem is that the nature of Christianity in terms of practical behaviour and attitude must always evolve and develop. But for some this has not happened; morality has been frozen in a pre-scientific age with different understandings of the nature of the world and humanity itself.

For me, an ordinary person, getting old but still with strong opinions, there are striking clashes of vision that will affect our nation and the wider world in future years. It is at the level of community and nationhood we find the problem. We are a broken and divided nation. We can, like the high priests and their followers, put our hands over our ears and pretend all is well, but it is not.

Stephen and the Jerusalem hierarchy could not talk to each other. In the Bible, for obvious reasons, we have Stephen as the wronged person, as indeed he was. But was there another way?

Gillian Rose, the Jewish philosopher, who died at a young age, wrote about the 'Broken Middle'. She converted from Judaism to Christianity on her death bed and profoundly influenced the thinking of Rowan Williams, our former

Archbishop of Canterbury. The 'Broken Middle' is a recognition of our broken society, of differing world views.

I used to teach practical theology. The students would identify a problem in their life of work or leisure and analyse it from a Christian perspective, teasing out the issues that made decision making difficult in a complex world. Facile answers would not do.

Instead of shouting each other down with slogans, sound bites and bad behaviour, violent or otherwise, we must try to bring opposing visions together, and look without prejudice at what they really mean for our world, what they will lead to. This is not just about a political 'middle way', but about the realisation that our world is too complex for narrow views. Rowan Williams has tried to work within our own Church of England to hold together the warring factions, living in the 'Broken Middle'. Many think he failed. The story this week might support that. But the story of Christianity is, in one sense, about failure. Success is not found in simple mantras, but in suffering and endurance. The 'Risen One' beckons us to follow him with our cross to the broken heart of our world and seek the healing we all need.

Knowing to Unknowing

Acts 8.26–40 John 15.1–8
"He asked, 'Do you understand what you are reading?'
He replied, 'How can I, unless someone guides me?'
Acts 8.30-31.

Being lost or bewildered, in some sense, is a universal experience. We all need guides, mentors, in many areas of our lives. Understanding ourselves and the world we live in, is a normal human goal. Yet paradoxically, although we seek understanding, what we may find is something very different. That may seem 'Double Dutch' and you may or may not understand what I mean in ten minutes time!

The Ethiopian eunuch was reading the Bible. He needed help to interpret it. Philip came to the rescue. One of the most important gifts of any guide is to help us make connections, sometimes without being aware of it.

This week I have had to read bundles of documents. I was fortunate to have a guide to help me and others through their convolutions. That has been of help to me. Our daughters telephone quite frequently. They need their mother to bounce ideas and concerns off. One of my sons sometimes lets off about hospital politics and medical frustrations. I am not sure he listens to anything I might say but it may help in clarifying the mind. These are ordinary familiar things, but of some significance. We can all produce numerous examples. Often without realising it; we are guides to people and we, in our turn, are guided.

School teachers are guides to us all. Many of us remember our teachers, including their eccentricities and the impact they had on our lives. We want our children to have guides outside their family; and many of us want that guidance to have a spiritual dimension that helps them connect human experience with the Divine.

Jesus was the guide to his disciples. Gradually, as they walked with him, they began to understand what he was about, but their understanding increased dramatically after he was gone. What we call the Holy Spirit continued to enlighten them. People like Philip felt the call or summons of the Holy Spirit to go and help others. The movement, started by Jesus, grew and continued to develop.

We now have had two thousand years of time, of thought, insights and continuing guidance. The journey goes on for each generation. Whatever religion we follow, many people in this world have lost their bearings. Many have opted out of the tradition they were born into; others have become confused and disillusioned by the diversity of the interpretations and guidance they hear. What is the right understanding of this or that? How do I know what to believe? Would it not be better just to do my own thing? Or, if I come to church to worship, all I need to do is worship, not understand. God is beyond understanding.

These are difficult issues and not easily solved. What I want to try and say is that it is a good thing for us to try and understand, according to our God given capacities, but we never will have total understanding. That sounds a real paradox, I know. Strangely, if after a lifetime of trying to understand the ways and works of God you conclude that you understand nothing, you have actually arrived. But the journey had to be made. To make no effort would have led nowhere.

On arrival at non-knowing, one finds that it is strangely and powerfully reassuring. Another way of putting this is that the purpose of all our journeying, all our guidance, is to see God. Then nothing else matters. We may well go up false trails, with bad guides. But we can return.

Job had bad friends, but he got there. His early life must have helped him. At the end of all his struggles, he was able to say: 'I had heard of you by the hearing of the ear, but now my eye sees you; therefore, I despise myself, and repent in dust and ashes.' (Job 42.5-6). T.S. Eliot, in a number of passages in the *Four Quartets*, puts us in touch with these issues in a different way. In some way the whole of this poem is an exploration of the circularity of time. Thus, Eliot says that the end of a lifetime of exploration is to return to where one started, but with a new 'mystical' understanding or knowledge that has no content. Following on from that, perhaps we realise that our arrival has little to do with rationality but with the emptiness of silence. Little Gidding is in Essex. I found the place and the church memorable. We are here in St Paul's Healey, but the message is the same. All the guidance, all the talking and thinking pass away in the end. We pass beyond our own limited reality into the presence of God.

Going Out

Readings Zephaniah 3.14–20 Matthew 28.1–10, 16–20
"Go therefore and make Disciples of all Nations."
Matthew 16.19.

At the heart of Christianity has always been the summons to preach the gospel to all people. How we understand this command and carry it out varies enormously. I find the emphasis on the word 'go'. It does not imply sitting in a church building and waiting for people to come. It does not even imply that being in a church is a sine qua non for discipleship. Like everything about Jesus, it is radical.

At one end of the spectrum is the objective of 'bums on seats'; bring more and more people into church. But in general, the evidence suggests that if this is a desirable strategy it is not working. By and large the number of people attending church is dropping in the developed world. If this is an indicator of success in disciple-making it suggests there is something very wrong.

Yet last week it was possible to go to a Ministry Division selection conference as an educational selector and spend time with a number of young people in their twenties who were offering themselves for ordained ministry. They had youth, energy, talent and conviction on their side. They were also connected with their generation. They were young people who related to their peers, regardless of belief. They were able to communicate with people and had the usual interests and enjoyments that young people have. In simple language they were not 'square'. Professional 'holy people', unless they are of remarkable stature, often turn people off. Nor does holiness equate with being out of touch with the thought forms and culture of the young, or indeed those of any age. These young people thankfully had a broader view of what Church is.

I admit that I am not a particularly 'churchy' person. I have spent my ministry on the edge of the Church at work and in other non-religious settings. I must say I have never felt it to be particularly difficult to discuss religious issues or whatever words we want to use with other people. But I think there are some important principles that have to be followed if outreach is to have any real meaning.

I do not consider talking about religion or faith, or whatever words you might wish to use, carry any weight in a vacuum. We are asked to go, and in going we must not understand our task to be explicitly increasing the congregation of this church or any other. Indeed, we have to ask ourselves what the nature of Church should be in this generation. If we had our time again would we create a Church over-dependent on clergy, and to a large extent alienated from the world around it. People are genuinely nervous about going into a church building. They feel 'foreigners in a foreign land'.

At the heart of going out is befriending, being genuinely interested in people, entering into a relationship. Only then can a dialogue start. We cannot know where that will lead. This needs a wide variety of people, with differing personalities and different backgrounds, to engage with people in friendship. At the heart of any outreach, any work for God, is risk, and what

I would want to call 'giving up control'. So often we are risk-averse and also want to have everything controlled by ourselves, including the outcome. In our engagement with each other there should be no determination about the outcome; that is up to God.

At our conference, our secretary gave an address about risk. The candidates took a risk in offering themselves; they were risking possible non-acceptance, and even if accepted they were taking a big risk entering ordination training. It would be likely they would not come out from this thinking and believing quite what they did when they entered. The selectors took a risk for God in recommending someone who they were a little uncertain about. There can be no sitting on the fence. It is better to take a risk than mess around.

As a church we must learn to take risks with all sorts of things. We have to be open to new ideas, new ways of doing things, we have to challenge some of our 'sacred cows'. Different sorts of people have to be part of the risk taking. No church has ever really flourished if the vicar, poor person, does everything.

At the heart of Creation is risk. We only have to look around to know for certain that in exploring creative potential and possibilities there are risks. There is the risk of things going wrong at the heart of molecular genetics. The very fabric of the core and mantle of the Earth is such that earthquakes are normal, and we may be in the way of volcanic eruptions or earthquakes. We make a big mistake if we think God is a control freak. He lets go. He sets us free. He takes risks, very big ones. Everything may not work out, but if there is no risk there is no creation.

We may put ourselves into composing a piece of music,

writing a book, painting a picture. It is our piece of creation, but we take a risk that it will not turn out as we hoped, that it will end in a bin or a loft.

If we return to the text, we must take risks and use our imagination in how we see the Church or ourselves 'going out'. Some plans may not work out. Some attempts fail. Some people may get cross. But that is the nature of moving forward. If we do nothing we go backwards.

God knows who his disciples are. Our job is to work with the one element in creation that transcends everything, including the things that go wrong, and that is love. It is love not words that makes disciples. Love is the primary motive for everything. Some of us are fortunate enough to have easier lives than others. We do not have to struggle about basic things. We have a greater responsibility to go out and be for others, regardless of the cost and with no expectations about outcome. The words success and failure are irrelevant.

Misunderstanding God

Acts 1.6–14 John 17.1–11

"Lord, is this the time when you will restore the kingdom to Israel?"

Acts1.6.

The early part of The Acts of the Apostles contains some fascinating issues, and this is one of them. What did the apostles mean by this question? On the surface they seem to have continued to misunderstand the nature of the ministry of Jesus. Like many other Jews they remained locked into a misunderstanding of messiahship. They were preoccupied with the restoration of a free nation to the people of Israel, an overthrow of Roman rule. They wanted a quick fix. Jesus gave them a gentle rebuke. He told them to forget about such things and to go out and be his witnesses to the ends of the earth; witnesses to the richness of life that could be found in following him in his way while on earth, lived in the presence of God.

Misunderstanding the nature of God and imposing on God our vision of what we want He/She to be is commonplace in our own age. Quite often our misunderstandings are based on a distortion of Biblical understanding that we attempt to use to reassure ourselves that all will be well as we live out our lives; that God will protect us, keep us safe, heal our diseases. Such a view is in direct conflict with the experience of many in this life. If we persist in thinking like this, we ignore the realities of human existence.

The Bible is not a systemic account of everything we need to know about God. It is patchy. It contains contradictions. Someone might say: 'look, the Bible tells me that if I ask it will be given me, if I seek, I will find.' That sounds very attractive. But set this alongside the suffering of Jesus himself, the difficult lives of early Christians, the words 'take up your cross and follow me'; our own lives that we live today. It is self-evident that it depends what we ask and what we seek; fullness of life does not mean an easy life. We must live realistically, and we must avoid triumphalist assumptions that Christians are special and have special protection.

I have seen far too much human suffering not to acknowledge that the supreme Being or Prime Mover we call God is not a god of quick solutions, relentlessly intervening in human or cosmic affairs to 'put things right'. God is present in all of his creation, suffering with us, affected by our sorrows, but just as Jesus rebuked the apostles, he does not provide us with quick fixes, put things right the way we want them.

This week we have been in the south, being with a sick daughter in hospital. My mind naturally turned to the reality that our world is full of diseases that have a profound impact on our lives. The example of Stephen Sutton, the courageous young man who raised millions as he was dying for the benefit of other teenagers whom he would never know, has moved many. We remain capable of responding to such examples of self-giving that put our own moans and groans in perspective. As I think Stephen said himself, life is not about longevity, but what you put into the world while you are here.

I still remember a young woman we will call Sarah. She first came to see me when she was taking her A levels. She was a devout Roman Catholic. Sarah was diagnosed with multiple sclerosis. The disease progressed rapidly. She never made it to university. In a year or two she became helpless, paralysed yet shaking all over too, her mind badly affected. Yet somehow in her short life she drew people to her. She was much loved in her profound impairments. There was no family anger about all this; only a profound dignity in the face of encroaching loss. She died just after a group managed to get her to Rome to be blessed by the Pope. The photograph of Sarah, her parents and the Pope remains over my desk and will continue to do so.

Those early disciples were told to go out and spread a gospel of love and forgiveness, leading to new life. They were not offered certainty, protection. They were told to get stuck in and to stop thinking what might happen to their own country. The mystical figure of Jesus, for me, always standing by the shores of Galilee, but perhaps for you somewhere else, summons us to 'launch out into the deep', not to hold back; he asks for commitment as we walk into the unknown. As he told the disciples, we do not need to know what will happen. We need to follow him. Peter was told to 'launch out into the deep' after a night's fruitless fishing. This was surprising as fish in Galilee were normally caught at night in shallow water; but he did it and his life was changed. That can happen to us.

The Affirming Flame

Acts 1.15–17.21–26 John 17.16–19
"They do not belong to the world, just as I do not belong to the world."
John 17.16.

Those words are taken from what has been called the high-priestly prayer of Jesus. Jesus appears to be saying that neither himself nor his disciples belong to this world. On the surface this is a very negative statement about the world we spend our lives in. One might call it 'world negating'. It would seem to be in direct contrast to the statement by God in the book of Genesis that creation is good. To try and understand this we have to discover the use and meaning of words used in the Bible and the various strands of thought that may have influenced statements such as this one in John's Gospel.

It should not surprise us that there are fashions in the understanding of Jesus' approach to the future of the world. One view is that he considered the created order would end imminently and that therefore engagement in the world was pointless and it was mandatory to prepare oneself for the coming judgement and new order. However, as the years passed this view became increasingly dubious. Nothing had happened and over two thousand years later we are still firmly imbedded in this world.

If we look in other parts of the Bible, we discover that the words 'world' and 'flesh' are connected with materialistic pre-occupations as opposed to spiritual. Someone who is wedded to materialistic concerns like wealth creation, power, influence and so on is regarded as 'of this world', whereas those whose interests are concerned with unconditional love and service are 'not of this world'. The implication is that when one is over-attached to material things one is worldly.

This type of understanding does not exclude the belief that creation is basically good, rather it is the misuse of creation that creates the image of someone bound to materialism. However, I cannot really go further before introducing another idea prevalent in early Christianity and possibly an influence in John's gospel, and that is the ancient form of Christianity called Gnosticism; believed to be deeply heretical by orthodoxy. In Gnosticism the creation is not good but deeply flawed. God himself, the perfect, undivided one, did not create the world; a demiurge did. This demiurge has various names. The human race is trapped in creation and the object of existence is to return to God. In each person there is a spark of light longing to be freed and return to the divine light. Those who are 'enlightened', who have special knowledge, are liberated; they are 'not of this world'. This is a highly negative view of the created world and it is possible that there are some of these negative elements in this Gospel.

I think most of us would prefer to see creation as positive, good, something to be cherished and loved. Our world is full of natural beauty although sometimes we find it savage and unforgiving. Creation is to be enjoyed. There is absolutely no evidence that the Jesus we find in the gospels of Mathew, Mark and Luke was a miserable world-hating person. He enjoyed table fellowship, he was a good communicator and in his statements about spiritual values he used the world around him to paint vivid pictures. The word incarnation implies world engagement. We are all, as Jesus was, incarnate in the world. What matters is that we love and look after our world with reverence, avoiding abusing what we have been given, and claiming ownership of resources that are a gift.

Last week we had three days away in a country hotel having a reunion with lifelong friends. We were surrounded by natural beauty, providing the perfect environment to reminisce about our families, our lives together as young people, full of enjoyment and exploration. These were good days, exciting days, world affirming days. The life of children shouts excitement, joy in living and exploring. They are the constant antidote to despair, to the feeling that the world is a sorrowful place to be endured, escaped, negated.

This verse in the Gospel of John has to be interpreted as meaning that we must always understand that the Love of God is at the root of creation and enjoy what he has given us, the gift of life, that reaches its fullness in loving care in contrast to ownership and manipulation.

War provides the ambivalence we all feel sometimes about existence. I am going to end with a well-known poem by Siegfried Sassoon. He pictures hope in the midst of despair. I often use it on Remembrance Day.

Everyone Suddenly Burst Out Singing

Everyone suddenly burst out singing;
And I was filled with such delight
As prisoned birds must find in freedom

Winging wildly across the white
Orchards and dark green fields; on; on; and out of sight.

Everyone's voice was suddenly lifted,
And beauty came like the setting sun.
My heart was shaken with tears and horror
Drifted away... O but everyone
Was a bird; and the song was wordless; the singing will never be done.

Ascended

I Peter 4.12-14, 5.6-11 John 7.1-11
"But now I am no longer in the world."
John 17.11.

On Ascension Day last Thursday and this Sunday, we mark the passing of Jesus from a specific historical context. The Jesus of history becomes the Christ of faith. That is a massive leap we need to dwell on. Using metaphor, Jesus ascends to the right hand of God the Father. Today and the next two Sundays mark key points in the development of Christian structure. I am referring to Pentecost and the work of the Holy Spirit, and Trinity Sunday when we reflect on the nature of God and specifically on the concept of God three in one — Father, Son and Holy Spirit. That all sounds rather abstruse. In some ways it is, and it has a controversial history. We are dealing with worthy attempts to explain the continuing power of Jesus to win disciples and the feeling that he was more than a man. What was his connection with God? The answers to these questions have provided doctrines, developed over centuries, which orthodoxy has adopted. We do not find them fully developed in the Bible.

In the Acts of the Apostles the ascent of Jesus is described in dramatic, pictorial language. In the Gospel of John, Jesus simply states he is leaving the world. The central question is how do you connect with an historical figure after he is dead? The classic Christian response is that Jesus is not dead but alive in the hearts and minds of his followers. He is not present in the world physically, but his spirit is with us.

The words 'His Spirit' need unpacking a little. The orthodox Christian doctrine of the Trinity is that God the Father, God the Son and God the Holy Spirit are coequal and coeternal. That means that all aspects of God existed before time and the Cosmos we exist in. These statements are attempts to express the inexpressible. They are not empirical.

The Holy Spirit or the Spirit of God has always been present in our world if it is present at all. It was there in the time of the prophets as it is now in the twenty-first century. The technical word for this is imminence. So, if this is the case, what is the difference between The Holy Spirit and the Spirit of Jesus that makes us feel he is still with us. I do not think it is possible to separate the two. The Holy Spirit is focused in the experience we have that Jesus is still with us inspiring and guiding us. Jesus said: 'When the Spirit of truth comes, he will guide you into all the truth.'

One way of looking at the person of Jesus in this world is that he was a 'spirit-filled person'. He was full of the Spirit of God. He held out the possibility that we could be spirit-filled too. One way of looking at the purpose of our lives is that we should seek to become spirit-filled people, although we find this path to 'Becoming' difficult beyond measure. In leaving the world at Ascension he points us again to the presence of the Spirit; that aspect of God that can enter all of us as it was present in Jesus. We are called to live in the presence of the Holy Spirit guiding us.

As I have intimated before, we move beyond mere reason

when we speak of the Spirit of Jesus or God or the Holy Spirit in our lives. Somehow, we must free ourselves to experience a presence that lies beyond the daily grind. The word mystic or mystical might imply something that lies beyond the experience of most ordinary people. I do not think that is so. In a myriad of ways, varying from person to person, we are all able to sense that presence beyond ourselves. Christianity or the Church does not own it. The Holy Spirit, the spirit that animated Jesus, is open to all and is in all.

We describe Christianity as an historical faith. In some sense, all faiths are historical and founded on the presence of an historical figure that probably lived: Abraham for Judaism, Jesus for Christianity, Mohammed for Islam, Gautama the Buddha for Buddhism. However, none of them claim, in their purist forms that these people are divine, except Christianity.

In making the exclamation *Jesus is Lord and to be worshipped* we are saying something different. He was not worshipped in his earthly life. Since he left the world, he has been worshipped down the ages as being the human aspect of God in its pure form and therefore worthy of worship and being at the right hand of God. He is ascended.

Pentecost and Trinity Sunday

These two Sundays of the liturgical year differ strikingly. Pentecost represents a fundamental experience for the Christian; the core experience that the Spirit of Jesus was with his early followers. Whether this is communicated in dramatic language or in quieter mode is immaterial. Pentecost marks the beginning of the Way that took early Christians by storm and enabled them to live again with hope and purpose.

Trinity Sunday is less easily connected with the simpler but driving force of experience. Trinitarian doctrine as expressed in the historic creeds lacks the immediacy of Pentecost. It purports to express in propositional language the experience that Jesus was more than a man; that the Holy Spirit is an emanation of God, the One, the source of all, and that these three experiences come from an undivided God that is named the Trinity. Many find this proposition fails to match their response to God in Jesus and their awareness of God, present throughout creation. The inadequacy of language makes any attempt to reduce God to propositions a failure, as all endeavours to describe the ineffable fail. The doctrine of the Trinity requires a more dynamic understanding, reflecting God's flow from the eternal to the temporal, exploring the essential fluidity of the Divine as opposed to the more static 'Three in One' picture that does not assist the image of God as 'One'.

Go Out for God

Acts 2.1–21 John 20.19–23
"He breathed on them and said to them, receive the Holy Spirit."
John 20.23.

Today is an important occasion in the Christian year. One could say it marks the beginning of the Jesus movement, the Way, the Church. A very small movement located within Judaism gradually spread beyond the borders of the Jewish faith and homeland. During the fourth century CE the adoption of Christianity by Constantine resulted in its spread throughout the Roman Empire that changed the religious map of the world. We meet here today because of these events and the generations of Christians that have preceded us down the ages.

We read in the Bible that something special appears to have happened at Pentecost, but with our modern minds we may have difficulty in grasping what this really was. The blessing of the Holy Spirit has divided Christians. On the one hand, it is that aspect of God, always present in the world, that we can apprehend if we are open to God. On the other hand, some consider that an outpouring of the Holy Spirit in drama is a pre-requisite of a true conversion to Christianity.

I think this difficulty is less important than it might seem. We cannot see the Spirit of God; we can only experience it.

There is no proof of its presence. Yet all religions in some way refer to a spirit presence in the world. Just as the Sufi mystic in Islam is spirit-filled so is the charismatic Christian in a European Church. Yet these dramatic indicators of the Holy Spirit are not the most important manifestations. If they were, millions of Christians would feel deprived.

There is diversity in how we experience God and in reflecting on the Holy Spirit we must start from our own experiences. I think it is probably important to say that we experience the Spirit of God with our entire being. We realise that we are rational and emotional beings that live in the world with others. It is in our daily lives that we are most likely to become aware of God's presence with us. We can refer to this, as the Bible does, as the Spirit of Jesus, the Holy Spirit, the Spirit of God or any other words that convey our awareness of the Divine in our lives.

Sometimes, people feel they need to authenticate their experience. I do not think this is a weakness, but Paul warned that it should not dominate people's lives and be regarded as the sole criterion of genuine spirituality. The majority sense the Other, the Divine, in quiet moments and sometimes in times of personal crisis. Perhaps, most importantly, we see the presence of God in others. That is unsurprising as the fruits of the Holy Spirit are love, care and understanding.

All our language about God is metaphor and that is the case with the Holy Spirit. Elijah used the phrase 'a still small voice' to describe his experience of God. Lucy Winkett, now Rector of St James Piccadilly, has written a book entitled *Our Sound is our Wound*. One of the problems we face with sound is the cacophony of sounds in our world of every type. Some sound is very personal, like tinnitus or the sound you hear through your earphones as you walk across the street, not hearing the traffic! Other sounds assail us as a community. There is a danger that the noise of our world blocks us from tuning towards the silence of eternity and thus the Spirit of God. I think both silence and sound can intimate the presence of the Spirit of God in contexts that are appropriate for us as individuals. The musician, the contemplative, the mother, the patient, the carer, may all experience God's presence in innumerable ways. We are caught unawares. We do not order a dose of the Holy Spirit; the Spirit comes to us unexpectedly.

I want to end with the word 'involvement'. Jesus 'breathed' on his disciples and sent them out to do his work. When we stand back from the work of God in our community, we lose our connection with others, with the world we are born to live in. We are born to serve and help others in a process of engagement in a certain historical period and location. If there is not any commitment we atrophy as people and our spiritual awareness declines, whatever our religion.

So, today we are called to 'Go Out for God' into our world, engage with others and make a difference for God manifest in the Holy Spirit.

An Alexandrian Battle

2 Corinthians 13.11–13 Matthew 28.16–20
"The grace of the Lord Jesus Christ, the love of God, and the communion of the Holy Spirit be with all of you."
2 Corinthians13.13.

This phrase appears to be an early Christian benediction. It does not speak of the unity of the Godhead, Three in One, that is the core of Trinitarian doctrine. Mathew 28 verse 18: 'Go therefore and make disciples of all nations, baptising them in the name of the Father and of the Son and of the Holy Spirit', is a later adaptation by the Church. We need to look to a much later stage of Christian development to discover the central battle ground for the development of what we call today, the Trinity.

Once upon a time there lived in the great city of Alexandria in Egypt, two priests. Alexandria was one of the great intellectual centres of the ancient world and a lot of clever people lived there. There were Christians and Jews, and much of their thinking had been influenced by Greek philosophers.

One of these men was called Arius and the other Athanasius. Athanasius was younger and rather ambitious. These two, like many others, tried to work out the nature of God. The foundation of Christianity, based on the person of Jesus of Nazareth, and the gift or presence of the Holy Spirit made it necessary to ask questions. Who was this Jesus and what was his connection to God the Father first made known by the Jewish people? They did not obviously seem to be the same, yet Jesus was said by some to have pre-existed before he ever came into the world.

Arius and Athanasius did not get on. They did not agree as to how to express these difficult issues in some theory of God and his nature. Matters became very tense. Constantine, the Roman Emperor, wanted to adopt Christianity as the religion of his Empire, but he did not want a lot of bickering. He wanted a clear-cut outline of this new religion and he called for a special synod to agree a creed. This council eventually took place in Nicaea in 325 CE. The views of Arius looked, at one stage, likely to prevail, as some powerful bishops supported him; but eventually Athanasius and his party won the day. Arius was athenamatised or cursed and the Nicene creed was born; subsequently, slightly modified at the council of Chalcedon in 481 CE.

Their differences were much less than might appear from subsequent history that has managed to vilify Arius as the archetypal heretic. What was all the fuss about and how does it impact on people seeking to worship God today?

What these two and many others were trying to do was to produce a framework, couched in technical language, that would adequately account for Christian recognition of God as Father, God as Holy Spirit and God as present in Jesus. This is an impossible human task, because all agreed God is essentially unknowable. We experience God in a number of ways, but no one has ever succeeded in tying God down. That is why the doctrine of the Trinity although useable and useful must be incomplete.

How do we experience God the almighty, the

unknowable, the first person or aspect of the Trinity? We experience this aspect through awe, wonder, the utterly beyond us. You will recall the response of Isaiah at the beginning of his prophecy. He is called by God and is overcome by a sense of awe, fear, and unworthiness in His presence. This aspect of God is almost alien. It is the primal and essential characteristic of deity that we respond to by worship. Before any defined religions existed, this was the experience of early humans; God or the gods were to be feared, worshipped, even humoured. We find this tendency to humour God in the Old Testament. People mistakenly gave God human attributes, such as jealousy and anger, but the essential response is awe in the presence of the *Entirely Other*.

But God was understood also to be Spirit, present in the world. The New Testament gives an account of the gift of the Holy Spirit to the disciples, but the spirit of God was present at the creation and even our creed states that he spoke through the prophets. Jesus spoke of the Spirit being present in our world instead of his physical presence. God, if he is to have relevance in our daily lives rather than be entirely remote, must exist always and in all places. The Holy Spirit is the 'Go between God', a phrase used by John Vernon Taylor. The Spirit of God stirs our imaginations, leads us into truth as we go beyond the surface of life's events in our search for meaning. And contrary to the traditional view that God is impassable (unaffected by human vicissitudes), the Spirit of God suffers with our spirits. Indeed, the Spirit is within us as it is in all creation.

And so those early thinkers came to Jesus; by far the most difficult issue for them. They had to find a way of accounting for the resurrecting presence of Jesus in their lives, driving them to found the early Church. In fact, the early Christians did not formulate the nature of Jesus clearly. You will not find the doctrine of the Trinity in the Bible. There are one or two elements in the Gospels that begin to refer to it, one quite clearly a later addition and looking totally out of place; a study of Gospel texts shows a lot of inconsistency about who Jesus was.

The best starting point is to experience God as uniquely present in Jesus in a fullness that suggests a new form of creation; sometimes referred to as the second Adam. Some branches of Christianity emphasise that Jesus points the way for us all in terms of spirit living; if we follow him, we can live life fully in the Spirit; even become as him. The word incarnation refers to the presence of God in Jesus, but we can reflect also on the Spirit in us.

It is not a huge leap to move from God as uniquely present in Jesus to the words 'Son of God', to imply the same thing. That is not difficult. And now I return to Athanasius and Arius. Arius could not accept that the son, Jesus, was coequal with God the Father. He thought Jesus was in some way begotten or created. Athanasius insisted that Jesus was coequal, co-eternal and unbegotten. He considered that nothing less could account for the impact of Jesus. In this disagreement, we have the heart of the problem of expressing the inexpressible in words; neither formulation is satisfactory.

But there are three aspects of God and the idea of a Trinity is helpful. There is the remote, unknowable aspect of God. There is God present throughout creation and beyond as Spirit. There is God experienced as incarnate in human form, in Jesus and in us, if we recognise the Spirit within us and seek to grow in grace.

Ordinary Time

This period refers to the Sundays between Trinity and Advent. Sometimes, referred to as the Sundays after Trinity or Pentecost; although nowadays the calendar range for each Sunday is specified. Trinity rather than Pentecost is the preferred referent nowadays. Ordinary Time is kept also on the Sundays before Lent and Advent. Although there may be special festivals during this period, such as: All Saints Day, Harvest, and Christ the King, the majority of Sundays have no particular theme, and the Gospel readings follow the triannual cycle of Mathew, Mark and Luke. It would be impossible to include a comprehensive selection of sermons for these Sundays. Therefore, I have selected a small sample. I have included a sermon on Harvest and Christ the King. I have omitted specific saints' days other than a reference to Barnabas, not a major saint. Ordinary Time provides some occasion for the mind to be loosened from the discipline of seasonal themes, although this does not necessarily reduce the risk of repetition. As usual I have not given the specific Sundays in the cycle. The reader may discover this from looking up the lectionary readings. There is no specific order followed.

Sermonising

Romans 12.1–8 Matthew 16.13–20
"He said to them, 'But who do you say that I am?'"
Matthew 16.15.

When anyone preaches a sermon, they have to reflect on what the purpose of a sermon is. There is no one answer. Is it meant to inspire and to challenge? Or is it a source of teaching, including what is termed exegesis, the expounding of the meaning of scripture when it was written; and then seeing if there is relevance to today's world? At what level should it be pitched? Should it seek to stretch the mind or be a piece of reassuring banality?

That may seem a strange way to begin this or any other sermon, but it is a real issue. No congregation is united about this. Some want it over as quickly as possible and do not want anything at all complicated; others think very differently. At the end of the day the preacher can only be himself or herself. There are too many opinions and viewpoints to satisfy everyone. I have said this now because this passage from Matthew is notorious for its difficulty.

Let me paraphrase it for a moment. Jesus is recorded going to Caesarea Philippi. If you look at an ancient map it was some twenty miles north east of the sea of Galilee. It was an area ruled over by Philip, son of Herod the Great, after his death in 4 BCE. It was relatively out of the way and might have been a good place to have a discussion about what people thought of Jesus. Was he John the Baptist come back from the dead? Was he Elijah or some other great Old Testament figure? Or was he like none of them, a unique figure, the Messiah. Jesus asks what people think of him; rather a strange thing to do if he already thought of himself as Messiah. Simon, soon to be called or nicknamed Peter, the rock, names Jesus as the Christ (anointed one) and son of the living God.

Jesus immediately affirms Peter. He calls him a 'rock' and predicts he will be leader of the Church. Moreover, he will hold the keys of entry into the Kingdom of Heaven. Finally, Jesus tells the disciples that they must not tell anyone else about his being the Messiah.

Matthew's account is based on a similar passage in the Gospel of Mark. That means that Matthew may have copied from Mark or used the same source. Mark is the first Gospel to be written. Mark sets the context of Peter's confession in a different setting, still in Caesarea Philippi, but after a blind man is healed in a pool in Bethany. Perhaps he means to symbolise the opening of the mind to spiritual insight. In Mark, there are no words Son of Man or Son of the living God. There is no discussion of the Church. Indeed, it is almost impossible that Jesus could have used the word Church, as he was a Jew. The real translation refers more to the word 'assembly' and could even refer to the synagogue, although the synagogue was not well developed until after the fall of Jerusalem in 70 CE.

Mark is the main source of the so-called Messianic secret. The instruction by Jesus to keep their discussions to themselves. No one has really offered a satisfactory explanation for the secrecy. One reason offered is that Jesus was very concerned about misinterpretation of his mission. He did not wish to be identified with the Zealot party of the time, or with any form of political extremism. The kingdom he taught about was the end point of a spiritual journey.

I have just touched the fringe of exegesis here. I have done it on purpose to point out that behind the words we glibly read, there are many layers to uncover and ponder about. Whether we want to think further and how we think are governed by many things. Apart from disinterest, some of us are put off by fear. We just want to read the Bible as the Word of God and leave it at that. We do not want to examine inconsistencies, consider alternative meanings or question what is written in the Bible in any way. We may think the authors of these books may have been men, but they were guided directly by God. This book cannot be looked at like any other piece of literature. Yet however you feel, I would want to encourage you to study the Bible and the forthcoming study series will be a start.

For me, the central question from this passage is the one that we all have to try and answer in our own way. 'Who do you think I am?', says Jesus. What do we say? We do not have to hide behind the right formula of words, the whole question is deeper than that. We might want to say nowadays that Jesus is our saviour although Peter did not at the time, only later. But, if that is our experience, we need to try and sort out in our minds in what sense that is true for us today. How has he changed our lives?

If we say that Jesus is the Son of God, what do we mean by that and how does that statement impact on us? He is not a son in any biological sense as we know it. When we say Jesus is born of the Holy Spirit, we are not using empirical, scientific language. We have entered the language of metaphor. Do we mean that the relationship of Jesus to God is exemplary and gives us all hope of becoming sons and daughters of God, or does this thinking undermine the uniqueness of Jesus? Is Jesus a supreme teacher of wisdom, remote in time and place from us, but stimulating us to follow a way of living that taken seriously is very different from the cultural emphasis of any age? Is to follow Jesus, always to be an outsider?

Perhaps, we are steeped in the mystery of it all. We see in our minds eye a remote figure standing by the shores of the Sea of Galilee, asking people in a compelling way to follow him. He still calls us in many very different ways. It is our challenge to respond and live out his calling. I find that exciting. We need to present the call of Jesus as exciting. It is never dull. We will not know where it ends. Follow me; he beckons to us.

Global Perspective

Romans 11.1–2a,29–32 Matthew 15.21–28
"I was sent only to the lost sheep of the House of Israel."
Matthew15.24.

A rather provocative statement! Certainly, it was an unsettling one to the Canaanite woman from the region of Tyre and Sidon. Yet she persisted and because of her great faith her daughter was healed.

Any intelligent reading of the Bible requires interpretation and I have deliberately chosen this statement by Jesus for some exploration. On the surface, it appears to negate any notion that Jesus was interested in non-Jewish people. To have any understanding of the situation we need to know something about the person who wrote Matthew's Gospel, who he was writing to, and the social and historical context at the time of writing. In addition, the Old Testament or Jewish Bible forms the bedrock on which Christianity developed. Reading the Old Testament in church, and alone, is of great importance and if we had read Isaiah today, we might have been enlightened a little.

I am going to have to read some of it now from Isaiah 56.6–8: 'And the foreigners who join themselves to the Lord, to minister to him, to love the name of the Lord, and to be his servants, all who keep the sabbath, and do not profane it, and hold fast my covenant — these I will bring to my holy mountain, and make them joyful in my house of prayer; their burnt-offerings and their sacrifices will be accepted on my altar; for my house shall be called a house of prayer for all peoples.'

Here we find a global perspective, but in the context of a Jewish faith open to others, and this is what we find in the Gospel of Matthew if we understand it properly. In Matthew, Jesus is the new Moses and the Messiah understood from a Jewish perspective. The Jewish picture of messiahship contains two broad pictures. The first is that of the Davidic Messiah who will establish a new kingdom based on Mount Zion in Jerusalem and restore Israel, inaugurating a universal kingdom of justice and peace. The second picture is aligned to the Son of Man figure recorded in chapter seven of the book of Daniel, coming 'on the clouds' to establish a reign at the end of time.

Any phrases such as Son of Man or Son of God in Matthew are understood from this perspective and did not refer to Jesus as the unbegotten Son of God. We must read John's Gospel for the mystic eternal Jesus, the light of the world. That is the Jesus developed in the historic creeds. It is not Matthew's picture.

Matthew was a Jew, writing to Jews. He wrote after the fall of Jerusalem in 70 CE and at this time Rabbinic Judaism, exemplified by the Pharisees, who had decamped from Jerusalem to Jamnia, was reviving an active proud Judaism that sought to exclude this small Christian sect within it. Christianity in the Diaspora, the burgeoning world of Paul, was escaping its identity within Judaism. In Matthew, Jesus was the Jewish Messiah; to enter his kingdom and follow his ways required entry into Judaism, its initiation rites and laws. The Law was not overthrown but transformed by the coming of Jesus.

Even Paul, the apparent enemy of this kind of Jewish Christianity, as recorded in such writings as the epistle to the Galatians, acknowledges in the epistle to the Romans (11.2) that 'God has not rejected his people whom he foreknew.' Matthew is the Christian Gospel to the Jews and Jesus is presented as a rabbi, a teacher, as the Sermon on the Mount amply demonstrates.

Because we are citizens of Paul's world, non-Jewish, often anti-Semitic, minimising our Jewish heritage, we may find ourselves more comfortable with the Gospels of Luke and John. But that would be a shame. The Canaanite woman of Mathew is a type. Tyre and Sidon were pictures of evil and the Canaanite Gods, Baal and Ashtaroth, symbols of idols and evil practices. Concerns with Canaanite religion abound in the Jewish Bible.

But this lady's experience tells us that no one is beyond the grace of God. Remote as she was from the Jewish faith and this new sect of Jesus' followers, she was not beyond the reach of Jesus. The reluctance Matthew inserts into the story is there to expose the dramatic nature of her faith, her persistence and courage; the possibility of transformation.

People in need cry out to be saved. They look for someone to draw them towards a calm shore, embrace them in love and care. We have just read of a woman like that in Mathew.

Elaine Pagels, the distinguished American professor of early Christian origins was jogging on a Sunday in New York. She was deeply distressed. The night before she had been told by a cardiologist that her young son with congenital pulmonary hypertension would die. He did. She had long ago abandoned the evangelical and literal certainties of early years and had not been in a church for a long time. She was drawn into a church by the music, creating a sense of joy, and she found an unconditional welcome. Here, she found she could be an explorer. She did not have to sign up to dogma, but she was loved. Just as in this building now, different people in that church believed different things or did not really know what they believed. Her experience led her to believe strongly that God is in each of us. The light of the world is in all of us. Salvation is to discover this and bring it out into the lives we lead.

There is something particularly compelling about the image of a lone person, in desperate need, seeking love and acceptance. This passage in Matthew tells us that it does not matter who you are, or where you come from; there is a place for you in the arms of God. You can be joined to the source of everything.

Competition and Equality

Acts 5.12–16 Luke 22.24–30
"For who is greater, the one who is at the table or the one who serves? Is it not the one at the table? But I am among you as one who serves."
Luke 22.27.

This brief episode in the Gospel encapsulates much of what it means to be a Christian. Put very simply the core of following Jesus means a life of service. Jesus uses the image of the one who sits at the table and the waiter or waitress. He draws a distinction between the two and is hinting at a radical reversal of normal social structures.

If you have any experience of French dining, you will know that the height of rudeness is to shout out 'garcon' to summon the waiter. The one who serves is to be respected, an equal, practising a refined art. He or she looks after you at the table but in no way is inferior. They should be consulted politely and referred to as Monsieur or Madame/ Mademoiselle.

Should we therefore be looking at a society where everyone sees themselves as a servant of others? Is that a utopian dream? In theory it is realisable. In practice we are far away from a universally adopted life of service.

The disciples were criticised for competing for greatness,

fame or importance. Those who actively seek recognition are moving away from any concept of service. Self-aggrandisement is anathema to any noble ideal. Any highly-developed society tends to have a hierarchical structure, and this even applies to the Church. Unfortunately, there is a tendency for those at the 'top' of the hierarchy to be deemed or to deem themselves as superior to those lower down. This is unfortunate because there is no reason why they should be if they adopt the role of servant as they undertake their tasks in life.

T.S. Eliot in the poem *East Coker*, part of *The Four Quartets*, famously referred to self-importance and the reality that we all reach the same level through the equality we find in death. It reduces us all to a mysterious base and those who are famous are shown to be victims of a transitory vanity that has no meaning. Merchant bankers, men of letters, presidents, prime ministers, princes and princesses, Olympic champions, headmasters and bishops, all end up equal.

Today happens to be St Bartholomew's day. We know very little about him. He is certainly one of the least known of the Apostles. He is named in Matthew, Mark, and Luke but not in John. However, most scholars identify him with Nathaniel, 'in whom there was no deceit', brought by his friend Philip and linked with Philip in the Synoptic Gospel listings. Early traditions have him travelling to India, Armenia and Mesopotamia. He was thought to have been martyred in Armenia. As far as we know, his life was one of service, and we remember him today as a little-known servant of God who followed Jesus. I think he fits in today with our theme of unpretentious service.

One might ask whether service and competitiveness are

incompatible. In our passage the disciples were competing with each other. We know that human nature has a competitive element. How can we marry the two; service and competition? An extreme view is that all forms of competition are inconsistent with Christianity as revealed in the Bible. This exposes one of the main problems about the development of Christian belief and ethics. Do we ignore the realities of human and animal nature? Are we of a mind that we will all be transformed into non-competitive beings when some level of competition is at the heart of survival? Ten people apply for one job, one person gets it. Only one athlete wins the race. There is the inevitable reality that we are not all born with the same abilities or intelligence. Sometimes, we only discover what is right for us by competing.

The most convincing perspective on this problem is that we should all strive to be the best that we can be in life without undermining the chances of others by causing injustice. Any just society must promote equal opportunity and seek to provide a more equal environment for those who are deprived. Jesus undoubtedly sought to overturn the social hierarchies of his day. He was biased towards the poor and sick. He did say that very rich people had a problem seeking the Kingdom of Heaven. There is no doubt that very intelligent young people from poor backgrounds still suffer disadvantage, despite progress.

It is possible to do one's best yet value your neighbour or colleague as yourself. As the New Testament constantly tells us it is what lies within our hearts and minds, the motives we have, that ultimately decides whether we are living for God and others rather than ourselves. We have just sung one of my favourite hymns. Let's just remember some of the words:

Brother, sister, let me serve you,
let me be as Christ to you;
pray that I may have the grace to
let you be my servant too.
We are pilgrims on a journey,
and companions on the road;
we are here to help each other
walk the mile and bear the load.

What is a Christian?

Romans 12.19–21Matthew 6.21–28
"If any want to become my followers, let them deny themselves and take up their cross and follow me."
Matthew 16. 24.

These challenging words stand out as a stark reminder of the nature of Christian discipleship. There was no Church when Jesus lived, no Christianity; and today, many people in the world would want to admire and follow Jesus but not join the Church. That is a reality we must recognise. A recent book entitled *The Invisible Church* by Steve Aisthorpe, draws attention to the increasing number of people who would claim to live a life of discipleship outside Christendom. There is a strand of opinion that Christendom is finished, has destroyed itself. But Christian discipleship is not finished. In a global environment, the structures, limitations and boundaries of the Church may hinder, not enhance, the mission of Jesus. I am sure there is truth in that, but it is an extreme view. However, if we want to look at the challenges our text brings for today, we need to look far beyond the 'walls of Christendom'.

It is difficult to place these words of Jesus into a precise historical context. Did Jesus have the insight to predict his own sufferings and death and therefore was challenging the disciples, if necessary, to follow in his own footsteps? Or was Matthew, the writer, living in the time of early Christian persecution and martyrdom, encouraging his readers to follow Jesus in his creative editing of the Gospel narrative?

There are two important elements in the challenge of Jesus to his disciples. The first is: 'Take up your cross', the second is: 'Follow me'. Whether Jesus was directly challenging his disciples to follow him to crucifixion, or some other form of death, cannot be the primary interpretation for us now. We need to look beyond the literal meaning of these words to explore any eternal relevance. *To take up one's cross* implies a determined decision to follow a path regardless of the consequences. The words imply difficulty, certainly not a way for the fainthearted. If we place these words at the heart of Jesus' discipleship, they imply a level of commitment that is not universally found within the Institutional Christian Church. Indeed, I have implied that many follow Jesus outside the Church and within other faiths.

Jesus is a figure of universal significance, but we cannot assume that he is the only figure of salvific note in human history, and what he stood for and the way he lived may be exemplified by other historic figures, some of whom may have explicitly followed him. That is not surprising. To give modern examples: Mahatma Gandhi remains an exemplar of non-violence, while seeking freedom of his people from the yoke of British colonial rule. In a similar way, but not without violence, Nelson Mandela committed himself to the freedom of his people from white racial domination. Both these figures took up their 'crosses' and took a difficult path for a specific purpose. Interestingly, Gandhi was very sympathetic to Jesus, but not Christianity. His experience of Apartheid in South Africa turned him away from the Institutional Church. He famously said: 'To be a good Hindu also meant that I would be a good Christian. There is no need for me to join your creed to be a believer in the beauty of the teachings of Jesus or try to follow His example.'

I regard Gandhi's remark as a profound insight into the modern problem of Christian discipleship. Although Christendom claims some two billion followers worldwide, the vast majority of people globally are outside the institutional Church. Within Western civilisation there is disillusionment, and many would agree with Gandhi that they can follow Jesus and his teachings without ever entering a church.

We know little about Nelson Mandela's religious views. We know that he went to a Methodist Sunday school and that chaplains from various denominations prayed with him in prison. He never spoke out like Gandhi and he knew that with the Dutch Reformed Church, a pillar of Apartheid, any attempt to unite his beloved country was best done without the support of formal religious structures.

I think it is possible to construe that both Gandhi and Mandela took up their '*crosses*' and followed Jesus explicitly or implicitly, while neither would openly wish to align themselves with formal Christianity. Both would have been deeply unhappy with the barriers erected within Christian structures that were inimical to the life and work of Jesus.

Moving beyond this, if one goes back to early Christian worship, before the dogmas of the Creed were formally developed, the essential aspect of Christianity was to worship Jesus as 'Lord'. The words Son of Man or Son of God in the Gospels of Mark, Matthew and Luke do not refer to Jesus as God, as understood later, but refer to titles in the Hebrew Bible related to kingship or the Jewish Messiah. The worship of Jesus as 'Lord' does carry with it divine connotations. So, the essential question for us is: Do we take up *our crosses* and follow Jesus as a great exemplar or do we do so because he is 'Lord' as well for us? The latter provides a deeper link between us and the figure we seek to follow.

'I live my life in God, in the mysterious ethical divine personality which I cannot discover in the world, but only experience in myself as a mysterious impulse.' Those words may help us to worship Jesus as 'Lord'. They come from some of the last comments of Albert Schweitzer, musician, theologian, doctor, humanitarian. If we start with God, as described in that quotation, we can move to Jesus, a spirit filled person, a God-centred person. We can see the person of Jesus as symbolising for us the kind of people we should seek to become in this world. We may then worship him as the focus of God's presence in the world and follow him. There are no diktats about the details of our lives, only a way to follow. Schweitzer said that Gandhi, who was the most 'Christian Hindu' of the century, once acknowledged that he got the idea of 'ahimsa' or nonviolence from the commandments of Jesus: 'You have heard that it was said, "You shall love your neighbour and hate your enemy." But I say to you, "Love your enemies and pray for those who persecute you, so that you may be children of your Father in heaven."'

Most of us want 'to make a difference' in the world we live in, however small and anonymous that difference may be. Schweitzer was a distinguished theologian, a Bach scholar, yet he was not satisfied. He felt he needed to be of practical help to others and decided to do this through medicine. He ceased to preach and felt that his undogmatic decision to follow Jesus needed to be lived out in the face of poverty and disease. We cannot all be 'Schweitzers', but his example of response to the call of a Galilean preacher is a reminder that we can all respond in our own ways.

Difficult Decisions

I Timothy1.12–17 Luke 14.25–33
"Whoever comes to me and does not hate father and mother, wife and children, brothers and sisters, yes, and even life itself, cannot be my disciple."
Luke 14.26.

This is one of the hard sayings of Jesus. Can he really mean this? We have several alternatives. First, we can take it as we read it and then work out what it means for us. We can consider that Jesus is using hyperbole to make a point. We can consider that the writer has inserted this when he wrote his Gospel around 90 CE. We can conclude that Jesus was a mad extremist and we should completely ignore this and indeed everything he says. I suppose the final alternative is a gross mistranslation. After all they do occur.

One does need to look at the whole chapter. It is unwise to take things out of context. The parable of the great banquet that precedes this passage can help us. 'But they all alike began to make excuses. The first said to him, "I have bought a piece of land, and I must go out and see it; please accept my apologies."' There followed other excuses. Jesus was talking about the banquet of the Kingdom of Heaven. There could be no excuses for not attending.

Put in a nutshell, Jesus is saying unless you take the search for the Kingdom of God seriously you cannot hope to reach it. Following me is radical and if you are sidetracked by anything in this world that distracts you and dominates your life, such as property, wealth, fame, whatever that enslaves you, there is no possibility of really reaching any kind of spiritual enlightenment.

But taken literally the remarks about family remain challenging. There is some evidence in the Bible that Jesus' own family found him mad. After all, he had left home, his livelihood, his village, and embarked on a lifestyle and mission that seemed extreme. Perhaps Jesus is saying that you have to follow your call regardless of your family and any objections they may have. Further, are we really being asked to 'hate' our lives, give them up? That is what Jesus did and others after him.

My mother was a committed Christian, but when Rene and I offered to serve as medical missionaries in India she became hostile. We would be taking two children with us; life would be hard, and the stipend was minimal. We would abandon our careers for what? Disease in India was rife in those days. Although she believed in overseas work this was 'too close to home'. We had to ignore her, and once we were seen to be determined, she relented. Yet there is little doubt she tried to stop us going. I think that provides some insight into what Jesus was saying. As it happens, I became extremely ill in India and could have died. I regret nothing about the experience. It changed our lives; it certainly undermined my health, but that happened to many people who travelled in those days.

The issue all this exposes is the nature of commitment. If you decide to be a Christian, what does commitment mean? It can imply many things, but it does not necessarily mean a total change in where you live and what you do. It is more connected with how you see the world and all that is in it. The decision to follow Jesus does require that you seek to avoid selfishness, seek to help others and detach yourself from domination by material things. That does not suggest you cannot enjoy a good meal, or a night at the cinema, but it does mean that nothing should become a god in your life that you cannot do without.

You do not give up the job or way of life you have unless your relationship with God guides you to change. What your commitment means will change as you grow older. I am no longer the young man who could travel and work in India. That was fifty or more years ago. Commitment, within the framework of our lives, is for us to work out at any one time what, if anything, inhibits us from following Jesus.

There remains a question and it is important. If you are not a Christian and have not explicitly committed yourself to any formal religion, is it possible to live a selfless life in the service of others, without seeking reward, in a spirit of love? YES. But sadly, some Christians take a different view and point to the need to undergo the forgiveness of Christ on the Cross. Yet today we must acknowledge the world is a different place in terms of our understanding. Globalisation has taught us of many cultures, many ancient faiths. On top of that, we have the idealism of many who truly wish to serve but who do not adhere to any formal religious structure. Some have argued that the Christian ideals that have dominated the West for two thousand years have filtered through to society in general and to some extent have become detached from their founder. There is evidence that this is the case.

Jesus made it clear, in Mathew twenty-five, that if you are very religious it means nothing unless you visit the sick, those in prison, help anyone in need. For him these were the criteria that mattered. But without acknowledging the source of your inspiration, God and his Spirit present in Jesus, you miss out on something. You miss out on the community of God's children and you miss out on acknowledging that the fount of all being, whatever name we attribute to that power in and beyond the universe, is the source of everything. You are connected with 'God' in the mystery of Being. Other faiths point in that direction, but for the Christian our commitment is clear. We want to follow Jesus because he has challenged and inspired us; and in him, we see the human face of God.

The Uncommitted

Philippians 4.1–9 Matthew 22.1–14
"Once more Jesus spoke to them in parables, saying: 'The kingdom of heaven may be compared to a king who gave a wedding banquet for his son.'"
Matthew 22.1–1.

And what a parable! Weird, over the top! What on earth do we make of it? Here is a king and he decides to have a wedding banquet for his son. He invites the usual crowd and they turn him down. He invites them again after showing what a splendid feast this will be. They are just not bothered! Indeed, they kill his servants who give the invitations. The king is angry, so he sends his troops and butchers the citizens he invited. He lays waste to one of his own cities. It is mayhem. He then goes and invites anyone his servants can find. It does not matter what sort of people they are. Then something very odd happens. One of the assembled company is badly dressed. He does not have a wedding gown. The king just turfs him out into outer darkness.

If you think the Bible is an easy read, think again. What message can we derive from today's Gospel? The first thing to say is that it was not written for us. The people who wrote the books in the Bible had no inkling that we would be reading Matthew in the twenty-first century. This parable was put together by Matthew for a specific audience. If Jesus spoke this parable at all it was not in the form we find it.

Matthew was writing to Jewish Christians circa 80–90 CE. He was writing at a time when there was a small group of Christians within Judaism, but there had been a revival of rabbinic Judaism after the fall of Jerusalem. This parable is told against that background. It is allegorical. The king is God the Father. Jesus is his son. The first invitees are the body of the Jews. They want no part with Jesus. Their killing of the messengers refers to the rejection of the prophets and Jesus himself. I should say at this point, that the accusations may not be entirely fair, but they are dramatised for effect. The destruction of the people and the city refers to the laying waste of Jerusalem and the mass slaughter of Jews in 70 CE. Matthew sees this event as the punishment of God. I am sure this is not true, but it reflects the prevailing understanding of God at the time. Those who are invited are the few Jews who have accepted Jesus as Lord and Gentiles. God's son is rejected by his chosen people.

And then we come to the curious episode of the wedding garment. The custom at a wedding would be to provide a garment. One did not have to supply one's own. Therefore, there was no excuse for not having one. This implies that one could appear to accept the invitation to this messianic banquet, the fulfilment of God's kingdom, but not be truly engaged with it. Metaphorically, one could say that person was not clothed in Christ; had not entered the fullness of the Kingdom. You may remember the letters to the seven Churches at the beginning of the book of Revelation: 'I know your works; you have a name for being alive, but you are dead.' These are the straw people of T.S. Eliot's famous poem the *Hollow Men*; the uncommitted, the indecisive, the token followers.

We only have one life. We can drift through it, unthinking, not really engaging in anything worthwhile; or we can commit ourselves to a life that means something, has a content, involves service of others. The framework of true Christianity presents us with a model for living. We identify ourselves with Jesus of Nazareth. We seek to follow him, attempting to work out what that means in our age. Those originally invited to that wedding banquet found excuses not to attend. They avoided commitment and became bogged down in mediocrity; surely a lesson for us all.

The Secular and the Sacred

1 Thessalonians 1.1–10 Matthew 22.15–22
"Give therefore to the emperor the things that are the emperor's, and to God the things that are God's."
Matthew 22.21.

This reading follows on directly from the parable of the wedding banquet. The parable refers to God's rejection of his chosen people after they had refused the invitation to join the messianic feast of his son, Jesus. Followers of the Pharisees, accompanied by the Herodians, were sent to try and trick Jesus. The Herodians were a group who probably supported Herod Antipas, and this implied that they accepted the rule of Rome for convenience. The Herods were puppet kings of the Roman Empire. The Pharisees sought Jewish independence. The only thing that really united them was antipathy to Jesus.

Initially they flattered him; what a truthful and sincere person he was! Then they asked him their trick question, with no easy answer. Should one pay taxes to Caesar, the Emperor? This referred to the census tax, one denarius per person. If Jesus answers yes, he appears to be in collusion with Rome and that might be very unpopular with Jewish people. If he answers no, he could be seen to be promoting insurrection against ruling powers.

He asks for a denarius. On the one side of this coin it read:

‘Tiberius Caesar, august son of the divine Augustus.’ And on the other side, ‘Pontifex Maximus.’ Jesus confounds his questioners by asking them whose image is on the coin and follows it up when they confirm it is Caesar by the statement: ‘Give therefore to the Emperor the things that are the Emperor’s, and to God the things that are God’s.’ But what does that really mean? The beauty of Jesus' answer is that he both concedes payment of the census tax while subverting the reach of the emperor. If read one way, Jesus' answer is simply an affirmation of Christian submission to governing authorities. Yet if read from another angle, Jesus affirms the all-encompassing reach of God's ownership in a way that relativises imperial claims of right to rule.

Although this story in Matthew has a very specific context, it can lead us on to the perennial question of the conflict between so called sacred and secular authorities. If God is the God of all creation, everything is sacred. However, in practice, we know that humanity has modified and developed creation, and most of us realise that there is a deep tension between what we might call worldly issues and the spiritual or sacred. In the modern era, charting one’s way through this maze is a real problem.

Perhaps the first thing we have to realise is that we really do live in this world. This is the place of our being and we have to interact with it. The idea that we are not of this world, brief sojourners, who belong to another world with God, is unhelpful. From the early days of Christianity some have felt it impossible to live in the midst of the material world and all that implies. Initially some lived in isolation, in the desert, and subsequently monastic orders developed. But it is unrealistic, however we live, to deny our material existence and our responsibility to be part of the world we live in.

Jesus never rejected the Jewish law. He claimed to fulfil it, emphasising the spirit of the Law, rather than the letter of the Law. His attitude to Sabbath observance is one obvious example of this. Law is an inevitable consequence of society. We cannot live without law and perhaps Jesus recognised this in his response to the question of tax. But how we govern ourselves has always been a matter of debate and this continues to this day.

A modern-day response to the undoubted moral issues that are involved in political decision making is to privatise religion; remove it from the 'market square'. One reason for doing this is that Christians do not necessarily agree amongst themselves about some of the major issues that we have to think about. For example, some think that the whole issue of Brexit has ethical dimensions that are largely ignored. Others do not think like that. Politics at national and local levels is an ethical minefield. Surely some will say, it is best to keep out of it. I do not think one can if one is a Christian. The reason for that is that Christianity has to be lived in the world and is not just about obtaining a ticket to heaven. Interestingly, the fact that we have an established Church is a tacit recognition of the relevance of the Christian religion in the life of the nation. Whether that should continue is debateable, but at present our Church leaders do take the opportunity to speak out on our behalf on important issues.

The words, 'the religious Right, the religious Left', indicate that there are many Christianities. We have to accept that. So, what can one do? Jesus was a peripheral, political figure. He got into trouble because he was perceived to be a political agitator, but there is no real evidence that he was political in the usual sense of that word. However his teaching, most notably the Sermon on the Mount, and his attitude towards the poor and women, does raise major issues about how society should be organised.

Rowan Williams, now back in Cambridge, is an important commentator on how we should live in the world. In response to the phrase 'Christian values' he said: 'It's a phrase that's flung around constantly. The heart of Christian values has something to do with mutuality — a real commitment to and investment in the wellbeing of your neighbour, and the confidence that they are invested in your wellbeing. Not everyone shares these values.' He added: 'The job of Christian communities is to keep arguing, keep nudging… The Church is obliged to be both a good and an awkward neighbour to the state. It earns its place in a plural state by asking certain unwelcome questions.'

However difficult it may seem in the modern world, it remains a Christian duty to engage with the complexities of life. The prophetic voice must never be stilled in the world of the emperor. The state may govern us, but this is God's world.

Our Duty in the World

Ecclesiastes 11.12 1 Timothy 2.1–7
"The end of the matter; all has been heard. Fear God and keep his commandments; for that is the whole duty of everyone. For God will bring every deed into judgement, including every secret thing, whether good or evil."
Ecclesiastes 12.13.

That is a remarkably traditional ending to what is a very untraditional book. It is really necessary to read the whole book to have any chance of understanding what is going on. The Christian Church tends to quote snippets such as the famous 'A time to' passage, often used in funeral services, but this does not capture the essence of Ecclesiastes. It is part of what we call Wisdom literature and one of the books of Solomon. The other two are Proverbs and the Song of Solomon, both very different in approach to Ecclesiastes. The Song of Solomon is about erotic love despite attempts by those, who do not think it proper, to allegorise it. Proverbs is a collection of pithy sayings, generally positive in tone. Ecclesiastes is gloomy, fatalistic, cynical, with certainly no emphasis on the traditional Jewish stories of the Exodus and the arrival in the Promised Land.

One must not conclude that this book was written by Solomon as it was almost certainly composed much later, either under Persian rule or the subsequent Greek invasion. There are Persian and Aramaic allusions in the text. The 'Teacher' or 'Preacher' is indirectly indicated to be Solomon by dint of him being described as son of David and wise. Evangelical Christians either wish it was not in the bible or put a complex interpretation on it. Others regard it as one of the great pieces of world literature. Famous phrases have been taken from it: 'There is nothing new under the Sun', 'vanity of vanities all is vanity', 'fly in the ointment', 'eat drink and be merry', 'a chasing after wind'.

What the writer does is look at life without the encumbrance of religious dogma. He explores various ways of living for himself and observes others. The good life of wealth, possessions, sensual pleasure of any kind is in the end meaningless. Excess leads nowhere. Whether rich or poor, wise or foolish, the same fate of death awaits us all. This teacher is very much concerned with life now rather than some hereafter. On the whole it is better to be wise than foolish, but it makes no difference in the end. Everyone will be forgotten. Humans and animals are alike; they share the same fate. It is not that the teacher is an unbeliever, but he finds it difficult to see the indelible mark of God in creation. Unlike traditional Judaism, he finds no evidence that the righteous are rewarded and the wicked punished. He is a realist. He thinks the young should enjoy themselves, it will not last. Yet at the end he says: 'Enough, follow God's commandments.' Perhaps he is eventually saying that the 'Good Life' can be reduced to that.

I think we have to put this book in context historically. If, as modern scholars suggest, it was written about 350–300 BCE it is approximately contemporary with the philosophy of Aristotle and Epicurus. Both of these philosophers asked the question: What is the 'Good Life'?. Unlike the philosopher Plato they were not concerned so much with the eternal. Epicurus has been grossly misrepresented; he is now linked with high pleasure and even gluttony. In fact, he stated that the 'Good Life' was very simple; friendship, a glass of wine and conversation with someone you liked, were some of the highest pleasures. What he did emphasise was that it is a waste of time dwelling on death. It comes to all. Aristotle concluded something similar and emphasised the importance of the traditional virtues. I think our 'Teacher' does the same. This is far from the world of sacrifice to God or the gods that prevailed in the ancient world, and therefore is surprisingly modern.

There is an intellectual honesty here that is often missing from religion. If we distort reality, we distort our picture of God and impose false images upon Him/Her. If we look at the world in the twenty-first century, we see enormous variety, appalling poverty and sickening wealth, attempts to be at peace alongside extreme violence, the lust for power alongside dependence, the life of pleasure alongside deep sorrow. In the face of this it is very difficult indeed to use the word progress. Any good life has always been simple and not excessive. The moments we treasure are usually basic. If 'Wisdom' can teach us this, it is worth having, but it may be a very different insight than our world tends to admire.

Building and Protecting

Nehemiah 6.1–16 John 15.12–27
"I am doing a great work and I cannot come down."
Nehemiah 6.3.

"If the world hates you, be aware that it hated me before it hated you." John 15.18.

Nehemiah was under threat. He had been the king's cup bearer in Babylon after it was conquered by Persia and the king was probably Artaxerxes I; but there is some confusion about the names of the Persian kings. His task was to rebuild the walls of Jerusalem to keep the returning Jewish people safe from attack. Amongst their enemies were Sanballat and his cronies. These were regional governors under the Persians. They were representatives of some of the tribes who had been driven out of the promised land by the Jews previously. They had a vested interest in keeping Jerusalem in ruins. That is a very brief historical background; a city in ruins, the temple rebuilt by Ezra and Zerubbabel. Nehemiah, possibly helped by Esther, the Jewish Queen of the Persian King, was sent to make Jerusalem safe.

But I want to move beyond history and consider this story in a metaphorical sense. Building something is a great task. The question is always: What are you building and why? For a Christian the fundamental task is to build a world of love. In our Gospel reading from John we are enjoined to learn to love one another as Jesus loved. That, as I see it, is the primary task of Christianity distilled to its essence, stripped of dogma. As we see in the story of Nehemiah, who was toiling for his people's safety, there are always threats to completing a task, removing us from the path of love towards hatred and violence. I have used the quote from John to point to the eternal issue that just as Jesus was hated for what he tried to achieve, anyone who seeks to follow Jesus will face temptation and opposition in many forms.

I think we then have to move from metaphor to the world we live in, and immediately Aleppo comes to mind rather than Jerusalem, although that city has many problems of its own. I know Aleppo is not near home, but we cannot ignore it and it is becoming a focus for serious questions about the apparent deep-rooted cruelty of humans. People sometimes say humans are behaving like animals, but this is a gross misreading of creation and the beauty of our natural world. The ordinary citizens of Aleppo want safety. They want protection around their homes, freedom to pursue their way of life. This ancient city is in ruins. Why? Any brief attempt to dissect this complex issue is bound to be inadequate, but we can identify some of the strands and examine possible motives.

The Assad regime is dominated by Alawite or Nusayri religious affiliation, including President Assad. Alawites are an obscure religious sect with secretive practices originating in Shiite Islam, but viewed by many as a separate religion. They view Ali, a descendant of Mohammed, and the key figure in Shiite Islam, as a Jesus-like incarnation of God. They use bread and wine in their rituals, celebrate Christian festivals and acknowledge some Christian saints. They form thirteen percent of the population of Syria, predominantly in the province of Latakia in North East Syria. This was an autonomous pro-French area during the French mandate after the first world war. During the mandate, Alawites began to form an important part of the army. After the mandate ended in 1946 the Sunni-led government of Syria incorporated Latakia into Syria, and Alawite autonomy was lost. Historically, Alawites were poor and deprived. The French mandate increased their importance and as a result of Sunni infighting and purges, their influence in the army and the newly-formed pan-Arab Ba'ath party increased. They eventually achieved power through a coup. The Ba'ath party, despite pan-Arabic claims both in Iraq and Syria, has not pursued this policy and believes in a one-party state. The war in Syria results from increasing majority Sunni resistance to draconian and brutal rule, but as always, the Sunni opposition is divided, with extremist groups increasingly influential.

America and allies seek to remove Assad and create fair elections and a democratic government. Russia seeks to destroy any opposition to the Assad regime and keep Assad in power. Iran, taking the view that Alawites are a kind of Shiite, support the Russian viewpoint.

This situation exposes the awfulness of humanity to many cynics. How can we build a world of love and peace when the human race is basically nasty, aggressive, and perhaps beyond redemption? Religion appears to make matters worse; underneath it lies the desire for tribal power that uses religion. Interestingly, the Ba'ath party is secular and is much more tolerant of religious minorities, including Christians and the Druze.

Creating a world of love, peace and safety is a noble task but its achievement appears unlikely. What has Christianity got to say to this? When Jesus preached and spoke of the Kingdom of God or Heaven, he spoke of something longed for but far removed from the tragedy of much human experience. Theologians have debated endlessly what this can mean. Many consider that the Kingdom of God, a kingdom of love, peace and harmony can be partially attained in this world, but its completion lies elsewhere. Looking at our world from a very limited perspective indeed, it is difficult for us to see global harmony on the horizon. Rather like Nehemiah, we try to concentrate on local rather than global issues. We concentrate our efforts on our village or town because transformation of other societies is beyond us.

Therein lies an important issue. By transforming ourselves and our communities, we point to the possibility of safety and peace to others less fortunate. Why do people want to come to this country? It is because we are perceived to be tolerant, peaceful and safe despite our own significant limitations. The same applies to other countries in Europe. If we are able to behave according to Christian values, the fruits of the spirit, there is a hope that others will come to their senses. But if we behave with arrogance and contempt for human life, we will not gain respect. That is why being involved in bombing Aleppo, whatever the motive, brings with it grave risks for humanity at large. It is a human trait to want to interfere in the affairs of others, but we seldom have the knowledge and understanding to make a difference for good.

Hearts ache for children and adults without food and in daily fear of their lives. We can help with aid, accepting refugees, being sensitive daily to the needs of others far from our homes. That is a task worth sticking with, but bombs are another matter. The fundamental question always is: 'How do you build a world that is safe and dominated by love in the face of opposition?' We all struggle to unravel the moral complexities of our world. It seems beyond us; yet through the work of the Holy Spirit we must try.

Persistence in Searching

2 Timothy 4.6–8, 16–18 Luke 18.9–14
"Proclaim the message; be persistent whether the time is favourable or unfavourable."
2 Timothy 4.2.

"Then Jesus told them a parable about their need to pray always and not to lose heart."
Luke 18.1.

The parable of the unjust Judge is, in some ways, a strange choice for Jesus to use as a story about determination and persistence. The classic, genuine parable, unadulterated by later interpretations, is not allegorical but makes a point. The focus of this parable is on keeping going and not giving up. The interceding of the woman on behalf of her son would not have fitted well into our legal system. We do not know whether he was guilty or not. It is her determination and persistence that matter.

The quotation from 2 Timothy extols the early Church to be persistent in its message whether times are good or bad, whether there is persecution or not. 2 Timothy is one of the pastoral epistles with I Timothy and Titus. On the surface it was written by Paul but there is now widespread scholarly consensus that this epistle was written long after Paul's death.

The writer, probably from the early second century CE, was writing as if he was Paul, as the great evangelist was revered in the Church. Authority is given to succeeding Church leaders by their being commended and encouraged by Paul. The vocabulary in these letters is quite unlike other Pauline epistles and the Church structures referred to in the pastoral epistles did not exist in Paul's day. Some regard these epistles as unsuitable to be in the Bible. Certainly, they lack the freshness and vigour of Pauline work. Nevertheless, they make the important point that the early Church needed to persist in spite of opposition and persecution. Finally, the story from Genesis, although not read today, describes the struggle that Jacob had with a strange being during one night before he met his brother Esau, from whom he stole his birthright. Again, it is his unwillingness to give up that is at the heart of the story and he has a hip injury to prove it.

Can we apply these calls for determination and persistence to our own day? If we take the church of 2 Timothy as our starting point, there are, to my mind, some issues that should concern us when considering the Institutional Church today. We now know that early Christianity was far from harmonious. The pastoral epistles record people who were preaching a different kind of gospel, who were to be condemned. We are entering the early stages of the fight for orthodoxy that extended well into the fifth century Common Era. The opponents that Timothy referred to are not named, but they may well have been representatives of Gnosticism that began to flourish at the end of the first and through the second century CE. I cannot describe the essence of Gnostic belief now, but suffice it to say it took a very different view of the resurrection, the way to salvation and the nature of the created world. The best introduction to this is probably the Gnostic Gospels by Elaine Pagels.

The relevance for us is: What kind of persistence and determination are we referring to? If we are referring to what is rather glibly thought of as Christian orthodoxy, we must be very careful. It is certainly true that in the first five centuries there was a rigorous attempt to protect the Christianity perceived to originate in Jesus and the apostles. Alternative interpretations, claimed to result from the continuing work of the Holy Spirit, given by Jesus, amounted to fresh visions and gnosis imparted by the risen Lord, who was seen as a spiritual enlightener to the chosen few. All this culminated in the debate over orthodoxy resulting in the Nicene creed in 325 CE.

Yet it is naïve and incorrect to imagine that there have not been changes in our understanding of the Christian message down the centuries. Most of us no longer consider our world was created in six days. We now know that it is extremely unlikely that any of the Gospels in the Bible were written by apostles, but by disciples who were writing for local communities and perhaps using certain names to promote authority. Gradually, new knowledge has forced many to shift their focus from the miraculous aspects of the Bible towards the primary teaching of Jesus. What is known as Kingdom theology, playing our part in making the world come right, is increasingly important.

As has always been the case there are many Christianities. There has always been diversity. The difficulty Christians have always had is accepting this rather than spending much time and emotional energy condemning the variants they find objectionable. This applies also to our acceptance of other great faiths born in other cultures. One evening some time ago at a dinner at the bishop's house in Ripon, I sat next to a bishop from Sri Lanka. He was astonished to learn that many British Christians had a problem accepting the importance and status of great faiths living alongside each other, as they did in his own country. What is commonly called religious pluralism remains a problem for many Christians, even in the light of our global awareness.

What I am trying to focus on is that in our determination to follow Jesus, mirroring the call of those early disciples, we need to accept that our understanding of the gospel may well evolve. Indeed, it should, as we study and put effort into making our faith alive in the twenty-first century. It has to connect with life lived now and not two thousand years ago. This is inevitable if our Christianity is not to lapse into a form of escapism from reality, offering unreal comforts in the modern world.

When I was young, I was a traditional evangelical Christian, but never entirely comfortable. I had a questioning mind. Gradually, I altered my view of a number of things. I felt liberated and still able to pursue my spiritual journey within the framework of Christianity. Others I knew in a similar situation dropped away, partly because they felt the Church lacked the breadth of outlook to accommodate them. They became the 'Invisible Church', the title of a recent searching book about the decline in the Institutional Church.

Today, many young people are put off the Church because they find it, in many instances, judgemental, intolerant of other faiths, closed to people of differing sexual orientation, peddling a spurious confidence rather than genuine seeking. The youth of our generation are no less spiritual or idealistic.

I myself have moved from what I called certainty to

mystery. The determination and persistence we are called to is that of a continuing search for truth, perhaps embodied in the word pilgrim. A pilgrim searches and journeys, changing and being changed by the people he or she meets and the insights that continue to flood into our minds as creation unfolds through the work of the Holy Spirit.

Unforgiven and Persecuted

Romans 14.1–12 Matthew 18.21–35
"So, my Heavenly Father will also do to every one of you if you do not forgive your brother and sister from your heart."
Matthew 18.35.

These words sometimes bother me. Am I forgiving? Am I a hypocrite, inconsistent in my actions and behaviour? A crucial aspect of Christian discipleship or indeed any authentic human life is that when we are forgiven, we must forgive others. Matthew's parable highlights this and points out that if we do not forgive, our behaviour is inimical to God.

Unforgiving behaviour at an individual level leads on to something even more sinister; persecution. At the heart of persecution is a belief that a group of people, even a whole race, are responsible for something bad that happens. Throughout history people have been on the receiving end of a judgment applied because of an interpretation of events that exonerates the one part at the expense of another. We can use the word scapegoating whether applied at individual or group level. The seminal book *Scapegoat* by Rene Girard explores many aspects of this phenomenon. One example is the scapegoating of Jews in the fourteenth century in Europe at times of the Plague. As is often the case, historical documents of the time expose that this was scapegoating rather than justice.

If we take the example of the crucifixion of Jesus, we still hear the phrase: 'The Jews crucified Jesus'. A close inspection of all available records suggests a much more nuanced picture. The Roman rulers were involved. Any suggestion of undermining imperial authority was put down by them. True, a group known as The Sadducees, played a part in the arrest of Jesus. But to say Jesus, a Jew, was crucified by the Jews as a whole is a gross distortion and has done untold harm to Jewish people.

The original scapegoating symbolic act in Judaism itself, took place on the Day of Atonement when the sins of the people were metaphorically placed on a goat and sent out into the wilderness to die.

I have brought this up today because of the current crisis involving the Rohingya Muslims in Myanmar. Described by the United Nations in 2013 as one of the most persecuted minorities in the world, the Rohingya population are denied citizenship under the 1982 Burmese citizenship law. According to Human Rights Watch, laws effectively deny to the Rohingya the possibility of acquiring a nationality. Despite being able to trace Rohingya history to the eighth century, Burmese law does not recognise the ethnic minority as one of the national races. It is impossible to go into the detailed evidence surrounding this persecution, but one aspect is the blame attached to this group, who are perceived to be the aggressors in Rakhine state. Contrary evidence suggests there has never been acceptance of these people.

And so, we come to one disturbing aspect of persecution, individual and group; the role of religion. One of the worrying aspects of institutional religion, including Christianity, is the endemic existence of intolerance, leading to persecution within the structures themselves, and outwards towards various groups alien to that religion in society at large. I do not think I need to spell this out. It is self-evident. The establishment of orthodoxies inherently excludes those who do not subscribe to them. Paul noted this in the early Church and our epistle today emphasises the acceptance of difference.

The sociological studies of decline in church attendance and the examination of the faith of those who have never been to church, and do not intend to do so, has exposed the distinct possibility that Christianity, by which I mean following the example of Jesus and seeking to live an authentic life committed to service of others, will survive; but Christendom, that body created when Constantine and his acolytes chose an orthodoxy and thus created an institution, albeit splintered over the centuries, will not.

In Romans Paul says: 'Welcome those who are weak in faith, but not for the purpose of quarrelling over opinions.' Further: 'Do not pass Judgment.'

It is fairly obvious that here in Masham we will not fill the pews at regular services. Indeed, that should not be our primary purpose. We have a lovely building. We could and should make it more flexible as a resource for our community. The essence of what we are has to point outwards. I think some of the initiatives that have taken place inside and outside our building are very welcome. They have no strings attached to them; they are open, there are no entry requirements. I have been bothered for a long time about the demands of initiation imposed by the institutional Church. Some may wish to undergo them; some not. I believe we have to move beyond the cultic to exercise true openness.

I have not always been a great George Herbert fan, but I think this great poem draws us in the more we read it; for this is surely what we should all be about in the Master's service.

Love

Love bade me welcome. Yet my soul drew back
Guilty of dust and sin.
But quick-eyed Love, observing me grow slack
From my first entrance in,
Drew nearer to me, sweetly questioning,
If I lacked any thing.

A guest, I answered, worthy to be here:
Love said, You, shall be he.
I the unkind, ungrateful? Ah my dear,
I cannot look on thee.
Love took my hand, and smiling did reply,
Who made the eyes but I?

Truth Lord, but I have marred them: let my shame
Go where it doth deserve.
And know you not, says Love, who bore the blame?
My dear, then I will serve.
You must sit down, says Love, and taste my meat:
So, I did sit and eat.

Self-Righteous Anger

Jonah 3.10–4.11 Matthew 20.1–16
"And the Lord said, 'Is it right for you to be angry?'"
Jonah 4.4.

One of the great glories of the Hebrew Bible is that it is earthy. It is full of ordinary human emotion and prejudice. We are dealing with flesh and blood feeling. Sometimes, when we read the New Testament the words and people seem less real. The accounts are heavily overlaid with piety and theological language.

Jonah had a real dialogue with God. He wanted vengeance. He was furious when God fulfilled his worst fears and let the people of Nineveh off. After all, he had never wanted to go to the wretched place.

Behind the fantastical story of Jonah and the Whale is ancient near eastern history. A visit to the British Museum will remind us that the great civilisation of Assyria, which included parts of Iran, Afghanistan and modern Turkey, was a powerful presence around 700 BCE. Jonah was an Israelite and this part of the Hebrew nation was annexed by Assyria and vast numbers of the population taken from the Northern Kingdom and integrated with the Assyrians. There was much hatred between the people of Israel and Assyria. The remains of the Northern Kingdom became what we call Samaria. People refer to the lost tribes of Israel when they speak of the tribes of Jacob who disappeared into Assyria. Many people claim to be descended from the lost tribes, the best claim being the six hundred or so Samaritans that live in modern Israel, who practice a variant of Judaism with their holy place being Mount Gerizim.

Although the picture of God in the book of Jonah is primitive, and he is presented rather like a superhuman figure, there are lessons for us. What picture of God do we have? Is this a god who thinks like us and therefore someone we can expect to agree with our judgements about people? Many of us want to believe in a god who fits in with our wishes. We project a bizarre, distorted picture, onto God.

There is nothing wrong in crying out in anger to God when our own personal lives go badly wrong through no fault of our own; for example, inherited disease. But when we cry out in anger because other cultures and groups do not fit in with our perceptions or world views, we need to be very careful. If God exists, he is the God of all people not of any group. The whole idea of being a chosen people is unhealthy. God is not the God of Christians, he is the God of all; Muslims, Hindus and so on. Our understanding of God may differ, but that is our projection, not ultimate reality. I believe personally that this misunderstanding lays at the heart of what is wrong with all the extremisms and orthodoxies that divide people of different religions and cultures.

In the case of Jonah, he was angry with this warlike people, but forgot about the history of his own people as they migrated into Canaan. The idea that the Israelites had a divine right to occupy this land may have been useful to Hebrew identity, but on an absolute scale they were just imitating the behaviour of many other tribal groups.

Such anger is with us today. We must wonder whether humans have any capability to change. Many religious people have spoken of the transforming power of grace, but it is rarer than we might think. We use Jesus, Buddha, Nelson Mandela, Mother Theresa and Gandhi as models; but all of them in some way transcend specific religions. As soon as we think God is on our side, we cease to follow true religion. Our world is beset by historical anger and prejudice that we all find difficult to overcome. The worst aspects of Islam, based on a distorted interpretation of the Koran and religious exclusivism, take past historical injustices very seriously.

Christianity struggles to find an identity stemming from an 'open' understanding of cultural history and ancient myths. Christian orthodoxy itself was minted in the cultural setting of an accepting Roman Emperor looking for coherence over his sprawling empire. Now the world is different. Christian history is strewn with the evidences of appalling cultural and physical damage to non-Christian groups, and an exclusivism that sits very uneasily in the modern world. There is a vast difference between following Jesus and erecting a monolithic faith that thinks it is the only faith. I have no qualms in saying that we have to face up to it.

So, let us return to the self-righteous angry Jonah. He knew in his heart of hearts that God was not like him. He found it so difficult to feel merciful and tolerant. He felt so bad that he wanted to die. His whole world was crumbling around him. Many people still have what we call a 'world view'. This means that their lives are built up around beliefs and cultural settings that allow them to function and live out their lives. In many ways this is a good thing if those beliefs and the cultural settings are not harmful to those with other world views. One problem experienced by Jonah, is that when a view is challenged by a realisation that the world is not really the way one thought it was, there may be severe anxiety, dislocation, defensive behaviour, anger and bewilderment. When we are faced with this kind of challenge, we can do a number of things. We can collapse like Jonah and wish we were dead. We can accept the insights we have received and modify our world view. We can reject the insight and carry on as we did before; but we pay a high price in terms of internal peace and integrity. Finally, we can reject completely our previously held world view and adopt another.

Jonah is a modern figure in that he represents the challenges that we all face in terms of our interpretation of religion and cultural difference in the twenty-first century. How will we react or how have we reacted? Our future internal and external peace may depend on it.

Inclusiveness not Triumphalism

1 Samuel 24.1–17 Luke 14.12–24
"He said to David, 'You are more righteous than I; for you have repaid me good, whereas I have repaid you evil.'"
I Samuel 24.17.

I have always had some sympathy for Saul because I think he focuses some of the problems of triumphalism. Self-satisfaction at one's good fortune is inimical to spiritual health. Saul was a sick man but chosen for high office by God. Although one can never be certain about medical diagnosis from a distance, a well-documented example being the madness of King George the Third, it seems possible that Saul had a bipolar affective disorder, commonly known as manic depression. A key feature of this is an unstable mood with episodes of both mania and depression. There is a high risk of suicide and irrational behaviour, both verbal and physical. It requires specific treatment. In our introductory text, we find Saul full of remorse and guilt. He feels unworthy in the face of the apparent goodness of David.

For much of history mental illness has been viewed like epilepsy, as some sort of moral depravity. Indeed, illness generally has been perceived as some kind of punishment from God. Job was torn apart by unmerited disease but subjected by his friends to the taunts that it must be a punishment for sin.

God never answers Job or his questionings. But Job himself comes to terms with the way things are, although his life is made easier by having his health restored.

People today continue to say things such as: 'I've always lived a decent life, why should this happen to me?' I remember a man coming to one of my clinics and saying just that. He had a trivial condition and what made it more amusing was that he was eighty!

Saul may well have had a genetic disease. We now realise that many diseases result from having an unfavourable genetic makeup. A topical example is the gene for breast cancer, but more telling examples are the dramatic genetic faults that affect new-born babies. Bipolar disorder itself has a strong genetic linkage.

When serious diseases affect the body, they are nowadays seen as a sad affliction. When they affect the brain, people continue to be less tolerant because the consequences of the disease affect social dynamics. There has always been a school of thought that claims there is no such thing as mental illness. Modern neurobiological research shows that this is not the case. Mental illness has to be viewed like any other form of physical illness.

And so, we come to the core of why I have said any of this. What has Christianity got to say about people who are the Sauls of this world, or people labelled psychopaths in prison who have disorders of their XY chromosomes, a known accompaniment of some people with violent behaviour? There are many more subtle aspects of our personalities that make us who we are and these are genetically determined, but it is when illness takes us well beyond accepted norms of behaviour that we sit up and take notice. Is there anything to say?

It is often stated that there are two ways of doing theology, from above and below. What do I mean by that? I do my theology from below. I mean that we cannot ignore the real experiences of life as we dwell on this planet. What is real or unreal has to be filtered through the lens of human experience. This includes the many things that go wrong and are not put right, the devastating diseases and natural disasters that beset humanity, not stemming from human evil. Theology is always in danger of imposing on humanity beliefs or doctrines that are unsustainable to many questioning people. This endangers the Church's ministry, leading to distortions and harm. Conviction that everything that goes wrong can be put right is palpably nonsense. I hesitate to say this about an ordinand, but a good many years ago someone who was shortly to be ordained said to me that God would grow new fingers for people with leprosy if they had enough faith. I won't tell you what I said. Time spent in India made me very angry at such rubbish.

There has been very little good work done on the theology of genetic diseases. They are very good examples of 'mistakes' in creation that cannot be put right by prayer or any Christian act. Genetic therapy is in its infancy, but most of us who have genetic diseases know that we will spend our lives with them.

These 'illnesses' are not going to be cured by magic; they are not due to devil possession. They exist and will always exist unless we engineer them out of future societies. All we can do as Christians is to create the most appropriate environment, because apart from specific treatments that may be available, it is the environment that matters most.

We read in the book of Samuel that David played his harp and this soothed Saul. He came near to him. Perhaps he did not speak to him at all. For words are often very damaging in the world of mental illness. What we are seeking to provide in the name of the Spirit of God, manifest in Jesus, is inclusiveness. If we recall the New Testament reading tonight, one of the elements in that whole chapter is the fundamental commandment to bring to the fold all the disadvantaged.

Do you believe in your individual salvation? Many years ago, when a group of us were discussing this we brought up the image of a circle. We are all points on the circle. It can never be complete or whole without all the points being there. That is our task. That is an answer to the question.

When we celebrate the Eucharist or Holy Communion there is always something missing; we are incomplete. We must be there on behalf of everyone. We bring to communion all those who cannot or will not come. We bring our whole lives, and the desire for everyone to be included. Those who are part of the Church are not in some holy club where membership is restricted.

David is often held up as the ideal king, Saul the opposite. Both were flawed as we all are. By recognising our own failures and limitations we come closer to standing alongside all whom we marginalise in our world. God has given us free will. Creation is a huge risk. It goes wrong. It is up to us to commit ourselves to help making it come right. And even then, there remains the mystery, the unanswered questions that require faith to live with.

The Rejection of Grace

Philemon 3.4b–14 Matthew 21.33–46

"Therefore I tell you, the kingdom of God will be taken away from you and given to a people that produces the fruits of the kingdom."

Matthew 21.43.

In the presentation of the life and work of Jesus that we find in Matthew's Gospel we are confronted with the Parable of the Vineyard at the point when Jesus is in Jerusalem, teaching in the temple, and in angry conflict with the hierarchy of Judaism. A similar parable is recorded in both Mark and Luke, but they are not identical. The oral tradition that gave rise to these recorded parables has been modified and edited to suit the life of the early Church. Essentially, we find anti-Jewish leader polemic that accuses them of claiming religious righteousness yet rejecting the prophets of old and the Messiah. The result is not a condemnation of all Jews, but a diatribe against religious leaders. There is no specific condemnation of Judaism and indeed the vineyard will be inherited by the new Church both Gentile and Jewish.

There are sets of characters in this parable. The landowner is God. The vineyard itself is Covenant Israel. The tenants are the Jewish leadership of Israel; the slaves are the prophets, the Landowner's son is Jesus, and the new tenants are the new

Church whether within Judaism or non-Jewish. The fruit are what is owed to God. The punishment of the tenants is the destruction of Jerusalem.

It is important to remember that the author of Matthew is Jewish, writing to Jews. The date of the book is about 80–90 CE after the fall of Jerusalem in 70 CE. The book is steeped in Judaism and the Torah. There are numerous Old Testament quotes. Jesus is the fulfilment of prophecy. He is the new Moses/Joshua. It was written at the time when The Christian Way was still, to an extent, within Judaism and connected with the synagogue. However, the transition from Temple Judaism, focused on the Sadducees (the hereditary priests), to Pharisaic religion focused on the synagogue, had developed rapidly following the establishment of an academic group of rabbis at Jamnia after the destruction of Jerusalem. This was an aggressive movement seeking to establish a new united Jewish identity. But it was a challenge to the new emerging Christian Way within Judaism, even though Jewish Christians of that time believed that the law remained important for them. In addition, they had accepted the importance of broadening the Christian message to the wider world. There was an inevitable clash between the new emergent Jewish identity and this Christian sect within Judaism that would lead to the eventual separation of the two faiths.

This parable is really about false religion and true faith. The Judaism condemned in Matthew's Gospel does not match up to the kind of faith recorded as the basis of the Sermon on the Mount or as exemplified in the life of Jesus. Righteousness is not about rule keeping. It is about being spirit based and living for others. Rules are not enough. Religion can be used to manipulate people, undermine their autonomy and bolster the power of those in authority. People can very easily be made to conform to authority structures with the loss and destruction of their lives. This is very true nowadays. All religions contain within them the serious risk of distortion and misinterpretation of sacred scriptures to suit group or individual agendas. Both the Bible and the Koran can be understood in ways that are deeply damaging to individuals and society. Religious leaders now, as in the past, may lead many astray and create 'false faiths' inimical to love and service. That is why all faiths need constant renewal and re-examination as to whether they have lost their way.

One of the most telling parables about the potential evil of institutional religion is the parable of the Grand Inquisitor told by Ivan in Dostoyevsky's novel *The Brothers Karamazov*. This can be read separately from the entire novel and is well worth reading alone. Jesus returns to earth in Seville at the time of the Spanish inquisition. He meets ordinary people and performs some miracles. He is immediately arrested and condemned to death the next day. The Grand Inquisitor visits him in his cell. He tells Jesus he is no longer needed. He gave people too much freedom of choice, and in refusing the three challenges of the Temptations made a serious mistake. The Church has now linked up with Satan, although the Inquisitor does not use his name. Ordinary people cannot cope with choice or religious freedom. They need to be ruled by the few and told what to think and believe. Their lives will end in death and destruction, but in the meantime, they can remain happy with their taught illusions. Jesus says nothing. He gets up after a while and kisses the Inquisitor on the lips. The Inquisitor lets him go, if he does not return again. He wanders off into the streets. The ending is rich in ambiguity.

All a religion can do is provide a rough framework for living, providing that framework gives rise to the fruits of the spirit; love, peace and the other qualities we all recognise. The Jewish hierarchy had provided a framework, but it did not give rise to the fruits of the spirit. Faith did not need animal sacrifice or rules so rigid that their very existence stifled love. The Sabbath was made for people not people for the Sabbath. Serving others should never be prevented by rules.

Today we continue to be bedevilled by negative attitudes to women, same sex orientation, and faiths outside the Church, that are highly destructive. The very existence of so many denominations reflects our inability to see what real faith is. If you start to exclude people from sharing the Lord's Table because they do not meet the right criteria in your view, there can be no Jesus there. He will have walked away into the streets to be with the dispossessed, the outsiders. It is a sobering thought. What does the parable of the Vineyard say to our times?

Healing and Wholeness

2 Timothy 2.8–15 Luke 17.11–22

"Then he said to him, 'Get up and go on your way; your faith has made you well.'"

Luke 17.19.

One of my favourite books is by a doctor philosopher called *The Danger of Words*. Most of us are aware when we use words that there is enormous ambiguity in their meaning.

Two words in that brief text are a case in point. Do we really know what faith means, and what does it mean to say: 'You are well?' We can spend hours, days and months discussing them. Think about 'well' for a moment, apart from the other uses of the word.

'How are you?' We say that, mostly, not expecting anything other than a few platitudes. We may say in reply: 'I am well, thank you.' The person who responds may feel well or not, mostly they will say they are well however they really feel. Whether we are well or not is far too complicated to put into a few words. To discuss how we really are would be an awful bore to most people. Such phrases are now a part of introductory social discourse; they mean virtually nothing, but they are part of being polite.

The context of the word 'well' in the Gospel account of the story of the ten lepers is far from clear. This is not an easy story at all. It is a very good example of how Biblical interpretation is often very tentative. The whole idea that it is straightforward to know what the Bible is telling us is terribly dangerous.

We find Jesus meeting ten lepers, asking him from far off to take pity on them. What he tells them to do is go and show themselves to the priest in Jerusalem. They were cured on the way. The reason for Jesus' instruction is that in those times it was only the High Priest who could pronounce people free from leprosy; and thus, allow them to become integrated into the community again. It was a legal requirement. He did not ask for anything else. Why were the nine who did what they were told castigated?

There are a number of possibilities. First, is this a real story or is it some kind of parable? I think the latter is highly probable. The source of this material is from the sayings Gospel of Q that Luke and Matthew used, or the special source L peculiar to Luke. The other Gospels do not deal with it.

Another possibility is that the writer was careless and told the story incorrectly and messed it up: we can conclude nothing from it. A lot of critics think that, and we need to remember that these Gospel writers were using material, oral or written, that had been compiled by other people. They were writing Gospels for a specific audience and did much editing.

Even if none of these possibilities is correct, we continue to have the problem of how to interpret this story. It is worth asking some questions. What was different about the Samaritan with leprosy, and does the word 'well' in the context of Jesus' final remark cast any light on the deeper meaning of the word 'healing'? Ten people with leprosy are apparently cured of the disease. I want to leave aside the nature and significance of the 'cures' associated with Jesus. We must leave that to another day. What is important in this account is that one person chose to come back to Jesus and express gratitude; the tenth person, who happened to be an outsider. Jesus clearly saw in this act something that was missing in the others. At one level this is just a simple lack of courtesy. However, it appears that the Gospel writer, or Jesus himself, is using the event to point to a deeper reality. Namely, that there is a real difference between being relieved of a medical condition and being made 'whole'. The Samaritan has linked his healing with God and comes to thank Jesus, the messenger of God. That is the difference that Jesus noted and when he says: 'Your faith has made you well' he is speaking of more than the cure of the other nine people with leprosy. This man has been made 'whole' because he has put his life in the hands of God. In other words, this little story is not really about the healing of a disease at all, it is about 'wholeness' that stands apart from whether we have a disease or not.

I have spent my working life in a branch of medicine that is concerned with many people who have incurable diseases; malignant brain tumours, Alzheimer's disease, multiple sclerosis, Huntington's chorea, motor neurone disease, muscular dystrophy. Does one take the view that all these people could be cured if they had enough faith, just like the ten lepers? Or can they be made 'whole' with their disease? Like it or not the disease becomes part of the body image and life of the person with it. It is part of them and as time passes their life is shaped by the illness.

I don't know what you think, but I know that all those people whose lives touched mine were not physically cured. Most of them accepted that life is like that. Disease is part of existence as we have known it. Much medical progress has been made; much remains to be done. One thing is certain to me; Jesus is not a doctor who intervenes when human endeavour fails. One of the awkward things about being a doctor or a nurse is that one is exposed to a volume of experiences that are bound to have a deep impact on one's view of God's action in the world.

Being 'well' is of ultimate importance; but it is not about curing physical diseases that cannot be treated. It is about true integration. The person we are depends on many things; our innate personalities, our relationships, our acceptance of ourselves and acceptance by others. To achieve that is our goal in life. God is wanting us to be 'well' as 'whole people'; accept ourselves as we are accepted. And every time we come to the Eucharist, and we kneel or stand before God, we give thanks for the healing he brings us.

Gutsy Engagement

Galatians 1.11–24 Luke 7. 11–17

"When the Lord saw her, he had compassion for her and said to her, 'Do not weep.'"

Luke 7.13.

What I want to explore today is what one might call the contagion of Jesus. I suppose the word contagion brings into one's mind the idea of infection, particularly the rapid transmission of nasty diseases. But the word has wider uses, and I use it here in the context of the extraordinary pulling power of Jesus down the ages and the great importance of maintaining the contagion. We do not want it to die out or be controlled.

You might ask why I quoted the words that Jesus had compassion on the widow who had lost her only son. Well, that word is a very inadequate translation. It does not do justice to the Greek word. The word is 'Splanchnon'. Now, to those of us who have had to learn all about splanchnic nerves and arteries we know that the word refers to the 'guts' as well as rather demurer expressions. He was moved in his 'bowels' might be a rather stronger expression. He had real compassion for the woman who was alone. True, she was surrounded by a great crowd. We find large crowds in Luke often, but they were more interested in Jesus or had just gathered in curiosity to witness the procession. The lady was alone.

This kind of gutsy involvement and compassionate caring is at the core of the contagion of Jesus. He did not draw people to him just by speaking, it was more about who he was and how he lived. That is at the core of his contagion.

We do not know a lot about Paul as a real person, but he tells us that he never knew Jesus. We first meet him when he was called Saul and he was persecuting the early Jesus movement. He was present at the stoning and death of Stephen, the first Christian martyr. Paul considers that his turning to Jesus was due to direct revelation as he had never been an original disciple. That may be the case, but perhaps his experience, watching with apparent approval the stoning of Stephen, had a deep effect on him. The contagious courage and commitment of this man would have had a profound effect on a sensitive mind.

I think that idea is important because the witness of Stephen rather than Jesus was operative or could have been operative. Jesus left this world, but he left behind other people and the Holy Spirit transformed them. Their job was to continue the contagion of Jesus and through caring compassion change the world. That is the ultimate challenge for Christianity.

There is a recent book by the monk Sebastian Moore, recently deceased at age over 90. It is called *The Contagion of Jesus: Doing Theology as if it Mattered.* For all our musings and thinking to matter, they have to be truly incarnational; earthed in this world.

We are told that numbers in the church are dropping. If that is correct, why? Is our worship sterile, disconnected from that visceral compassion that drew people to Jesus? The future of the Christian movement does not depend on Jesus now, but us. We are the successors of Stephen, Paul and many others. It is only if our Christianity really matters that the spirit of contagion can continue.

Some of the views of young people about the Church, as gathered in a survey, should challenge us. Many young adults felt that their experience of Christianity was shallow. One-third of survey participants felt that going to church is boring. Twenty percent of those who attended as a teenager said that God appeared to be missing from their experience of church. The study found many young adults do not like the way churches appear to be against science. Over one-third of young adults said that Christians are too confident; they know all the answers.

Some felt that churches are too simplistic or too judgmental when it comes to issues of sexuality. Seventeen per cent of young Christians say they've made mistakes and feel judged in church because of them. Two out of five young adult Catholics said that the Church's teachings on birth control and sex are out of date. Another reason the study gives for such an exodus from churches is that many young adults struggle with the exclusivity of Christianity. Twenty-nine per cent of young Christians thought churches are afraid of the beliefs of other faiths, and feel they have to choose between their friends and their faith. The last reason the study gives for young people leaving the Church is they feel it is unfriendly to those who doubt. Over one-third of young adults said they feel like they can't ask life's most pressing questions in church and twenty-three percent said they had significant intellectual doubts about their faith. This is another fundamental issue and it exposes the problem that we seldom discuss our beliefs openly and honestly. Doubt is a fundamental and entirely reasonable feature of any religious or spiritual journey.

The contagion of Jesus is about engagement. We should engage with each other, our children, and be available to talk with the young in our community. Explore with them. Discuss honestly the big questions in life. Somehow, we have to escape from dead tradition and unconditionally relate to people, mentally and emotionally.

Put simply, he had compassion for her. He was engaged. This was the Contagion of Jesus. It should be our contagion.

Knowing God

Hebrews 11.1–3, 8–16 Luke 12.32–40
"And he set out not knowing where he was going."
Hebrews 11.8.

What a funny thing to do! The fellow must have been a fool. Who would ever start out on a journey not knowing the destination? Would you?

I took a course once in neuro-linguistic programming. The words themselves suggest absolute 'mumbo jumbo'. What the course was really about was developing self-confidence. You were encouraged to identify what your current situation was, where you wanted to get to and plan how you were going to achieve your goals. A very different picture to Abraham setting out on a journey at the call of God without any idea of the outcome.

The life of faith or Journey of faith as symbolised by the picture of Abraham can be a great puzzle for us all. Can it be true that we are called to a life of reckless abandon, following the whims of the Holy Spirit whenever it prompts us? I put it like that to draw out the point that there is a very narrow line between the 'The life of faith' that is farcical and one that represents a genuine journey open to the Spirit of God, with the ultimate goal of knowing God, rather than achieving any temporal goal.

I was brought up in Sussex and attended a very evangelical Baptist Church. There were many good things about it, not least the friendship of other young people. Most of us were filled with the natural idealism of the young and that could make us very vulnerable to false witnesses. I recall a certain evangelist who exhorted us to give up our jobs and our training to follow God in the life of faith; to abandon all security and just see what happened. God would supply our needs. He was a fat man and as he 'challenged us' in a house group after church one Sunday night, he did so consuming large numbers of cream buns thoughtfully provided by his host! He was a fraud, a dangerous person. Fortunately, most of us took a dislike to him and realised that he was not a sound adviser.

We need to remember that the story of Abraham has its own context. Abraham and the people of his day and age were nomadic. It was usual for them to wander in search of pastures. In the Old Testament account, we have a picture, told as sacred history, of the gradual passage of a nomadic people to a more settled existence within the land that we used to know as Palestine. They were not the only peoples there, but the Bible recounts their particular sacred history and their relationship with God and their journey towards knowing God.

What is knowing God? It is nothing to do with knowing things about God. In a modern scientific world we tend to translate all knowledge as factual; knowing things about something or someone. But God is not in particular things. In our Old Testament reading the Children of Israel made the profound mistake of thinking that God could be known and appeased by rituals. The passage makes it clear that this was not the way to come into any relationship with God. Cease to do evil and learn to do good, was what God was looking for.

At the heart of true religion, the life of faith, is knowing God. That comes before everything. From true knowledge of God stem actions and ways of living that lead us to the promised land, the Kingdom of God.

Today many people find the rituals, dogmas and hierarchy of traditional religion unhelpful. They are not people without desire for a spiritual life, although we are all tainted by materialism in our world. For them, religion appears to get in the way of the spiritual life. That is not a new notion. Meister Eckhardt the twelfth century German mystic and teacher was a committed Christian. But he realised that religious practices are not knowing God, nor are they a substitute for knowing God. He did not reject the liturgy, but it was only important if it acted as a means to knowledge of God. Through many years of thought and prayer Eckhardt propounded what he considered to be the direct route to God. This involved the journey into our deepest beings to discover the core of our own existence. There, God could be found as pure essence stripped of all the projected furniture that we surround him with. For Eckhardt one of the main problems was the human projections as to what God is like; all of them false. God cannot be described in propositional language. He is not a person. Words, images, are all frail when it comes to God. But God can be known; known in purity. We can have a great shock when we come to know God and that is at the heart of the unknown journey of the life of faith, the journey of Abraham.

We discover a purity that is simple and yet beautiful. It does not provide explanations. It is not specifically about comfort and how God can answer our problems and make us feel better. God is not a prop. If we can truly say that we know

God that allows us to start on our way. We need have no expectations about life that will disappoint us. We should seek nothing in this world for its own sake. We need no rewards at all.

Not knowing where he was going? Perhaps not so stupid after all. Know God. We start with ourselves and what lies within us as God's creatures. Although words do not suffice once we arrive, we can begin to understand the experience of T.S. Eliot that after all the exploration we undertake, we return to where we started and begin to glimpse the ultimate for the first time.

Being A Disciple

Philemon 1–21 Luke 14.25–33

"If anyone comes to me and does not hate father and mother, wife and children, brothers and sisters—yes, even their own life—such a person cannot be my disciple. And whoever does not carry their cross and follow me cannot be my disciple."

Luke 14.26-27.

"So therefore, none of you can be become my disciples if you do not give up all your possessions."

Luke 14.33.

Strong words indeed. I have chosen them intentionally as our Gospel reading appears to be unambiguous and rather alarming for most of us. Would we not all line up with that rich young man who wanted to follow Jesus, but just could not see his way to giving up everything? Can these readings mean really what they say?

In our epistle we read of the ageing prisoner Paul, writing a letter to Philemon to recommend a former slave Onesimus. Paul had given up much for the gospel. He tells us he did! He gave up a settled life, a comfortable existence as a Roman citizen to spread the gospel despite suffering and persecution. Paul was famous for saying that 'We are all one in Christ

Jesus.' He took little account of status or possessions, although he did use his Roman citizenship when it was useful to him.

This model of giving up all to follow Jesus is at the heart of much traditional evangelical teaching. It appeals to the young and the idealist. Human history is full of people who have seemingly abandoned all to serve God.

The whole monastic movement is, certainly in part, based on the idea that possessions of any kind bind us to this world, increase our egos and prevent us from finding God. The temptations of the world must not interfere with our discipleship. In the pictures we have of John the Baptist and Jesus we find people dedicated to a vocation or mission from which they did not swerve, although we know very little about their personal lives.

Perhaps the most disturbing words in the Gospels are those that apparently encourage us to hate mother, wife, children, brothers and sisters to follow Jesus. Can these words really be true? The simple answer is no, and they have been the subject of much distorted thinking. They expose the dangers of an over-literal interpretation of the Bible and taking one passage apart from the life and teaching of Jesus as a whole. The Bible has an eternal message, but to understand it we do need to make an effort to explore the historical context.

Being a neurologist, I cannot resist pointing out the danger of all words and language. Words are just symbols. There is a huge capacity to misunderstand what has been said, and an even greater difficulty in finding words in the first place to express our thoughts and emotions. Having said all that, it is important to try and look carefully at this Gospel reading.

The first point to make is the context. The literary context is a work produced by the disciple called Luke sometime towards the end of the first century. Luke used other literary and oral sources. He brought his various sources together to make an account. In this chapter apparent teachings are linked with parables. We cannot be sure that all these words were said at the same time. The Synoptic Gospels themselves tell similar stories at different points.

The next point to remember is that we are dealing with a translation from the original Greek used by Luke. The word 'hate' is an interesting example of translation problems. The Semitic meaning here is 'love less' rather than the active meaning of hate, which we use in a completely different way today.

Having stated that, there is no doubt at all that Jesus did call some people to leave their families and follow him in establishing a new Israel under the heading of the Kingdom of God. This was a supreme calling in response to a spiritual vision. Jesus chose twelve apostles and he called them to leave all and follow him. They were his inner circle; Peter, James and John, the core of this group. We can be in little doubt that these people were summoned to leave their families for the importance of the Kingdom, and the urgency of the message required nothing less. A larger group of people, the seventy, were called to travel and take the message of the Kingdom. We do not know that either group was on the road all year. It is possible that in the winter they returned to Capernaum where many of them lived.

Jesus spoke of a life without regular comforts or property. He certainly saw riches as a barrier to the Kingdom. But there is no evidence he summoned all to leave their homes and follow him. His special friends Martha, Mary and Lazarus provided hospitality and others would have supported the itinerant group financially. Common sense would tell one that if everyone abandoned their homes there would be chaos. This was a special ministry, and particular vocations have been part of the Christian story ever since.

What underlies the call of Jesus to us all is that if we make any material thing our god, we can no longer follow *God.* This can mean different things to different people. We are gifted our lives and all the things we touch in life should not be seen as personal property. They are trusted to us to be used wisely. We are accountable for their use. As soon as the possession or retention of something becomes the centre of our existence, we lose the plot and cannot serve the one true God. This could be money, power, property or personal beauty.

There is no real doubt that many prevailing values mitigate against the gospel. As the philosopher John Paul Sartre pointed out, many of us fail to reach authentic freedom because we follow the customs and norms of the day. We try to fit in with the people around us, because we are afraid of being seen over against them as different or odd. Sartre was an atheist, but what he said can apply to the call to follow Jesus whatever that may mean for us as individuals. We must be prepared to be free to make the right decisions, not swayed by the masses.

Today we all need to consider what is required to be authentically Christian. That is very different from being 'churchy'. In every generation we need to be challenged and to count the cost of true discipleship. Our Gospel records parables about counting costs. As we are human, there will be a cost of discipleship because we no can longer think of ourselves. That is difficult for us and the challenge of the call of Jesus is still uncompromising. It does call for change.

Inner Transformation

Ephesians 3.14–21 John 6.1–21
"To know the love of Christ that surpasses knowledge, so that you may be filled with all the fullness of God."
Ephesians 3.19.

What does it take to make you full? Last weekend we had a meal in the Cotswolds with one of our sons and daughter-in-law. The meal was overpriced; elegantly presented, but the portions were very small. For our son at 6 feet 4 inches and in need of plenty of calories, one felt that a post prandial visit to the 'chippie' might be required.

Neither of these two readings is really about our dietary needs. We know we need food although not too much of it, and preferably the right sort of food for a balanced diet. Food in itself can present many moral problems for all of us; too much for us all in the West. We feed ourselves too well and become ill as a result. Elsewhere, people starve, have a poor diet and are hungry most of the time. They are not full in the physical sense, far from it. And no one should start preaching about the fullness of the spirit in the presence of a starving person; that is obscene.

The story of the feeding of the five thousand in John's Gospel or similar stories in other Gospels can be seen at more than one level. This Gospel is regarded by many as being compiled over time by a number of authors. We find variation in the approach to miracles or signs as they are referred to in John.

There is, in John, what we call a 'signs source', or collection of miracle stories used by this Gospel; these indicate the miraculous actions of Jesus. But there is also within the Gospel a layer that is later; that rejects the idea of signs. In John 4.48 Jesus states: 'Unless you see signs and wonders you will not believe.' In response to the question in John 6.30: 'What sign are you going to give us then, so that we may see it and believe you? What work are you performing?' Jesus replies: 'I am the bread of life.' There is ambiguity in the Gospel. There is one layer that accepts signs, but there is another that turns these stories into metaphor. Signs are no longer acceptable. This reflects a movement in theological opinion and development.

If we look briefly at the loaves and fishes story, we can note a number of features. We are dealing here with poor people. To buy food for them all would have been beyond anyone's means. The bizarre question that Jesus asks Andrew seems to draw attention to Jesus' exceptional status. In John, Jesus seems no ordinary man. The story concludes with the people regarding this as a miraculous sign. But a sign of what? They completely misunderstand the nature of Messiah as Jesus understood it. They say: 'Surely this is the prophet who is come into the world.' Jesus understood they were looking for a temporal leader, one who would free them from Roman bondage. He withdrew.

The many discourses in John refer to inner change that brings satisfaction and fullness. Much of the Gospel attempts to get away from crude miracles that really have no meaning in isolation, and point to the deeper meaning of stories; the Gospel is ripe with metaphor. The implication of the 'loaves and fishes' is that we are made full and satisfied by Jesus: 'I am the bread of life.' This is the way our lives are transformed. We can go through life without bothering about our inner health or spiritual health; but if we do that, we are only half alive. Whatever the appearances of prosperity and success we may be able to parade, we are not alive in the true sense of the word. Many people realise this even though they do not subscribe to a specific religion. Many seek to be filled 'with the fullness of God' as Paul puts it, but they want to express it in a different way. They may talk of being close to nature, in touch with themselves and others. They may not use the word God, but their aspirations are similar even if not tangibly expressed in God language.

With the erosion of traditional religion, and deep mistrust and irritation with the institutions of religion, we all need to be more open to the aspirations of others, even if not couched in traditional ways. Unless we listen to their experiences and hopes, regardless of their religious affiliation, and regard them positively, we can never be true ambassadors for Jesus.

I do not think Jesus ever wanted to be the founder of a new religion. He wanted to go beyond religious institutions and speak of the transformation of the heart. We may call that Jesus living in us, us living in Jesus, the Spirit in us, God in us.

The core of it all is that life is more than just living, it is to be experienced and lived in a way that does honour to God and others and ourselves, and the ethical dimensions of that are obvious.

We may worship here daily, weekly or monthly or anywhere else, but unless there is this inner life that satisfies, and for us Christians that is found in following Jesus, we are essentially empty and unsatisfied.

In the Eucharist, as the Gospel of John implicitly recognises, the need for transformation and indeed the renewal of inner transformation takes place. External elements of bread and wine are transformed into the 'bread of life' and the 'life blood' of our inner existence. These symbols or metaphors or actualities, however you see it, are at the heart of our recognition and submission to Christian transformation.

Faith and Works

James 2.1–10[11–13], 14–17 Mark 7.24–37
"For whoever keeps the whole law but fails in one point has become accountable for all of it."
James 2.10.

The epistle of James is an unusual document in terms of the New Testament canon. It was not mentioned seriously as a part of scripture until the fourth century and the earliest references to it as writing worth heeding is in the third century. It was probably written around the end of the first century at the same time as works such as the Shepherd of Hermas, not eventually included in the New Testament.

There are at least two James's in the Bible, notably James the apostle and James, Jesus' brother, who was a witness to early events in Jerusalem and was, on reasonable evidence (see Acts and Galatians), leader of the Jewish Christian Church in Jerusalem. This James is the one that this book is ascribed to. In fact, there is no evidence that he wrote it, but the book contains an early view of the Jewish Christian sect. James was the bane of reformers such as Luther who promoted justification solely by faith, and it is this issue that I want to dwell on.

You will recall that Paul places major emphasis on justification by faith rather than works. The faith is in salvation through the atoning death of Jesus. This is the lynch pin of the Reformation and much Protestant theology. Works do not justify or bring salvation. The law is superseded.

A good deal of early Christian debate and argument was about the place of the Jewish Law in the new Christian messianic sect that emerged from Judaism. In his epistle to the Galatians Paul is very uncomplimentary about Judaising Christians, even paranoid. There is evidence that there were plenty of Christians who thought that the law was not outdated and should remain part of Gentile Christianity. The Jerusalem Church, led by Peter and James, was of this opinion; although there is some evidence, not entirely conclusive from the historical point of view, that they reluctantly came to some kind of agreement with Paul, and for his part Paul is certainly less aggressive about the Law in his epistle to the Romans; although this book is the core document on the early theology of justification through faith.

The epistle of James, we will call it this for simplicity, takes an interesting view. Although we cannot call it definitely an anti-Pauline polemic, it does not agree with many people's interpretation of what Paul said. James states: 'For whoever keeps the whole Law but fails in one point has become accountable for all of it.' (James 2.10). He also says: 'So speak and so act as those who are to be judged by the law of liberty.' (James2.12). This latter quotation is interesting because it is clear that Paul would not have been entirely happy with such a statement.

Early debate in the Christian movement had some polarised positions. At one end was someone like Marcion, who had many followers and rejected the whole of the Hebrew Bible as evil and would only advocate the letters of Paul and the Gospel of Luke. On the other hand, there were Ebionite Jewish Christians who wished to follow the Law and considered it essential to Christianity and that Jesus never overthrew the Law at all, but was, on the contrary, a perfectly respectable Jew.

Now you may ask why I am regurgitating this boring rubbish! The answer is severalfold. We ought to be aware of the many debates that took place in early Christianity and the different arguments that are contained within the New Testament, even though much of early literature has been lost. The issue also has practical implications for us as Christians today. Paul soon found that his theology of justification by faith alone had problems. People took him literally, particularly in the context of a view that envisioned the end of the world and the rapid return of Jesus. It led to the 'anything goes' attitude. You are saved by faith; you need not worry about what you do. The moral framework for living disappeared. We can see the problem in some of Paul's remarks to the Corinthian Church.

It was unrealistic for Jewish Christianity to imagine that the culture of the Greco-Roman world could cope with the entire Jewish Law, just as it is a problem for most Christians today. But we do need a moral framework to live by and we can use, with benefit, the outline Ten Commandments, and the golden rule, 'Love your neighbour as yourself', quoted in James.

James makes the important point that the Law gives freedom. Because one is following some precepts one is in fact liberated in developing a system of how to live. It is true that one can become a slave to those precepts, but as a general guide to the way we live they are important. This is why James states: 'What good is it, my brothers and sisters if you say you have faith but do not have works? Can faith save you?' (James 2.14). For James faith without deeds is useless. It took generations for many Protestant theologians to take this on board and I have noticed a change for the better in my lifetime.

In this epistle passage we read James is concerned about unequal treatment of rich and poor. This is at the heart of any great religious tradition. If rich people are treated differently to the poor there is something seriously wrong. We would do well to dwell on that as we consider our vision for this church.

James does not discuss the nature of salvation. Much of the New Testament concentrates on the few days surrounding Jesus' death and resurrection. But we need to remember his life, his teaching, if we are to balance our view of the Christian Way. Modern progressive Christianity tends to emphasise Jesus, the creative teacher and first century leader of a messianic movement. Traditionalists emphasise the salvation and redemption through the Cross and Resurrection, however we understand these events. These are not mutually exclusive.

James is little read. It is worth reading; I commend it to you.

Setting Free

Galatians 5.1,13–25 Luke 9.51–62
"For freedom Christ has set us free. Stand firm, therefore, and do not submit again to a yoke of slavery."
Galatians 5.1.

The epistle to the Galatians is by far the most severe indictment in the New Testament of the Jewish Law. It is generally agreed that it was written by Paul. It represents the kind of view that eventually led to the split of the early Gentile Jesus movement from the Jewish form of Christianity that continued to follow the Law and took a different view of Jesus.

This letter is also rather different in tone from the more conciliatory accounts of the relationship between Paul and the Jerusalem Church. We have to wonder what lay behind this letter. There is enough evidence that Judaisers were present in the Galatian Church, and that Paul's polemic contained in this letter against Jewish Christianity was, in part, inspired by rival versions present in the community at the time. One of the great conundrums in early Christian / Jewish studies of this period is the question of what Paul really thought about the Law. Is this an exaggerated account of his views?

We are the inheritors of the brand of Christianity that Paul developed, and many early versions of Christian theology completely rejected the Old Testament, regarding it as an evil document whose God was totally different from the God of Love in the new Testament. Marcion in Rome around 150 CE was the most notable.

The Jewish Law here is called the *Yoke of Slavery*, a very hard saying, and there is no evidence that Jesus thought this way. By many he was regarded as fulfilling the Law and not abolishing it. There were many different views of the Law in his day and Galileans in particularly were notoriously lax in keeping it.

We all have frameworks that we need to live by, and it is how we use these frameworks that matters. Paul spoke of Jesus releasing people to live in freedom, but he did not mean that living in the spirit meant 'anything goes'. This was not always understood, and we only have to read his first letter to the Corinthians to realise that people thought this freedom in the spirit meant that they could do and behave how they liked.

Paul's understanding of freedom in the Spirit seems to be this. We are freed by God and his Spirit through Jesus to be ourselves. In Christianity, being ourselves means living in the presence of God. If you live in the presence of God, what you want to do and be will coincide with the will of God, and Paul lists the fruit of the spirit that we are familiar with. Throughout his writing he emphasises the primacy of love, as that is the nature of God, and love leads us in the right direction in human living and behaviour.

The ultimate challenge is that few if any achieve perfection in this life. It is very interesting that Jesus and the Buddha have much in common. Neither of them preached a life of extreme asceticism. Both emphasised that the core of human suffering was desire and attachment to things in this life, so that our true nature or ego was grossly impaired by selfish concerns and addiction to material matters. Jesus emphasised that following him involved letting go. In the Gospel reading today there are various hard sayings. If we think of them in a metaphorical way rather than as literal examples, we can see what he is saying. He is advising against attachments that prevent us from following him. The Buddha and his teachings, using the concept of Enlightenment, come to a similar conclusion. Enlightenment sets you free from bondage.

Because we are all in need of a framework, we are unable to follow the path of Jesus or the Buddha without a set of rules. Jesus followed the Law but not perhaps as a Pharisee. The Ten Commandments have remained at the core of much of Western morality. The various paths of Buddhism are the guide for those who follow his way. In every generation we have to work out how to live. The generations live in different worlds. Cultural patterns change and much religion is related to culture or fashion.

One change we have all had to face up to involves the way couples live together before they are married. That is not something entirely new, but in conventional so-called respectable society, there has been a striking change of practice. This includes young Christians. It is an interesting example as to what kind of interpretation can be applied to the freedom Paul spoke of in his day. We live in a completely different culture, but young people may try to say that they value commitment despite living together without marriage. They may say that marriage can be sign and symbol of that commitment, but it is not exclusively the case and has no value at all without commitment and love.

Whether you agree with that or not this issue demonstrates

that we all have to work out for ourselves what life in the Spirit means in practice. How do we live? In what sense are we addicted to things of a material nature that ruin our lives? It is how we are attached to things that matters. Our lives can be destroyed by meticulous adherence to a set of rules such as the Law, or perhaps money or power or anything that we feel we could never do without.

We have been set free, but we have to use our own minds to work out how we live now. Certainly, we realise that there is no magic book of rules that tells us what to do in any particular situation; so, we do depend on the freedom of the spirit and our own traditions and wisdom to chart our way through life's puzzling journey.

Do not be a Fool

Colossians 3.1–11 Luke 12.13–21
"And he said to them, 'Take care! Be on your guard against all kinds of greed; for one's life does not consist in the abundance of possessions.'"
Luke 12.15.

Luke provides us with some of the most arresting of Jesus' parables. The account of the rich fool is one of them. The parable comes in response to a question about the division of an inheritance. Jesus does not want to get involved with that, but he is concerned to say something about pre-occupation with possessions and tells the parable.

The heart of the parable is the teaching that human happiness is not, as it might appear, really dependent on wealth or possessions. Many religions, including Hinduism and Buddhism, teach that 'attachment' to things in this life causes suffering in this world. In themselves, money or possessions are not evil, but if one becomes so wedded to them that their surrender is impossible or extraordinarily painful then they are deeply damaging. Both Jesus and the Buddha taught that enlightenment or salvation depended on letting go of dependency on things that are ultimately ephemeral. Jesus taught that those who seek to save their lives will lose them. He means that if you think about yourself all the time you will never actually become a real person.

Take the rich man in this parable. We do not hear that he had any interest at all in the outside world. He does not seem to be concerned about the poor, his neighbours, his friends. All he seems to be interested in is self-gratification, and then it is all over. He dies before his time. All that wealth was nothing. Perhaps this is a caricature, but it makes the point.

What does the story say to us today? Recent economic events have made the stupidity of greed all too clear. The concept that making money as an end in itself is an appalling distortion and deeply damaging to those involved in such enterprises. The creation of wealth must have a purpose that relates to human wellbeing and the wellbeing of our planet.

The world is full of starving people who have no shelter, no schooling. Their whole lives are spent wondering whether they can survive. Their existences are beyond the experience of most of us. The reasons for this may not be simple, but at the heart of the problem is the parable of the rich fool. We are too concerned with ourselves and what we have. We cannot let go. Our governments constantly refer to the need for us to go out and spend more! It is a crazy world. Leaders in developing countries are sometimes corrupt; aid never reaches those in need, it is appropriated and stashed in overseas bank accounts.

We all know that our world is in a mess. Many people feel deeply dissatisfied with the values we live by. More and more we need exemplars to challenge us and provide role models for less selfish existence. It is possible to come across people past and present who change our lives and our way of thinking. My wife and I have a missionary background ourselves and we were inspired first by Jesus, but by others, amongst them Albert Schweitzer and Dr Bob Cochrane a senior colleague and renowned leprologist.

We lived in a large hospital community. We were provided with free accommodation. We worked in the hospital. There was no major differentiation in people's wages. We received a packet each month from Calcutta with an allowance. There was nothing much to spend it on except basic food from the market and paying the lady who helped us. Life and entertainment centred around people. When we returned through ill health it was like re-entering another world, a harsher world, a greedier world and an infinitely sadder place.

In the developed world we live amidst fierce competition. The structure of society is such that when things go wrong for people disaster strikes. A couple with a mortgage and large family lose their main job, mortgage repayments become impossible, the house is repossessed, the stress and lack of money cause family fragmentation. They disappear from their established social network like a sinking ship. The waves roll over them. 'I wonder what happened to them?', someone says.

Who is my neighbour? Our neighbour is anyone who responds to our need. The parable of the rich fool is the opposite of the story of the Good Samaritan.

Giving is not just about money, it is anything that we can give of ourselves in terms of time, talents and practical love. The rich fool was isolated and that was his greatest tragedy. He lived his life alone. We are greatly blessed being able to live together. May God help us all to be generous with our lives as She/He has been generous to us.

Following the Seventy

Galatians 6.1–16 Luke 10.1–11
"After this the Lord appointed seventy others and sent them on ahead of him in pairs to every town and place where he himself intended to go."
Luke 10.1.

The passage that we have read in Luke is from what we call the Q source from the German word 'quelle'. There is general agreement that this source, now lost, was an ancient sayings document of early date that was used by Matthew and Luke. This implies that it was a real document that once existed, and many believe it to be a reliable early account of Jesus' ministry.

What we read here is an account of early evangelism appropriate to the culture of the day. Apparently, Jesus would send out a team of people to prepare for his coming, rather as a mass evangelist might do today. This kind of preparation to enlarge his following was felt to be the most efficient. He told his followers to give a simple message; The Kingdom or reign of God is near or at hand. How would Jews have understood this? Remember that this message was only to Jews. I think the most likely understanding would refer to the coming of the Messiah. There was great hope that the Messiah would come and rescue Israel in this time of trial and subjugation. All sorts of prophets and holy men and movements were springing up.

At one extreme were the Zealots with military aspirations, at the other extreme, the Essenes, the authors of the Dead Sea Scrolls, who had opted out of society and lived a community life on the shores of the Dead Sea.

The message of the Jesus group seems to have been that the kingdom over which the Messiah would reign was near, it was breaking through. The message was greatly misunderstood, but that seems to be the reason why the Jesus movement became so popular. Something that tuned in with the popular imagination of Jewish culture outside Jerusalem was on offer. Jerusalem was rather different. Politics held sway. The Sadducees were powerful and had reached a kind of rapprochement with Rome. They were not interested in petty movements from Galilee, at least not until they became a real nuisance.

This was a simple, rural world, in Northern Palestine, where people went in and out of each other's houses. Visitors such as the seventy may not have been that unusual. Hospitality rules were very different then. There was much greater social obligation to provide food and shelter to strangers. Society was less fragmented, and privacy was not the totem that it is today; a very different world indeed.

If you are a Christian in today's world you subscribe to the view that the Messiah has come in the person of Jesus. Of course, we present this in the language of Christian theology. We tend to the view that although there is no observable reign of God on this Earth at the present time, two thousand years later, there is a duty incumbent on Christians to go out and tell of the Kingdom just as those seventy did. If this is the case, how do we do it? Is it really worth it? This is the essential challenge for Christianity today in a world torn apart by human behaviour.

There are no easy answers. First, the Church is a problem. It is divided and extremely hierarchical. Its true purpose is easily strangled by its own structure. Countless movements have tried to put this right by returning to simpler forms. The 'House' movement is an example, but even these have foundered on their own disciplines and those who seek to impose them.

We can see from statistics that Christian discipleship is falling away in the West. The only way I think it can recover at all is by connecting with people's basic needs and aspirations. One has to question whether this is even viable since many are welded into material concerns. We have to start with communities, with friendship and with help in times of trouble. We have to teach our children about ultimate values. This is at the heart of making the world a better place and that is or should be the basic purpose of all religion. It may be comforting to be reassured that you will be all right when you are dead, but if that is seen to be the main purpose of religion it is distorted and useless. Whatever language we use to describe our hopes for this world, if we stick to the core values, we are doing what we can. Going to church is a reflection of a community. We come together in worship, but that should be because we are a community anyway. We belong to it. The people we sit next to should mean something to us. If people do not respond to us we can do little about it, but we should remain there willing to connect in God's name if the opportunity arises.

The Church now has a movement called Fresh Expressions. It is a movement concerned in discovering new ways in communities of 'being Church'. In many ways this can mean being less ‘churchy’. It means that people who belong to the Church need to think the unthinkable and use their talents and imagination to bring the essential message of Christianity to our communities. An essential question for us all now is how we can do the work of those seventy who were sent out so long ago.

God in the Ordinary

2 Corinthians 12.2–10 Mark 6.1–13

"Prophets are not without honour, except in their home town, and among their own kin, and in their own house."

Mark 6.4.

We often find it quite difficult to get a 'handle' on Jesus' humanity. From the human point of view, we would like to know more about him. This little cameo in Mark's Gospel is very revealing and something we can all connect with.

Jesus did not make much impact in his own town. They thought he was a jumped up so and so. We read he offended them in the synagogue. They knew his family. His sisters were in the congregation, and Mark names his brothers and sisters. As far as local people were concerned, Jesus was just a local lad with no particular qualifications or authority. They were not going to be lectured to by someone like him. He was far too ordinary. After all he was no different to them or some of them were superior. He could not really be as wise and powerful as he appeared to be.

We read that Jesus was amazed, taken aback. He does not seem to have been expecting this! We get a sense that even his family did not appreciate him. It's interesting, and it has the ring of truth about it. Yet having said all that we have to get behind the mind of the person who wrote this Gospel. It is important to remember that the Gospels were written for a Christian community. They are not simple recitations of facts.

One of the most important puzzles the early Christian community had was why the Jewish people did not recognise Jesus as the promised Messiah. Mark, at the beginning of this passage, records the grudging admiration at 'the words of wisdom' uttered and the 'mighty deeds', but it was not enough to persuade the hearers. The local conclusion about Jesus is eventually mirrored by the wider community. He was not the Messiah. He did not fit in with some stereotypical picture of what a messiah should be.

It is a fact of life that often we do not recognise the wisdom or messages of those we are close to. Children naturally rebel against their parents; they need others to guide them at some stages in their lives. We see people we have known all our lives differently than the distinguished person who comes among us. We have difficulty seeing the special in those who are familiar. We find it difficult to see anyone as being very special if they are under our noses. Of course, we do see our children as special in their own way but seldom as spiritual gurus.

Beyond all this is the very human tendency to project our own images of God and our messiah based on our own set of prejudices and opinions. In the Old Testament, Elijah searched for God in whirlwinds and mighty manifestations, but God was a 'still small voice'. In Isaiah we have a messianic picture of one despised and rejected of men, a man of sorrows and acquainted with grief.

Jesus was born into an age when there was a very definite Jewish establishment. The Sadducees are an example of this. A messiah was meant to be a king-like figure not a local carpenter; a person of status and education, not an artisan.

What would we expect now if we are honest? Would we look for a saviour from just down the road? Would we listen to someone without official status? We would probably call that person mad, or after money or bent on some devious purpose. Would we take notice of something very ordinary or expect loud noise and publicity to accompany something really important?

Times have not really changed. It needs an opening of the mind and heart and removal of our false projections to glimpse the truth. Peter's sudden flash of spiritual insight when he named Jesus as Messiah was a breaking through of the barriers that limit our vision. He was able to move beyond the image of the carpenter's son, as we have to move beyond our image of Jesus as a remote primitive Galilean who lived two thousand years ago. Even then, Peter's image of Jesus was distorted, incomplete.

When the scales suddenly drop from our eyes for a moment during our own journeys through life, we enter a still moment, a space of pure light. That may well be precipitated by something very ordinary, very local, and unaccompanied by a label that it is important. After all God is very near to us. He is present in the mundane if we can look and see.

The Golden Rule

Hebrews 9.11–15 Mark 12.28–34
"You shall love your neighbour as yourself. There is no other commandment greater than these."
Mark 12.31.

We were on holiday in France. My wife had visited the supermarket and when she came out we decided to have a coffee at a nearby café. I looked very dubiously at the chair at the table. I thought, am I ever going to get off this? I sat down anyway! A little later I tried to get up with Rene heaving me, no success. Immediately, a group of French people rushed to our aid and with a lot of effort they got me up. We were very grateful. I decided to be very careful where I sat next time! That little story, seemingly trivial, sums up quite a lot about the best of human behaviour. We go and help people. We would almost certainly hope they would help us in a similar situation.

It is a simple, practical example of what is known as the Golden Rule. We find it here expressed in the text: 'Love your neighbour as yourself.' The Golden Rule has been used in many cultures and religions through the ages. We find it in Confucius, Islam, Judaism and so on. It can have positive or negative expressions. Treat your neighbour as you would want to be treated or do not treat your neighbour in a way you would not want to be treated. It is at the core of any caring sort of life. Here Jesus attaches it to the other great commandment: 'Love God with all your heart, mind and strength.' The juxtaposition of the two commandments here suggests that the one follows from the other.

But can we argue that a caring virtuous life is indelibly linked with religious belief? Jesus lived in an age when nearly everyone believed in God in his community. It was difficult to separate religion from daily life. In mediaeval Christian Europe, the Europe of The York mystery plays, the same applied. Secularism was still uncommon at the time of the first great modern philosopher Rene Descartes in the seventeenth century. But by the eighteenth century, with the rise of science, came the development of Scepticism. The famous Scottish philosopher David Hume was an atheist, but he was widely regarded as a good man. The French loved him and called him 'le bon David'.

Here we have a problem developing. A good life, a caring life, does not appear to depend on loving God. Perhaps one can argue that society had been infiltrated with Christian values; people were just beginning to forget about God.

One of the great questions about human nature is what kind of nature do we really have? and this is linked to the development of the idea of sin, even original sin. We have built into us a tendency to be violent and selfish as well as loving and caring. Religion may have been part of society in medieval times, but there was much violence around; the Crusades are a good example. It would appear that in the process of our becoming the species Homo sapiens, we have developed the ability to reason and choose, but we have not lost our aggressive instincts. Most people would argue that an animal is not rational and does not choose in the way we do. We would not call a violent animal, such as a tiger, evil; the tiger kills to eat as we do. It will kill if threatened, but it does not justify its actions. This is what a tiger is; it has no moral philosophy.

It would seem that the human race is in the process of development, but this development is uneven. There is the possibility of evolving into a caring and loving race and the possibility of going in the other direction. Looked at from our very limited perspective it is difficult to assess whether we are more caring now than we used to be. What I think one can say is that if people commit to a loving God and to a genuine faith in Being beyond themselves, they can find the inspiration to live in a loving way, and we are more likely to evolve into a just and harmonious race. Jesus, whom we call the human face of God, becomes our exemplar, and we should follow his wisdom.

A very interesting book, called *Love's Endeavour, Loves Expense* by W. Vanstone describes the arrival of a priest on a new housing estate to found a church. He is struck by the fact that everyone seems very ordinary and pleasant, but they do not seem to need church. The book is a description of how he works through this problem and some of the conclusions he draws. One of his conclusions is that the God of love is about in this world whether we recognise God or not, whether we acknowledge Him/Her or not. God longs for our love and acknowledgement, but when people behave in a loving and caring way, they are in touch with his love although it is not explicit to them.

Jesus made it very clear that true religion is not about how often you attend church or how pious you are. What matters is that you follow the Golden Rule. In Mathew twenty-five he tells people that unless they helped the poor, visited the sick or visited those in prison there was no place in the Kingdom of Heaven. You could be as religious as you liked, but without the life to go with it, there was no relevance.

We rightly get angry with the silly machinations of the institutional Church. We hear that people will not agree to things because of their individual consciences concerning women or gay couples. Jesus tells us quite clearly to stop being judgmental and get on with it. 'You shall love your neighbour as yourself. There is no other commandment greater than these.'

Friendship

I Corinthians 9.16–21 Mark 1.29–39
"Let us go on to the neighbouring towns, so that I may proclaim the message there also; for that is what I came out to do."
Mark 1.38

Jesus was an itinerant preacher and teacher and a charismatic healer. Great emphasis is often placed on Jesus' healings, but as our text reminds us his primary purpose was to proclaim good news, the message of the Kingdom of God. We know from other literature that healings were not unusual at that time and that Jesus used familiar rabbinical formulae in his healings. We should not divorce healing from the overall context of the gospel message. The kingdom of God would be characterised by an inward change of heart and would be a kingdom of love and as such, be a healing experience.

We are not itinerant preachers and teachers. We have not left our homes and families. That is a very special kind of ministry. So, can we answer the question: If we are to be followers of Jesus today, how do we translate his teaching and actions into our culture and time? Put another way how do we connect all this with ordinary life?

When I said to someone last week that I had not decided what to say, that person said, 'talk about friendship'. On reflection that seems a very good thing to touch on. Real friendship is holy, sacred and at the heart of God's purposes for us. We may not think of it as being terribly religious, but it is at the heart of the Kingdom. Friendship can be profoundly healing. Acts of friendship may be brief but most of us think of friendship as something that endures, that grows over time. Both are important. One of the best things about enduring friendship is that you do not have to explain yourself, the one to the other, you are 'known'; a metaphor for how God knows each one of us.

I suppose if we were to outline some of the characteristics of friendship, we would emphasise caring, faithfulness, practical help and communication at an I-Thou level. These are holy things and they are truly healing. We can never underestimate the healing power of a true friend in times of trouble and ill health.

Sometimes we use derogatory phrases like 'fair weather friend', meaning that it was no friendship, because there was no one there when we needed that person. In understanding the gospel song: *What a friend we have in Jesus*, we recognise that his friendship is mirrored in us when we encounter human friendship in this life.

Emily Bronte was a gifted young poet. One detects a sadness and perhaps disillusionment in this comparison between the constancy of friendship and the fickleness of romantic love. We know she liked bleak things and we have to forgive her disparagement of the rose-briar. It is called *Love and Friendship*

Love is like the wild rose-briar,
Friendship like the holly tree —

The holy is dark when the rose-briar blooms
But which will bloom most constantly?

The wild rose briar is sweet in spring
Its summer blossoms scent the air;
Yet wait till winter comes again,
And who will call the wild-briar fair.

Then, scorn the silly rose wreath now
And deck thee with the holly's sheen,
That when December blights thy brow
He still may leave thy garland green.

It would seem Emily is thinking about the transient nature of romantic love. We can understand that she sought enduring love in friendship. But although we value the constancy of long-term friendship, we would never wish to devalue those transient contacts of love and care that touched our lives for the better but were not meant to be long-term. We realise that Jesus touched many lives in his ministry, but he moved on, as our text tells us, leaving behind a permanent mark.

We may recall the care of a nurse at times of great need; the willing, practical help of someone when we needed it in a strange place. We are called to this ministry as well.

I remember the help of a colleague once. We were on an ethics conference together. I was taken ill in the night. I managed to get to the porter. He went upstairs and woke my friend up. Without complaint, he came down, confirmed my diagnosis, and drove me to his mother's house in Newport. He was going to drive me all the way, but he was not really awake and filled the petrol car with diesel! So, my wife had to drive over. He delivered the cleaned car later on! A week or two later I remembered his friendship with enormous gratitude. We seldom meet now but I do not forget him. He was part of my healing experience.

In the book *Loss and Gain* by John Henry Newman, a central character is Charles Reding. He travels by train from Oxford to London and meets, briefly, a priest, who talks with him and provides him with an introductory letter. The priest's attire is strange and foreign. Reding learns nothing of him.

'By the time they had reached Paddington; and before the train had well stopped, the priest had taken his small carpet bag from under his seat, wrapped his cloak around him, stepped out of the carriage, and was walking out of sight at brisk pace.' This person's background and thoughts were unknown to Reding, but he entered his life for a brief moment and gave great and lasting assistance. We can all tell our stories.

Part of our picture of the healing power of the gospel is that it must be an inclusive picture. Can we ever be healed truly when others remain isolated, uncared for, outsiders? That is why friendship is not just for an inner circle. We seek to include all in the circle of God's Kingdom, regardless of background or culture. Yes, we have our circle of friends, but we have to look beyond cliques, to bring in others: the stranger at our door, the one who seems very different to us.

Sometimes, in our friendships we feel helpless. We are human. We do not know what to say or do. All we can do is stand and be there, hang in there. We may be able to say little. We are called to be silent but our presence may be healing. Metaphorically, we can stand with someone at the foot of their personal cross. Jesus himself did not offer the quick fix. We misunderstand his ministry if we think of it as a chain of miracles. We only have to remind ourselves of the temptations to realise this. The power of God can be manifest in such moments of apparent failure and vulnerability. God does not wave a wand over us, but he calls us to be faithful and to fulfil his purposes in the friendship and love we can offer others and receive ourselves.

Fulfilling the Law

1 Corinthians 2.1–12 Matthew 5.13–20
"You are the salt of the earth; but if salt has lost its taste, how can its saltiness be restored? It is no longer good for anything but is thrown out and trampled underfoot."
Matthew 5.13.

"Do not think that I have come to abolish the law or the prophets; I have come not to abolish but to fulfil."
Matthew 5.17.

In its historical attempts to detach itself from Judaism the early Church seemed to forget the words of Matthew. We often gloss over the clear divide between Jewish Christians, sometimes given the pejorative label Judaisers, and Gentile Christians, ourselves, the offspring of Pauline preaching that came into conflict with the Jerusalem Church over the keeping of the Law. Two classic examples are circumcision and dietary laws. The early Jewish Christians, sometimes called Ebionites, used something akin to Mathew's Gospel because of its significant Jewish orientation. The Law is not condemned it is fulfilled. It did not become irrelevant overnight.

The Law was not only religious but cultural, and we need to remember that the structure of all religions is inevitably embedded in culture. Jewish identity, constantly threatened over the centuries has survived because of its unique culture that stems from the Law, however interpreted. After the death of Jesus and the sacking of Jerusalem in 70 CE, Judaism did change, as all religions change with world developments. The Temple was destroyed. Cultic worship, dominated by a hereditary Aaronic priesthood, supported by the Levites, disappeared and synagogue worship and the role of the rabbi dominated Judaism. The Pharisees became predominant. They moved to Yavne, historically known also as Jabneh or Jamnia, a city in the central district of Israel, and Judaism was redeveloped through the work of scholars.

So, although the statement that not one jot or tittle of the law would pass away, the study of Jewish law has been and is a dynamic and living process varying in interpretation between orthodox and more liberal Jewish perspectives.

It is unsurprising that a similar process has taken place within Christianity under the leadership of theologians based in universities rather than the Church hierarchy. It should be so. The salt does lose and has lost its savour in the presence of new knowledge and cultural shifts.

Let me just list one or two issues that have caused theological adjustments within Christianity and indeed other faiths. The first is the theory of evolution that has placed humans firmly in the natural world, arising from it. The second is the scientific world view itself; this identifies us as living on a small planet in a vast universe, possibly containing other life forms. The third is our realisation that ethical decision making is now sufficiently complex that any naïve certainty about 'what to do' in a complex situation is foolish. The Bible has never been a textbook of ethics.

Judaism and Christianity have much in common, but,

interestingly, it is probably Christianity that has had the greater problem adjusting to modern knowledge. The question of the salt losing its savour is highly relevant for us today. Although we hear a lot about strategies to grow the Church, sometimes using modern communication techniques, these do not always address the fundamental problems Christianity faces in a postmodern, post-truth, scientific world. Christianity for many is tasteless.

I think three things are very important to the future survival of Christianity if it is not going to degenerate into a meaningless rump. The first is the word relationship, meaning that people are drawn to Jesus through others who have a caring relationship with them. True friendship is the salt that makes our lives worthwhile. Thumping out messages devoid of relationship does not work.

The second is that the decline in young people's involvement in Church stems from a divorce between the words they hear and the attitudes they perceive, disconnected from their concerns. The Churches latest report on sex is a disaster. Young people do not share the British Anglican Church's view on sexual orientation and gender. I am old enough to say these things. The Church has struggled with human sexuality since its inception; for centuries a male dominated bastion, divorced from the real world.

Thirdly, in a postmodern world there are no systematic answers. Dogmatic theology does not work. People do not respond, in general, to being told that to be a Christian they must subscribe to a very specific set of beliefs. I recall being presented with a piece of paper to sign as a student to join the intervarsity Christian fellowship. It stated various pieces of Christian dogma and they required my signature at the end to confirm that was exactly what I believed. I declined to sign it. We require a looser framework for Christianity that concentrates on living discipleship rather than intellectual constructs.

Jesus said he came to fulfil the Law. I think what he meant by that is that the Law, and for us, the inheritance we have from Judaism and the Christian framework, are to be mined for the spirit they enshrine rather than their intellectual content. We all recall that Jesus healed on the Sabbath and was condemned for it. He responded that surely it was better to do good.

One could extend that kind of argument in many directions. Is it better to marry a same sex couple in Church and affirm their love for each other, or to say to them you have my love, but I cannot help you?

You are the salt of the Earth? The Jews were and are a small nation with massive global significance. Christianity has changed much of the world, sometimes through good, sometimes through evil. If our faith is to have any influence for good in the future it can only achieve this through unconditional love and acceptance. No one is outside the reach of God. Sadly, we too often give lip service to that conviction and at the same time turn people away, crippled by convictions that produce the antithesis of love.

Production and Harvest

Deuteronomy 8.7–18 Luke 12.16–30

"For the Lord your God is bringing you into a good land, a land with flowing streams, with springs and underground waters welling up in valleys and hills, a land of wheat and barley, of vines and fig trees and pomegranates, a land of olive trees and honey, a land where you may eat bread without scarcity, where you will lack nothing, a land whose stones are iron and from whose hills you may mine copper. You shall eat your fill and bless the Lord your God for the good land that he has given you."

Deuteronomy 8.7-10.

This passage, describing all the good things awaiting the Children of Israel in the land of Canaan is a picture of shalom or flourishing. For the people of that age it was linked to a covenant with God. Obedience to the commandments of God was a prerequisite for shalom. The 'Good Man' flourished, the 'Bad Man' did not. Throughout history it has proved difficult to throw off this link between prosperity and behaviour whether it be good health or material wellbeing. In the Gospel of Luke, however, we find a subtler treatment of the issue. It would seem the rich man has prospered despite ignoring God and indeed others. He is doing very well, but suddenly his life ends before he can enjoy his spoils. He has created wealth for his own enjoyment and his stupidity is exposed. There follows a poetic injunction not to over concern ourselves about material prosperity. God will provide. We can see the picture painted in Luke as an illustration of harvest divorced from the needs of others, and the environment we live in.

There is an increasing realisation that we have a duty of care to all around us. This has raised many ethical questions about what we produce and how it is produced. Harvest brings with it contrasting themes and questions. Celebration, in a rural economy, that the products of the earth after hard work are good, is fundamental; but that is set alongside questions about the production of goods that we cannot ignore. Was the means of producing a bountiful harvest or product line justified? Is the actual product of intrinsic value in the world? How are the products distributed in a planet beset with inequality? These are big questions and we must let them lie for the most today. They provide much to reflect on.

The philosopher Schopenhauer considered that there are three elements that dictate human behaviour; egoism, compassion and malice. Malice itself may be understood to be incorporated into egoism much of the time, because pure malice is rare. Schopenhauer was a nihilist and is not fashionable, but he pointed out that compassion struggles to express itself in the presence of egoism and malice. It is amazing that it does at all, says Schopenhauer. There is a constant struggle in the world to overcome egoism and malice. Some of the fundamental questions of religion centre around liberating compassion from the traits that destroy it.

In the rural economy, farming methods, the treatment of animals and the land itself have given rise to ethical debate. One reason for this is the realisation that we are part of the natural world and not set over against it. We are animals just like other animals in many ways. Recent work on the brain of Neanderthal Man suggests that the capacity of the human brain to think in special ways does not or should not separate us from everything else. We were and are not as unique as we think we are. Issues such as climate change have focused attention on the human ability to damage the natural world and the systems that maintain it. In theological terms, the instruction to be good stewards of creation are abandoned. Put in another way we alienate ourselves from all that is around us when we concentrate our attention on short term benefits for our own species.

We are all aware that mass production of materials may harm us apart from our environment. The misuse of child labour in this country in the Victorian era continues elsewhere in the modern age. Cheap labour and abuse of human rights continue to mar the apparent successes of unfettered capitalism. Human health continues to suffer in production processes in many parts of the world.

There are many ethical theories; and it is evident that in a complex world, solving moral dilemmas is extremely difficult. A crucial element in deciding what is right or wrong has always been the question: Does the means justify the end? Let's take a simple example that I have isolated for the sake of debate. Suppose that battery chicken farming is highly efficient in terms of cost and the production of large quantities of meat or eggs for human consumption. This is seen to be highly desirable because it provides cheap food for consumers and therefore makes the product more accessible for poor people. However, the opponent of battery farming will say that the means of production is morally wrong. Chickens are abused, removed from their natural environment and live a miserable existence. Intensive farming, in general, may impair the health of the animal and lead to increased amounts of greenhouse gases. The simple statement of opposition to intensive farming is that animals are sentient beings and should not be treated in this way. One of the major proponents of this argument against intensive farming has been Peter Singer, the Australian philosopher. Here are two quotations:

'Forests and meat animals compete for the same land. The prodigious appetite of the affluent nations for meat means that agribusiness can pay more than those who want to preserve or restore the forest. We are, quite literally, gambling with the future of our planet — for the sake of hamburgers.'

'To give preference to the life of a being simply because that being is a member of our species would put us in the same position as racists who give preference to those who are members of their race.'

Harvest can never be a simple celebration. It is a time for reflection. There is ample evidence that our remote ancestors treated animal life with reverence, while accepting their own nature as meat-eating animals like other species. We should do the same.

For people of all faiths or none, the core belief that should unite us is reverence for life in all its forms. In Christianity that attitude stems from a belief in a creator God. Not all religions believe that creation is good, but it is a core element in Christianity, albeit with a recognition that there is an element of fallenness because of human behaviour. Those who understand Jesus as the second Adam, who restores us to a pre-fallen state, may no longer restrict their understanding to the restoration of humanity, but extend that understanding to the whole of creation harmed by the interaction of humanity with it.

I do not pretend there are easy answers as to how to live and how to produce. All we can do is make every effort to understand the consequences of human action in the world, as we chart our way through the moral maze of modern life. Reverence must be the key. This quote is the final challenge to us from Wendell Berry, the distinguished American writer, poet and farmer, writing from a Christian perspective:

'We have lived by the assumption that what was good for us would be good for the world. And this has been based on the even flimsier assumption that we could know with any certainty what was good even for us.' May the Holy Spirit guide us as we seek shalom in our promised land.

Christ the King

Ezekiel 34.11–16, 20–24 Matthew 25.31–46
"And the king will answer them, 'Truly I tell you, just as you did it to one of the least of these who are members of my family, you did it to me.'"
Matthew 25.40.

In this famous passage, a key to Christian behaviour, Jesus is pictured as king and judge. If we put our text alongside the equally well-known sentence: 'My kingdom is not of this world,' we arrive at the question, what sort of king is this Jesus? We know that a recurrent theme in the Gospels is the quest for the Kingdom of God or Kingdom of Heaven. How does one enter it and what is it about? Is it about the present, the future or both? The Kingdom of Heaven is not a place; it has no geographic boundaries; it is not part of space and time in any ordinary sense. It reflects a state of being that stems from a way of life that God summons us to take up.

As the Gospel of Matthew points out entry is not about religiosity but how we treat others. Unconditional love and care are at the core of this kingdom that Jesus reigns over.

If you ask the question: What is piety? you might come up with answers connected with a life of devotion to your god or gods of a particular religion. If someone never went to church, you would be unlikely to call them pious. But you might be wrong if you take this passage in Mathew twenty five seriously. God does not need our worship; worship is a response to a state of being that is aligned with the life God calls us to. Without that it is worth nothing.

I like reading the dialogues of Plato. They are very readable and stimulating. I have recently read one of the shortest and it is called the Euthyphro. This is a dialogue between Socrates, about to be tried for impiety, and Euthyphro a respected theologian. At issue is the meaning of piety. Socrates ties his debater up in knots and by the end we begin to wonder if we know the meaning of anything. For a Christian who argues that God is good, God must love and cherish what is good. But then we ask what is good? Fortunately for us Jesus makes it clear that for him what is good is not necessarily frequent worship, but whether we treat others selflessly and with generosity in life, regardless of who they are; in prison, hungry and destitute.

The message of the New Testament is counter cultural. There are no 'gongs' handed out for any form of self-aggrandisement. We have to seek out the needy in our lives and help them regardless of cost. It provides a stark contrast against prevailing cultural norms in any age and is meant to be challenging. Our worship and recognition of Christ as king of our lives is only valid if we respond to his call to serve. Jesus says when you were helping others you were helping me. The Bible is full of stories that bear this out. Perhaps one of the most telling is the parable of the Good Samaritan, a story told against piety of the wrong kind; the hero is not a proper Jew but a Samaritan.

I have just completed a novel titled *The Archbishop.* As a piece of literature it could be better, but its interest lies in a fictional account of the first female Archbishop of Canterbury appointed in 2019. The novel exposes a tension that lay between her agenda of service to the needy and the government agenda of unrestrained capitalism. There is a sinister plot to undermine her credibility through personal attacks on her morals and integrity through the press; none of it credible. Her mission was counter-cultural.

One of the dramatic changes in modern society compared with the time of Jesus is the rise of individualism, particularly in the West. External forces dominated the lives of those in pre-modern cultures. Life was generally short and hard with no concept of privacy. People had minimal control over their destinies. Since the seventeenth century there has been a gradual rise in individual autonomy, accelerated in an extraordinary way in the last hundred years by the rise of science and increased longevity through an ability to treat disease. Our expectations have risen dramatically. We now think we can control our planet. But the I of individualism has taken us away from the call of Jesus to follow him and be servants. We can look at our TV and see images of people dying of ebola and malaria and be relatively unmoved. Our personal wellbeing pre-occupies us.

Every generation has to ask the questions: What am I going to do with my life now that God has blessed me with all that modern society can achieve? Who is going to be my king? Will I follow the *Servant King* and seek to be part of his kingdom here in this life or will I follow another god?'

We are at the end of the Christian year. A new cycle is coming around again. A new Advent for waiting, reflection and decision making; the possibility of fresh starts and opportunities awaits us.